For Love of Town and Village

JACK MAHON

explores the exciting success of the

AIB GAA Club All-Ireland Championships

BLACKWATER PRESS

ACKNOWLEDGEMENTS

In my journey around Ireland doing research for this book, I received nothing but courtesy *en route*. It was a labour of love. As with all my books since 1992, I'm indebted to Paddy and Florrie Barrett for their patience and efficiency in the typing and layout of the book and for all the glasses of home-made wine. My thanks too to Susannah Gee of Blackwater Press for her co-operation and enthusiasm. Finally, my gratitude to Adrienne Murray and Brenda Hurley of AIB without whose support this book would have been much more difficult to produce and I'd also like to thank Séamus Heaney and Bryan McMahon (*The Master*) for giving me permission to reproduce from their works.

Editor	**Layout**
Susannah Gee	Paddy Barrett
Design	**ISBN**
GS	0 86121 664 4

© - Jack Mahon 1997

British Library Cataloguing-in Publication Data.

A catalogue record for this book is available from The British Library.

Produced in Ireland by: Blackwater Press
c/o Folens Publishers
8 Broomhill Business Park,
Tallaght, Dublin 24.

CONTENTS

FOREWORD

The All-Ireland Club Championships have become such an integral and exciting part of the GAA, it's almost impossible to remember a time when they weren't there. The truth is, of course, that they are only 26 years old, but so great has been their impact that they have knitted very quickly into the fabric of GAA life.

This was brought home to me in March 1996 when AIB Bank hosted the Silver Jubilee Awards to honour the very best of the hurlers and footballers who had won All-Ireland club medals since 1971. It was great to hear so many players, drawn from different decades, reminiscing about the past. What made it all the more interesting was that the club, the core unit of the GAA, was the binding force amongst them all.

Jack Mahon has always been a well-known figure in GAA circles, both as a star player with Galway and Dunmore MacHales and as a writer on the game he loves with a passion. This book is a credit to him, combining as it does, so much detail with a deep and warm appreciation of what the club stands for within the GAA. It also represents another proud strand in the on-going development of AIB's sponsorship of the Club Championships.

I hope that, like the Club Championships themselves, this book will provide lots of pleasure for the many people whose lives are indeed based on the noble dictum "For Love of Town and Village".

Hugh Cawley,
General Manager,
AIB Bank

AIB Bank Manager

AUTHOR'S NOTE

It would have been so much easier to visit the National Library, get transcripts of games played over the past twenty-five years and interview selected people from the various clubs by phone. But then I wouldn't have met the people; seen the places; noted the grounds and facilities; and captured the spirit of the clubs throughout the land, who had by their achievements earned for their members a chapter in this book.

The title, "For Love of Town and Village", is, I feel, very apt. It is borrowed in a sense from the famous saying of Matt the Thresher in Charles Kickham's *Knocknagow* "for the honour of the little village". But the title must include teams from cities and the larger towns alongside the villages and small rural townlands which have won All-Ireland titles.

I travelled to every corner of this country to get the feel of the champion clubs. Many people helped me along the way like Tom Ryall (Kilkenny), Jim Cronin (Cork), Danny Murphy (Down) and Liz Howard (Tipperary). Memories abound. In the early hours of a sharp spring morning a fox led me all the way from Len Gaynor's house in Kilruane to the main road. I spent a delightful evening in Mick Minogue's home in Roscrea. Later on as autumn beckoned I found it so hard to say goodbye to all those lovely Loughgiel people assembled in the Pound Bar deep in the glens of Antrim. Meeting John Fenton of Cork as he proudly talked of his beloved Midleton was another milestone. Then there was a very pleasant evening spent in hallowed St Colman's College, Newry, one of the great football nurseries. I listened to Tony Doran talking with pride of Buffer's Alley; Tony Hanahoe on St Vincent's; "Fan" Larkin on "The Village"; Joe Cooney on Sarsfield's two-in-a-row triumphs; Tony O'Keeffe on Austin Stack's in Kerry's palatial GAA offices in Tralee and Timmy Delaney singing *Lovely Fair Ileigh* in the back kitchen of Biddy Stapleton's friendly hostelry in Borrisoleigh. These are but a few nuggets from a golden odyssey which took me through Ireland in 1996.

I'm grateful to AIB Bank and in particular to Hugh Cawley, General Manager, Dublin for their generous sponsorship of this book. They made a very wise choice when sponsoring the All-Ireland Club Championships some years back, for the AIB Club All-Irelands are growing in popularity annually. Despite their timing, which sees many of the major games played in dreadful conditions in the depth of winter, they have established a niche for themselves in the GAA calendar of events. St Patrick's Day has become

AIB All-Ireland Club Final day – the place to be on our national holiday. Being from the club Dunmore MacHales which first nurtured the idea and saw it through at administrative level, the establishment, gradual growth and present health of these competitions gives me immense pride. This book which was first mooted in a casual conversation with Mr Michael Marren, AIB Area Manager, as we crossed the GAA field in Corofin after the Connacht Senior Football Club Final of 1995 is my monument to the GAA club scene, the grassroots of our noble Association. Long may the AIB Club All-Irelands flourish and prosper. *Go n-éirighidh an bóthar leo.*

Jack Mahon
January 1997.

1
How It All Began

The club unit has always been the bedrock of the Gaelic Athletic Association since its foundation in 1884. In the early days the All-Irelands were contested between clubs representing counties, the first ever titles of 1887 being won by Limerick Commercials (Football) and Thurles (Hurling). This practice continued right up to the 1920s. My own club Dunmore MacHales (Galway) once contested a Connacht Final (Football) with Ballina Stephenites. From the 1920s onwards, counties were represented by selections from all the clubs in these counties and the club unit tended to count for less. As the inter-county All-Irelands increased in popularity, a huge debate developed which was often termed 'Club or County'. Inter-county players (or the élite) were getting plenty of games whereas the club players who supplied this élite were in the main denied the greater activity they craved. It was difficult to fit both into the same fixtures calendar.

DEBATE

That debate — Club or County — grew with the rising popularity of inter-county All-Irelands, especially after the arrival on the scene in 1938 of that marvellous radio commentator Michael O'Hehir. Shrewd man that he was, O'Hehir always did a thorough homework on players under his scrutiny, never failing to mention where they hailed from. I grew up in that era and thousands of youngsters like me became fascinated by names of places like Tullaroan, Toomevara, Ahane, Moycarkey, Cornafaen, Knockcroghery, Mullahoran, Mooncoin and all those lovely club names like Glen Rovers, Faughs, Cooley Kickhams, Young Irelands, Austin Stack's or Dungannon

Clarkes. How proud I was when he mentioned my own hometown Dunmore or the MacHales club when talking about Brendan Nestor or my next door neighbour Frank Fox. It was the 1938 All-Ireland Football Final between Kerry and Galway. Wirelesses were few in our street. Down the road from our house John Donlan had one and from about noon many people from our street converged on the Donlan home. The wet battery had been charged and a few youngsters with myself were told to sit quietly in a corner. I was a five-year-old and my memory of that day is hazy now but I do remember this clearly. Excitement was mounting. O'Hehir was painting an exciting picture. The man of the house stood beside the wireless set. 'A free to Galway. Brendan Nestor, the Dunmore schoolteacher, steps back. Up he comes....' All in the kitchen edged closer. Then a shout from the excited Donlan 'for Christ's sake stand back and give young Nestor a chance'. He scored and we all cheered. Míchael O'Hehir kept clubs in the centre of it all and his successor Micheál Ó Muircheartaigh has continued the tradition. A player is first and foremost a clubman. Club first, county afterwards. A certain conflict of interests has always existed.

EMERGENCE OF OUTSTANDING CLUBS

The move to re-establish club All-Irelands as such, grew in the 1950s and 1960s, mainly due to the emergence of outstanding club teams over the years. The legendary Mick Mackey won twenty Limerick Senior Championship medals with Ahane (fifteen hurling and five football). Christy Ring won fourteen Cork Senior Hurling Championship medals with Glen Rovers and one Senior Football Championship medal with St Nick's, a sister club of The Glen. Seán Purcell won ten Galway Senior Football Championship medals with the famous Tuam Stars. The emergence in Dublin of St Vincent's as a dual club in the fifties heralded a new dawn for the GAA in the capital city. It wasn't unusual then to have Dublin inter-county teams formed mostly of country lads from other counties working in Dublin, with few native Dubliners involved. You had to be born or reared in Dublin to play with Vincent's. The Vins as they became known took over in Dublin, winning title after title and in the process adorning the scene with such folk heroes as Kevin Heffernan (Heffo), Ollie Freaney, Dessie Ferguson (Snitchy), Jim Crowley, Mossie Whelan.... Many of these Vincents' men were dual stars like Heffo, Snitchy and Norman Allen. Years later the same club produced possibly the greatest ever dual star in Des Foley. In the 1950s they won nine

Dublin Senior Football Championship titles in a ten-year period. They took the capital by storm and in their heyday it was not unusual to have crowds of over 20,000 in Croke Park to watch them play against teams mostly comprised of players from other counties such as Westerns or Gárda. Tom Langan, Mayo's Team of the Century full-forward, once told me that one of his greatest thrills was to shoot a goal for Gárda against St Vincent's into a packed Hill 16 goal. Hill 16 was becoming Dublin's preserve even then. The epic Tuam Stars against St Vincent's confrontations of the 1950s were born and the equally hectic hurling tournaments in Munster featuring Mount Sion, Thurles Sarsfield's, Glen Rovers and hosts of other club tournaments throughout the land. In the 1950s and 1960s I remember travelling on enjoyable outings with my Dunmore MacHales club to Enniskillen to take on Omagh St Enda's in 1955; to Corrigan Park at Easter 1963 to play St Johns (the game being on a dreadfully wet Easter Sunday, was abandoned because of the conditions); and then on to Lurgan the following day to face Clann Éireann, Alf Murray's club. On another occasion we travelled to London for Easter, defeating London on the Sunday at New Eltham and the London champions Naomh Mhuire on the Monday. Crossmaglen Rangers, a brilliant club team in the 1960s were our opponents then too. Against that scenario the move to establish club All-Irelands took root. Winning a County Senior title was still a huge ambition for every club. It was and still is their little All-Ireland. But it didn't have to stop there.

PROVINCIAL GROWTH

Like many things in the GAA it wasn't easy to initiate change. The movement to set club All-Irelands in motion took off in three different provinces in the 1960s. In Connacht the idea took off after the Sligo Town GAA club Craobh Rua organised an unofficial Connacht title in the late 1950s won by Tuam Stars more than once. Dunmore MacHales now had a team powered by such well-known names as the Donnellan brothers, John and Pat, the Keenan brothers, John and Tommy, Séamus Leydon and Bosco McDermott. At the home of our Secretary, Bertie Coleman we often debated and planned strategies late into the night. In Ulster the movement was led by clubs like St Joseph's (Bundoran–Ballyshannon) and St Johns (Belfast) where unofficial Ulster club tournaments helped sow the seed. An official Munster club title was organised in the South.

WHEELS OF CHANGE

Motions to GAA Congress to establish club All-Irelands began to surface. Early in 1964 the *Gaelic Weekly* started a Forum requesting contributions from various writers on diverse topics of the time. One such theme was 'Should All-Ireland Club Championships Be Inaugurated?' Four regular columnists, namely Chris Phelan (Laois), Deasúin Mac Coiligh (Armagh), Séamus Ó Ceallaigh (Limerick) and myself, all came out in support. But the wheels of change were already turning. Our club delegate Bertie Coleman had convinced the Connacht Council to initiate an official Connacht Senior Football Club Championship in 1961 and this was finally completed in 1964 at O'Hara Park, Charlestown when Dunmore MacHales defeated Melvin Gaels (Leitrim) by 2-8 to 0-5 on Sunday April 28. I cherish the historic medal I won that day and a second one for 1966, won eventually on 15 April 1968 in McHale Park in Castlebar where we defeated Ballina Stephenites by 1-10 to 1-9. This official Connacht competition had its teething problems and tended to be prolonged.

BERTIE COLEMAN

All the time Bertie Coleman in his eager-beaver way was keeping the idea afloat and, just to prove it could be done, was the main motivator in organising an unofficial All-Ireland Senior Football Club Tournament in 1968. Dunmore MacHales successfully defeated St Nicks (Cork) representing Munster in a home and away series, total aggregate deciding the winner. The same procedure applied in the final against St Joseph's (Donegal) in Ballyshannon at Tuam Stadium. These were two epic games with St Joseph's coming out on top. More importantly the idea was sold to a wider public and the competition was hailed as a success both competitively and socially. That second game in Tuam is still talked about. I was nearing the end of my own playing career but in the first game in Ballyshannon, I substituted for the injured Jim Nestor when my immediate opponent was Donegal full-back Pauric McShea. The winners had a super team with players of the calibre of McShea, Brian McEniff, Declan O'Carroll, Séamus Granaghan and the present Donegal County Manager Mickey McAloone who was, after Martin McHugh, the best Donegal forward I have seen. His duel with John Donnellan in Tuam in 1968 was worth travelling miles to see. The club All-Ireland seed was now firmly sown.

GAA Congress 1970

GAA 1970 came to Galway for the first time in the first of a series of trips outside Dublin. It was the year that Waterford man, Pat Fanning, became President (at his third attempt). A Rules Revision Committee had most of its recommendations rejected relating to suggested changes in the solo-run, pickup and enlarged square. A suggested return of the hand-pass was firmly ruled out. After this, All-Ireland finals, semi-finals and provincial finals at senior level only, were to be of 80 minutes duration. On the Clár were two motions from Galway and Wexford calling for the introduction of club All-Irelands. I was a spectator in St Mary's College, Galway when Bertie Coleman stood up to propose the motion. First to oppose it were Cork, through delegates Weeshie Murphy and Denis Conroy. They were not really against the idea but Weeshie complained that they found it difficult to organise it in Munster while Denis, in his argumentative way, felt it would interfere with the *status quo*. The debate is best remembered for an altercation between the newly elected President and Cork delegate Denis Conroy with Con Murphy entering the fray to defend his Cork colleague. Despite all of this the motion was carried by 92 votes to 74. The day was won. The rest is history. The man who deserves the major credit for seeing the motion through was Dunmore's Mr Football, Bertie Coleman.

Iniskeen

Michael Hand, the well-known journalist, tells this story of his early days with the *Sunday Press*. He was sent to Iniskeen, County Monaghan to do a piece on what the people of his native place thought of native son, Patrick Kavanagh, poet and writer. So he set off all agog and entering one of the Iniskeen pubs on arrival made himself comfortable and then asked the barman what he thought of Kavanagh. 'The greatest amadán I ever met. Don't mention the so and so's name here. A luadramán.' He heard much the same from the other people in the bar. And the same story down the street later and elsewhere in Iniskeen. No one had a good word for the author of *The Green Fool* and *Raglan Road* and *Tarry Flynn*. Hand was mystified. So he retraced his steps to the first pub. He told the barman about his mission. Kavanagh was Iniskeen. Iniskeen was Kavanagh. Just why was he held in such low esteem in the area? 'Well it's like this, Gaelic football is big in Monaghan. Once ever in our history did the local GAA club Iniskeen

Grattans reach a County Final. There we were leading by two points and a minute or two to go, when our goalkeeper, Kavanagh — yes Patrick Kavanagh — left the bloody goal to get a mineral from a huckster behind the goal and while he was gone the other crowd got the winning goal. That's why Kavanagh, the bastard, will never be forgiven in Iniskeen. I can still see that empty goal.' That story is one of Tony O'Reilly's favourites. Mine too.

Bertie Coleman, the man who proposed the motion in 1970.

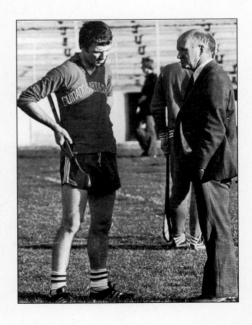

Christy Ring chatting with Jimmy Barry-Murphy at a training session.

Brian McEniff, another prime mover in setting up club All-Irelands.

Seán Purcell (right) won 10 Galway Senior Football Championship medals with Tuam Stars. Photographed here with the author, Jack Mahon.

13

2
Castlegar: Galway's First

It was entirely fitting that Castlegar, the club which tops the roll of honour in Galway club hurling with 17 senior titles, should win for the county its first club All-Ireland title in 1980. The club on the outskirts of Galway City embraces the area from Renmore to Ballybrit to Brierhill and all those villages of the sweet-sounding names Castlegar, Kiltulla, Breanloughane, Coolough, Ballynew, Killoughter, Twomileditch, Cloonacauneen and Bruckey. The men of 'Cashel' first made the headlines in the 1930s winning five-in-a-row of county senior titles in the period 1936–1940. I watched Castlegar play many games and the first men to impress me were Willie Fahy, Johnny Molloy, Mickey Burke, Pádhraic Nolan, Séamus Cullinane, Paddy Egan and the famous Connolly brothers. During all those years since, many families have become identified with wearing the famed green and white hooped jerseys of Castlegar — the Connors, Burkes, Corcorans, Shaughnessys, Fahys, Cannons, Murphys, Egans, Glynns, Coynes and of course the Connollys.

THE RACECOURSE

There has always been a close connection between the club and the Galway Racecourse in Ballybrit, situated as it is in the heart of Castlegar. The club often trained there prior to the acquisition of their own fine club grounds and facilities adjacent to the motorway between Galway and Oranmore. Many of the hurling families associated with Castlegar learnt their hurling there, pucking balls for hours on end on summer evenings.

The 1970s

As in the previous decades, the 1970s were good for Castlegar. The young Connollys were emerging. John returned from the US to help the club win out in 1972. Stalwarts then included Tony Gavin in goal, and backs, Tommy Broderick and Ted Murphy, while in the attack Mickey O'Connor and Noel Cummins led the way. The crown was annexed again in 1973. Then came 1979 with wins over Mullagh, Athenry, a lucky enough draw with Killimordaly in the semi-final before the replay was won at Ballinasloe. Finally, a good win over newcomers Kinvara in the County Final in Ballinasloe played early in December. Castlegar won their 16th title on the score 2-13 to 0-6.

The Rockies Of Cork

Castlegar went on to win the Connacht club title defeating Tremane of Roscommon in the final. Picture the scene in Kenny Park, Athenry, on Sunday 25 May 1980, when a crowd of 3,000 attended the meeting of Castlegar and the reigning All-Ireland club champions, Blackrock of Cork, who were firm favourites to win that All-Ireland Semi-final match. The Castlegar team was raring to go, trained by that effervescent character, Tony Regan, a man whose very presence is an inspiration. Blackrock had eight of the Cork Senior Hurling team which had just won the National Hurling League title on the previous Sunday in a replay against Limerick. They were further boosted by the presence of that brilliant Kilkenny mid-fielder Frank Cummins, who played at centre-half-back for Blackrock. I remember the names: blonde-haired John Horgan, the compact Dermot McCurtain, fleet-footed Pat Moylan, free-scoring Éamonn O'Donoghoe, the dual All-Star Ray Cummins and consummate hurler Tom Cashman. Castlegar tore the form book to shreds winning in the end by 2-9 to 0-9 in a game described by former Castlegar hero Willie Fahy as 'the greatest game I ever saw'.

The Connollys

Just as the Cooneys are still doing it for Sarsfields, the contribution of the Connolly family to Castlegar's All-Ireland Semi-final success cannot be underplayed. Five brothers, Pádhraic, John, Joe, Gerry and Michael, the captain, all played, while Tom entered the fray as a substitute in the third quarter against Blackrock, and Murt, the seventh member of the clan was also a substitute. J.P. Burke (*Tuam Herald*) paid them this tribute 'The Connollys dominated the scene with John at centre-half-back dictating terms in his own immaculate style, while brothers Joe, Michael and Gerry scored all but two points in their total.

'It was nip and tuck in the first quarter before Michael Connolly put Castlegar in front 0-4 to 0-3 in the 13th minute. Six minutes later Michael short-passed to brother Joe for a Castlegar goal and the home side led at half-time by 1-6 to 0-5. In the second half a long free from elder brother John fell to Joe, who scored his second goal, but Blackrock rallied to try and save their title in a thrilling finish with goalkeeper Tommy Grogan tipping over a fierce Frank Cummins penalty for a point.' J.P. Burke in his final paragraph tribute wrote: 'This was vintage hurling by a great club side.' He paid tribute also to 'the wholehearted hurling of Séamus Fahy and Tom Murphy at mid-field, the splendid displays of Gerry and Michael Glynn on either side of John Connolly, goalkeeper Tommy Grogan and John Coady, Pádhraic Connolly and veteran Ted Murphy, who were always reliable'. A Galway hurling team now seemed capable of going the whole way at last, with the final taking place in Páirc Tailteann, Navan just one week later against the Ulster champions Ballycastle McQuillans.

Champions Of Ireland

Castlegar hurling reached the pinnacle of success on 1 June 1980 when they deservedly beat Ballycastle McQuillans in the All-Ireland Club Final by 1-11 to 1-8 after a very tense struggle in Navan. They had to battle hard against a very capable Northern side back-boned by the Donnelly clan of Kevin, Séamus, Terence, Dessie, Brian and Eddie. Fifteen minutes after the start Ballycastle went ahead by 1-4 to 0-4 but the Galwaymen came back to lead at half-time by 0-8 to 1-4. In this period Joe Connolly popped over seven superb points from frees. It was Ballycastle who made the running in the second half but with Ted Murphy and Gerry Glynn scintillating, Castlegar held firm. The Connollys, Joe and John combined to send Jimmy Francis through for a vital point. Then came the important goal. Joe Connolly first-timed the ball into the goal area where Liam Mulryan was on hand to double on the sliothar and crack home a great goal. Ballycastle whittled the lead back to just one point 1-9 to 1-8 entering the last quarter. Neither side scored in a very tense ten minute period which followed. Then Gerry Connolly shot a point to relieve the tension and Joe wisely pointed a penalty to leave the score 1-11 to 1-8 at the end. Castlegar's huge support in the 4,000 attendance danced with joy as Michael Connolly received the Tommy Moore Cup.

CLUB SPIRIT

There has always been a magnificent club spirit in Castlegar. During my teaching days many future Castlegar stars passed through my hands including six of the All-Ireland winning team. Even as schoolboys they were very proud of Castlegar's hurling tradition and were pillars of the schools' hurling and football teams. This was the Castlegar team in the final:

Tommy Grogan

Ted Murphy   Pádhraic Connolly   John Coady

Gerry Glynn   John Connolly   Michael Glynn

Tom Murphy   Séamus Fahy

Jimmy Francis   Joe Connolly   Packie Connor

Gerry Connolly   Michael Connolly (capt.)   Liam Mulryan

Substitutes: Mike Murphy, Patrick Burke (who came on for P. Connor,), Gerry King, Tom Connolly, Pakie Long, Murt Connolly, John Connor, Christy Mulryan, Seán Broderick, Máirtín Ó Cillín and Seán Murphy.

John Martin covered the game for the *Irish Independent* under a heading 'Connollys Outdo Donnellys — Castlegar Win'. He didn't over-praise the standard of play, writing that the attendance of 4,000 'must have been disappointed with the general standard of play in a final in which both clubs were newcomers. In truth the scoreline should never have been so close and the responsibility here must fall on the Castlegar attack which never operated with any fluency'. Castlegar had 13 wides to Ballycastle's 6 and Joe Connolly (0-9) and Peter Boyle (0-7) contributed 15 points *en toto* from frees.

TOMMY EGAN

Tommy Egan, who was Chairman of the club at that time, is one of three brothers who wore the green and white jersey of 'Cashel'. 'At that stage in 1979 we were a few years waiting to win another county title, 1973 being our previous win. We put together a thirty-two-man panel to have a crack at regaining the County Cup. We eventually beat Kinvara well in the county final. We never thought we'd win the All-Ireland but we had a real trump card in Tony Regan as our trainer. It was the in thing that time to have a trainer and it was Jimmy Wall suggested we get the UCG man. We would never have won the All-Ireland without him.

'We trained in our own club grounds. The dressing-rooms and pitch were in operation. The Clubhouse was on its way up then and the official opening took place in 1983. The big achievement was the beating of Blackrock. In that Rockies game I remember one incident which really ignited Castlegar. Frank Cummins came up the wing soloing the ball. Ted Murphy came across and gave him a fair shoulder, putting him out over the line and against the wire and the crowd went mad. That happened after about ten minutes. It was the spark which set the team alight. Everyone in Athenry that day was a Castlegar supporter. Michael Glynn was the outstanding man but they were all brilliant. The contribution of the Connolly brothers was immense.

'Often in Castlegar we talk about the great ones and there is many an argument as to who was the greatest. I remember meeting Mickey Burke (Galway's captain in 1953) one Sunday and he told me Ted Murphy was the best he saw in the Castlegar jersey. More would say Johnny Molloy, or John Connolly or Tom Molloy, Willie Fahy or Jim Donoghoe.

'We were on such a high after the win over Blackrock that, with only one week to the final, we were nearly caught on the hop. The man who kept a cool head that day and helped us weather the early storm was John Connolly at centre-half-back. In the first ten minutes he stopped everything going through. Gerry and Michael Glynn took inspiration from him. It was fantastic coming home with the Cup. The next night we travelled round the parish with it.

'Every club has its own great clubmen. Some might never have hurled. Others did, and after quitting, devoted their lives to the club, often putting their hands in their pockets to keep the thing going. One such man for us was Willie Cullinane. He often gave us money from the till in his pub to get hurleys in Naughtons and at AGM time such monies never showed on a balance sheet. He was on the famous five-in-a-row team and won the All-Time Clubman Award given in Centenary year. Matt Hackett was another true blue, another five-in-a-row star. And Michael Giles has to be included.

He went everywhere on his bicycle and did great work with the juveniles and minors of our time. Men like Mark Heneghan, Wally Forde and Michael Broderick all gave great service. As to the future, we have a young promising team whose day of triumph will come.'

JOE CONNOLLY

1980 was a great year for Joe Connolly. As well as the club All-Ireland triumph, it was he who led Galway to the promised land after 57 years of endeavour. His victory speech tré Gaeilge after receiving the McCarthy Cup is now part of hurling folklore. Nowadays Joe is Sales Director of Connolly Sports Ltd, Claregalway, a thriving concern which gives him great pride. 'This is our 16th year in business and we employ 85 people as of now. There are three business sectors — corporate, tourist and the active sportswear sectors, with GAA jerseys a major part of the latter.' He has fond memories of 1980. 'We won everything in 1980. Even the County Junior Football title with Éire Óg. Somebody said we'd have beaten the All Blacks! I'll never forget the club All-Ireland victory. We knew we had a good team in Castlegar. There was a good club spirit. The big battle was with Blackrock. In choosing our home venue, it was expected we'd choose Pearse Stadium or Ballinasloe, the obvious venues, but any hurler will tell you the best and most favoured hurling venue would be Athenry. So we opted for Athenry.

'That was the greatest game I ever played in as regards hurling. Nothing will ever compare with winning the All-Ireland for Galway but that was the greatest game of them all. For sheer hurling, defiance, bit between the teeth from the first second and not relenting till the final whistle, nothing ever surpassed it. The crowd surrounded the "tunnel" as we came off from the gate up as far as the dressing-room. Literally a guard of honour which was composed of many erstwhile opponents who often shouted against us. We did not underestimate Ballycastle in the final. There were 10 minutes left in the second half of the final and the ball never left our backline. Liam Mulryan's goal helped seal it. I hit a 40 yard shot in, which was hopping and Jack Nicklaus with a 9 iron couldn't do better than Liam in pulling on it and rocketing the ball to the net.

'At that time most of us were still living at home in the family home. The greatest days were the days after a big game. My mother and sisters never went to games. It usually began to hum about 11 a.m. The hour or two after that was always great fun, full of slagging and codding, laughing and analysing. My mother would be happy if nobody got hurt. The boss would be there taking it all in, never a yard away from it all. We all looked up to John of course.'

Memories

'I remember in the 1960s when Races time came around, we operated a car park in front of our house that could fit about 12 cars. Our charge I think was half a crown and one of those days Jim Treacy of Kilkenny, pulled in. It was as if God arrived. I ran into the house to announce it. We all ran out to gaze at an All-Ireland medal-winner. Of course, we brought him in for tea. So you must remember where we came from to win All-Ireland medals and how much it meant to us. Nowadays I don't think the present generation of Galway hurlers appreciate the starvation years of Galway hurling prior to 1980. Now All-Ireland hurling titles, especially at lower levels and in the schools, are taken for granted almost. I remember driving along at the time and trying to convince myself that Castlegar was the best club team in Ireland. A magic feeling. About five years ago I was on a business trip in Cork and about to cross a pedestrian crossing on the Grand Parade. On pressing the button, I made eye contact with this man beside me and said hello. As we crossed the road he went ahead of me then turned around and said, "I shouldn't talk to you at all and where ye brought the Rockies 10 years ago." They still don't forgive us in Cork for bringing Blackrock to Athenry.

'The present club All-Irelands are generating great hype and have become settled into the GAA calendar, taking over from the Railway Cup. It's lovely to see new clubs like Éire Óg, Dunloy, An Tóchar, Baltinglass emerge from what might be termed weaker counties. The football All-Ireland between Éire Óg and O'Donovan Rossa, Skiberreen exuded intensity of endeavour (the drawn game of 1993). It gives a place to men who may never aspire to inter-county teams and this has to be good. In our business here we get great support from clubs and I'm proud to say we outfitted our sixth in a row of All-Ireland club champions. I'm always grateful I grew up in Castlegar and became part of a club with such a hurling tradition of winning defiantly. I remember looking up to the Egan family next door and the stars of my young days were Stephen Francis and Patsy Kelly.'

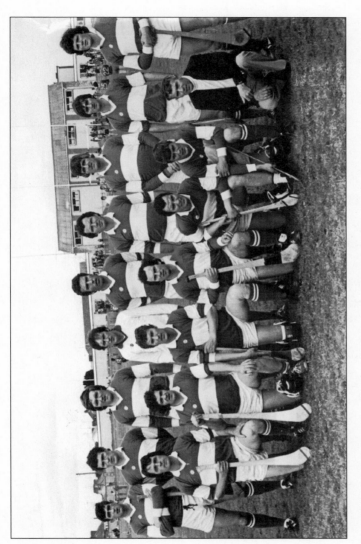

Castlegar 1980

Back row: Gerry Glynn, Joe Connolly, Liam Mulryan, Tom Grogan, John Connolly, John Coady, Ted Murphy, Michael Glynn, Seamus Fahy

Front row: Tom Murphy, Pakie Connor, Michael Connolly, (capt.) Jimmy Francis, Padraic Connolly, Gerry Connolly and Tommy Egan (Chairman)

___ 3 ___

The Village's Two Crowns

Tom Ryall is the great archivist of Kilkenny's GAA. He took me through the history of the James Stephen's club in Kilkenny City, winner of two All-Ireland Senior Hurling club titles in 1976 and 1982.

'James Stephen's was a native of Kilkenny City. The club came into existence officially, in the 1920s as a junior team, though there was an old James Stephen's side, which competed in the early days of the GAA. The area the club came from originally was Patrick Street and 60 years ago Kilkenny was a much smaller place of very few streets. The club is still centred in St Patrick's Parish but they can select players from any other part of the City in accordance with GAA rules. James Stephen's bought their own field in the 1950s which they have developed since and they now have a very impressive GAA complex opened in the early 1980s.'

SIX COUNTY SENIOR HURLING TITLES

'They have won six Kilkenny Senior Hurling titles in all: 1935, 1937, 1969, 1975, 1976 and 1981. "Fan" Larkin captained the 1975 team, while Jimmy O'Brien was in charge in 1981, both of these going on to annex All-Ireland crowns. Regarding the Village's stalwart players the first to come to mind would be "Fan's" father Paddy who, like "Fan" went on to captain Kilkenny and win All-Ireland finals, also "Fan's" uncle, Mick "Flip" Larkin, who like Paddy played in the famous three-game-saga of 1931 All-Ireland finals against Cork. After the great days of the '30s it took a junior title success of 1955 to bring a resurgence and Seán Tyrrell went on to captain Kilkenny to a junior All-Ireland success in 1956. Then came Phil "Fan" Larkin who started with Kilkenny in the 1960s and continued after a lull into the '70s, when along came Liam "Chunky" O'Brien, Mick Crotty, Brian Cody, Tom McCormack, Éamonn Morrissey. On one occasion the club had three representatives on the All-Star hurling team, "Fan" Larkin, "Chunky" O'Brien and Mick Crotty (1974) while Brian Cody won one in 1975 and 1982. Joe Hennessy, who came from a wonderful hurling tradition on both his father's and mother's side, also won All-Star honours. Georgie Leahy's contribution to James Stephen's was immense. He was the sole selector when "The Village" won the All-Ireland in 1976. The same Georgie, who later trained Offaly, Laois, Westmeath, Waterford and various teams in Kilkenny. He also trained Glenmore when they won the club All-Ireland in 1991. Pound for pound I suppose Joe Hennessy was the greatest hurler of them all. The Secretary of the club at the moment is Michael Moore, goalkeeper in both All-Ireland teams of 1976 and 1982. Michael is a grand-nephew of Tommy Moore, after whom the club All-Ireland Cup is called.'

THE 1976 SUCCESS

Before 8,000 people at Nowlan Park 'The Village', in Arctic-like conditions won their 4th Kilkenny Senior Hurling title with an easy win over Galmoy by 1-14 to 1-5. John Knox in the *Kilkenny People* gave top billing to Liam O'Brien whose 'trickery was marvellous to watch'. On 25 January in Dr Cullen Park, Carlow, St Rynagh's of Offaly were beaten in the Leinster Final by 1-14 to 2-4, where Liam O'Brien was again the star supreme, ably helped by goalkeeper Mick Moore and left-half-forward John McCormack. In the All-Ireland Semi-final James Stephen's easily defeated Ballygalget (Down) by 4-15 to 1-7. All was now set for the final against Blackrock on Sunday 14 March 1976. The venue was Semple Stadium, Thurles and in the *Irish Press* of Monday, 15 March, Pádraig Puirséal, that racy scribe from Noreside, under the heading 'Villagers go to Town. O'Brien Inspires' wrote about James Stephens' great win by 2-10 to 2-4. 'Despite trailing by five points at the interval, James Stephen's turned on the steam and the style when wind-assisted in the second half and deservedly brought home to the old city by the Nore the only All-Ireland hurling trophy Kilkenny had never previously won.' The Rockies had a super club team at the time powered by John Horgan, Dermot McCurtain, Frank Cummins, Ray Cummins, Éamonn O'Donoghue, and Pat Moylan. Pádraig Puirséal gave star billing to 'Chunky' O'Brien ably helped by 'the dedicated leadership of "Fan" Larkin, Brian

Cody 'a tower of strength when he blossomed in the second half, Niall Morrissey, Paddy Neary, Tom McCormack and Joe Hennessy'. This was the winning team:

Moore

Paddy Neary   'Fan' Larkin (capt.)   Niall Morrissey

Tom McCormack   Brian Cody   Jimmy O'Brien

Dinny McCormack   Mick Taylor

Joe Hennessy   Liam 'Chunky' O'Brien   John McCormack

Mick Crotty   Michael Leahy   Ger Tyrrell

Substitute: Michael Neary for J. O'Brien

'FAN' LARKIN REMEMBERS

'Fan' tells how he got his name. 'I have two first cousins also called Phil Larkin and my second name is Francis, hence the name "Fan" to distinguish me from the cousins. Years ago when the Village would be playing, the Patrick's Street Band would play the team and supporters across the City to the Park, (Nowlan Park) and do the same after the match on the return journey. From 1968 onwards was our greatest time. My first one was in 1969 when Mickey Dunne, my next door neighbour, was captain. His father "Sock" Dunne also hurled for the Village and my father Paddy captained both our first two title winning teams of 1935 and 1937. We had a few lads from the other side of town namely Mick Moore and the two Morrisseys. But most of us were Village people — Mickey Leahy, Mickey Dunne.... When we won the title in 1969 there were three Larkins in the full-back line, my brother Paddy, a first cousin, Phil Larkin and myself.

'Going back to 1975–1976 we were very lucky to beat Buffer's Alley in our first game in Leinster in Wexford Park. Tony Doran played at centre-half-forward on Brian Cody and that was a great duel. Mick Crotty played a blinder that day. A late goal won it for us. "Joey Boy", "Fan's" pet-name for Joe Hennessy, was good as usual. Mick Leahy, Georgie's brother, scored the winner. Georgie knew his hurling and we all responded to him. In the final it was a helluva windy day and Blackrock got a goal straightaway from Éamonn O'Donoghue, after only ten seconds. After another ten minutes they scored a penalty, which went in off my hand. So we were two goals

24

down in short time. I thought I had it and it spun off me into the net. I suppose they were the finest club team we ever met.

'That was the best win I ever enjoyed. Of all the medals I've won, that's the most cherished one. Maybe the first County Final one was just as good because I was bringing the Cup home to where I started. To the parish. We had unbelievable celebrations. A great night above in Delaney's, a pub in the middle of Patrick Street. Bill Cody, Brian's father was our Chairman then and a very shrewd man, who must get major credit for our success. Georgie, of course, too.'

Worked together

'A lot of us grew up and worked together as well. I'm a plasterer myself and we were all working in Cleere's. The Morrisseys, Niall and Éamonn were carpenters and my brother Paddy, God rest him, was a bricklayer. Michael Taylor was a painter. We were all together working by day and we'd train every night. Mickey Leahy came from the same street and never missed training. Joey Boy too. You could give a shout and we'd all be together. There were four or five of us on the county team. Joey Boy had a great game in that final. Didn't start too well in the forwards but when he came to left-half-back he was brilliant. Himself, Brian Cody and Tom McCormack in the half-back line really snuffed out Blackrock. The Patrick Street Band didn't escort us in that night because they were all at the match. There were about five or six Larkins in the Band. My uncles used to play in it and they couldn't do the two things together!'

THE 1982 SUCCESS

'The Village' were very proud to be the first team to take the Tommy Moore Cup out of Munster. They were to repeat that success in 1982. In the Kilkenny Senior Hurling Final of 11 October 1981 they beat The Fenians (Johnstown) backboned by the Henderson brothers Pat, Ger and John, Pat Delaney, Nickey Orr and Billy Fitzpatrick by 2-10 to 0-8. John Knox in the *Kilkenny People* gave the major credit to former All-Star Mick Crotty for his goal in the 15th minute of the second half ending 15 minutes of tension-packed deadlock to put the winners two goals ahead 2-6 to 0-6. He 'kept his head when others around him were losing theirs' and delivered the vital blow.

His man-of-the-match was the Mullingar-based Garda Denis McCormack, who was dynamic at mid-field. The St Patrick's Brass Band and Majorettes led the teams in the pre-match parade.

Afterwards in the Leinster Final they beat Faythe Harriers (Wexford) on Sunday 21 March at Athy by a bare point 0-13 to 1-9. Gerry McCarthy in the *Irish Press* praised the County Final hero: 'Dinny McCormack's accurate long-range shooting, whose four glorious points from play set a headline none of the forwards on view could emulate.'

In the semi-final 'The Village' beat Gort (Galway) by 1-13 to 1-8 in Nowlan Park on Sunday, 25 April, before an attendance of over 4,000. Sylvie Linnane had been dominant at centre-half-back for Gort in the first half and his team led at half-time by 1-6 to 0-7. Ned Kelly was sent in on Sylvie in the second half and this switch curbed Sylvie's influence. Gerry Lally goaled from a penalty after 38 minutes to square the game 1-7 each. Now Kilkenny panelist Billy Walton struck a purple patch scoring five points without reply and that was the end for Gort. In the other semi-final Mount Sion (Waterford) defeated Cushendall (Antrim).

For the final George Leahy, who had been the sole selector in 1976, was brought into the backroom team. Twelve of the 1976 team were in action again for 'The Village' while their opponents Mount Sion had won their 25th Waterford Senior Hurling crown in 1981.

THE FINAL

'The Village' won the final at Thurles again by 3-13 to 3-8 in a game marred by some heavy May showers. The fare was poor enough at the start and the losers led at the break by 1-5 to 0-6. Donal Carroll in the *Irish Independent* of 17 May 1982 paid tribute to a fine second half where the winners fought back from a deficit of seven points to win by five. Sharpshooter Billy Walton shot 0-10 in all (seven from frees). The half-back line of Joe Hennessy, the unrelated Martin Hennessy and captain Liam O'Brien was outstanding, while veteran 'Fan' Larkin was also a hero and the winners will always be indebted to three-goal-hero John McCormack and to Mick Crotty. The winning team was:

Mick Moore

Paddy Neary   Brian Cody   P. 'Fan' Larkin

Joe Hennessy   Martin Hennessy   Jimmy O'Brien (capt.)

Tom McCormack   Dinny McCormack

Billy Walton   Eddie Kelly   Andy Egan

John McCormack   Mick Crotty   John Joe Cullen

Substitute: Donie Collins for A. Egan

'JOEY BOY' REMINISCES

'"Fan" would be seven or eight years older than me and I looked up to him a lot. If a forward got around you, or went on a solo past you, you'd always know "Fan" would stand in his path no matter how big he was. As a youngster I was mad on hurling and as well as "Fan", I admired Liam "Chunky" O'Brien, and Ned Byrne, the former rugby player. I was twenty-one when I played in the 1976 club final. Once we won the county title in 1969 we felt the need for a new GAA complex. It went from a dressing-room to a prefab to a bit of a bar and when the club All-Irelands were won we made full use of it. I never drank or smoked. A visit to our complex is well worth making. The last bit of green in "The Village". Our complex is the focal point of the whole area. I always loved Gaelic football and won three Kilkenny Senior Football titles with the club.'

Hardest to win

'When asked to compare the club All-Ireland win with his other achievements he said, 'Hardest of all to win. Easier to win a Senior Hurling title with Kilkenny than the club title with "The Village". In all I've eight All-Irelands, one minor, two U-21, two club and three senior to my name. As to my greatest thrill — it had to be beating Blackrock in 1976. First you had to come out of Kilkenny — always pretty difficult, then Leinster and after that the best of Cork. The turning point of that 1976 game was in the second half when it was touch-and-go and we got a 21 yard free. Liam "Chunky" O'Brien had the bravery to go for a goal and get it. It was my best ever game I think.

'I'd like to pay tribute to Dinny McCormack and Niall Morrissey. Both of them were knocking on the door of the county team. They never missed training. We were always great pals. Bill Brennan, who died just a year ago at one of our games, was very much behind the building of our clubhouse in his spare time. Georgie Leahy too, who was completely in charge in 1976. Who in Ireland today, in any sport, would take on such a responsibility?'

The game

'There is far too much protection for goalkeepers now. It should be possible to tackle a goalkeeper. The whole scene around goal has gone soft. Referees get far too much abuse. Very few past players get involved because of this abuse. Hurling is a cleaner game than football. It's faster than football. The players haven't the same time to do anything else but hurl. I'm worried about the visors on hurling helmets leading to accidents rather than preventing them. I never wore a helmet. Hurling isn't a dirty game. I got some stitches alright but never anything really serious. As to the greatest "Village" hurler "Chunky" had great skill. His first touch was brilliant.'

'The Village' 1982
Back row: Michael Moore, Billy Walton, Mick Crotty, John Joe Cullen, Dinny
McCormack, Tom McCormack, Andy Egan, Brian Cody, Phil
"Fan" Larkin.
Front row: John McCormack, Paddy Neary, Joe Hennessy, Jimmy O'Brien
(capt.), Ned Kelly, Martin Hennessy, Tom Hogan.

4

Kiltormer's Three-Game-Saga

Sunday, 23 February 1992 was the date of the first game between Kiltormer and Cashel King Cormacs in their three-game saga which came to be compared to the four-game Meath against Dublin series of the year before. The score at the end was Kiltormer 1-10 Cashel King Cormacs 2-7. This was how the *Tuam Herald*, led in: 'While a draw on away-soil, in front of an 11,000 mostly partisan crowd, was a really good result, the visitors must have felt frustrated having led by eight points after only 20 minutes 1-6 to 0-1. It was all Kiltormer at that stage, Justin Campbell netting in the third minute and the whole team putting in a supreme effort led by the inspirational Conor Hayes, who was outstanding at full-back and who had the better of the duel with Cormac Bonnar, who also found Pakie Dervan a tough nut to crack when moved to centre-half-forward.'

CONNACHT TRIBUNE

John McIntyre's piece in the *Connacht Tribune* was headed 'Majestic Kiltormer Do Galway Hurling Proud'. He selected Conor Hayes as the weekly Sports Star of the week, while the *Tuam Herald* selected Justin Campbell as its man-of-the-match. John McIntyre wrote: 'It was so close to being Kiltormer's greatest hour. From a team performance aspect they never before equalled what they produced at Leahy Park, Tipperary last Sunday — they were breathtaking. The wonder is how they didn't win. In one of the greatest club matches I have ever seen, Kiltormer served up a feast of quality hurling in the first 20 minutes that had favourites Cashel mesmerised and hanging by their fingertips to keep up with the rampant Galway men.'

REPLAY

The replay in Ballinasloe ended in another draw after extra time on the score Kiltormer 1-14 Cashel 2-11. Michael Glynn's *Connacht Tribune* piece read: 'For some inexplicable reason Kiltormer have never done themselves justice during their various reigns as Galway county champions and over three decades there have been inglorious exits at the hands of the Roscommon and London sides... this time it is different. They have twice comprehensively outhurled Cashel only to see it all count for naught. In reality they might now be preparing for the final against Birr on St Patrick's Day instead of facing into a second replay with a side who have only once headed them in the course of 150 minutes of hurling. At Duggan Park they squandered a five-point lead on three separate occasions the last of these in extra time, when, after scoring 1-2, they failed to score in the final 17 minutes.'

ARISTOCRATIC HAYES

Played before an enthusiastic support of over 12,000 Michael Glynn paid tribute to 'the aristocratic performance of Conor Hayes, whose aerial command, surges from defence, lengthy clearances and four points from long range placed balls combined to total the perfect exhibition — a display so complete that it is difficult to remember one better even from his hey-day.'

There was much to gladden the heart from the Kiltormer performance not least the manner in which Cormac Bonnar was held scoreless by a series of markers. The excellence in defence of Brian McManus, Pakie Dervan and Ollie Kilkenny, the invaluable contribution of Tony Kilkenny, when brought to mid-field to complement the workrate of Aidan Staunton was vital and as Mike Glynn put it, credit too to 'the perception and finishing instincts of Justin Campbell and Damian Curley in attack'. Once again the *Connacht Tribune*'s Sports Star Of The Week award went to Conor Hayes.

THE SECOND REPLAY

The *Connacht Tribune*'s heading told it all: 'Kiltormer Slay the Kings'. Kiltormer 2-8 Cashel 1-8. John McIntyre wrote: 'In the end justice was done. Twice before Kiltormer had let Cashel off the hook, failing to put them away and fuelling fears that the chance of entering uncharted territory had once again eluded them. Perhaps forever. Curiously on a day when their superiority over Cashel was far less marked than in the first two encounters, the Galway champions finally earned an historic place in the All-Ireland final against Offaly's Birr. It is a long overdue achievement for a club which has dominated domestic fare since the mid-'70s. Appropriately it was substitute Tony Furey, the veteran of many a long campaign, one of hurling's great modern day opportunists, who put the Kiltormer fans on cloud nine with a priceless goal four minutes from the end of another absorbing encounter.' Martin Staunton rattled the net with a pass from his brother Aidan to leave Kiltormer leading at half-time by 1-3 to 0-5. 'Aidan Staunton rallied his team for one final mighty effort, leading by example and slotting over the equaliser 11 minutes from time.' Cormac Bonnar, who during the series had been eclipsed, levelled the scores at 1-8 apiece with four minutes remaining. Another long raking clearance from Conor Hayes found its way via Dermot Cox to super substitute. Furey for the match-winning goal. It was all over and Kiltormer's huge support in Croke Park on St Patrick's Day went mad. Conor Hayes was magnificent but the man-of-the-match was Aidan Staunton, who was in inspirational form. In the first half corner-back Brendan Dervan was superb and Justin Campbell, when switched to mid-field, was another ace in the pack.

THE FINAL—MARCH 29TH

On 29 March over 16,000 spectators came to Thurles to see Kiltormer triumph over Birr by 0-15 to 1-8. John McIntyre was there to record the triumph. 'They came from the four corners of Galway in support of Kiltormer and the Galway county champions didn't let them down. A great club has finally scaled hurling's Everest, reached the pinnacle of achievement and turned the dream into reality. Past frustrations, disappointments and even the odd disaster in the All-Ireland Club Championship were brushed aside as Kiltormer celebrated the club's greatest day when comfortably disposing of Birr's challenge in Thurles. Their historic All-Ireland win at the fifth attempt completes a memorable two years for the East Galway hurling stronghold during which they have captured two county titles, two Connacht titles, the All-Ireland sevens and now, the greatest prize of them all.'

THE TEAM

Kiltormer were handicapped by the absence of two key players Ollie Kilkenny and Brendan Dervan, two great servants of the club. Their top stars were Justin Campbell, Brian McManus, Damian Curley, Tony Kilkenny, Sean McKeigue and Gerry Kelly, who had been outstanding throughout the campaign. Great credit was given by all to the men in charge John Goode, Seán Cormican, Michael Callagy and trainer Tommy Lally. Veteran forward Seán Kelly summed it all up so well 'we wanted it more than they did'. This was the team:

Sean McKeigue

Brian McManus   Conor Hayes   Kevin Tierney

Fionán Curley   Pakie Dervan   Gerry Kelly

Tony Larkin   Aidan Staunton

Justin Campbell   Tony Kilkenny   Damian Curley

Seán Kelly   Martin Staunton   Dermot Cox

Substitutes: Tony Furey (0-1) for P. Dervan and Tomás Hanrahan for B. McManus, Ollie Kilkenny, Tommy Kilkenny, Kevin Tierney, Peter Staunton, Kieran Lynch and Cathal Curley

Birr's star players were Declan Pilkington, Brian Whelehan and Daithí Regan.

TONY KILKENNY COMPARES

'That club success is the greatest honour I've won. Because you're talking about a fully committed and united community on the move. The inter-county All-Ireland has much more hype and buzz to it but the intensity of a small community would be more meaningful than a county scene.

'We had this dream of emulating what Castlegar did in 1980 and felt we could do it. By the time it came to winning against Birr there were a lot more issues involved. It became a battle of wits between ourselves and Cashel at the finish. The Galway against Tipperary syndrome all over again. The final game versus Birr became only incidental after the three-game-series but that is meant to be no reflection on Birr, or Offaly hurling. On final day we were very vulnerable because it all seemed so secondary. 'We had marvellous celebrations after the third game against Cashel. We were all living on a high during the Cashel series. We had got used to winning and then it was draw after draw. We were almost on automatic pilot all the time. Recovering from one game, straight into another.

'It was great relief to win in the end. We just floated along and the supporters took over. Everyone was on the move in our area of Kiltormer, Clontuskert and Laurencetown. They all came together in a united front. People who had gone away from hurling were all of a sudden in the forefront. Having seen how the people of Galway can become so fragmented, all of a sudden all three areas were together in celebration with bonfires galore.

'The man who really got it going for us was Tommy Lally. He brought a new approach to GAA training — varied, interesting and a good series of manoeuvres, which actually freshened everybody up. All of it coming from a man who knew nothing about hurling but knew all about fitness. We all had a common purpose. John Goode was the player's man, who nursed us all along the way. Seán Cormican we all respected as a former stalwart and Mike Callagy, or Cal as we called him, was always there when the chips were down.'

HISTORY OF THE CLUB

History records a hurling team in Kiltormer in 1886 organised by Patrick Larkin. From 1917, a separate hurling team is recorded for Laurencetown. In 1957 the two clubs amalgamated. Success quickly followed with the winning in 1959 of the East Board Junior Hurling title and then the arrival in the Parish of former Clare star Father Jack Solon in 1959. The present Kiltormer pitch was purchased and developed in 1960 and immediately Father Jack started to organise juvenile hurling and sow the seeds of future success. Many of the senior stars who went on to win County Senior Hurling titles were first coached by Father Solon. Then in 1969 came the amalgamation with Clontuskert. Since 1970 the club has contested County Finals in almost every grade of hurling. The club won County Minor titles in 1972 and 1973, U-21 titles in 1972, 1973, 1975 and 1983, Intermediate in 1975 and the Senior County Cup in 1976, 1977, 1982, 1990, 1991 (five in all) as well as under-age and Primary Schools' County titles.

For a time the club also made great strides in Gaelic football winning the 1979 County Junior crown, followed in 1980 by the Intermediate League and Championship crowns and finally reaching the Galway Senior Football Championship quarter final of 1981 by defeating Corofin before losing out to Dunmore MacHales with the same panel practically as the senior hurling club squad. Splendid playing facilities were developed in Clontuskert and Laurencetown in the mid-1980s and I was present myself at the official opening of Kiltormer's magnificent club centre and playing field in 1988 when Liam Mulvihill (Árd Stiúrthóir CLG) and Bishop Kirby of Clonfert did the honours. The club is very proud of its two All-Ireland seven-a-side titles of 1988 and 1990 hosted by the Kilmacud Crokes GAA club annually.

CONOR HAYES

Conor Hayes is one of Galway's most respected of hurlers. A marvellous captain of Galway's All-Ireland winning teams of 1987 and 1988, the man had charisma and presented a fine image in his high profile capacity. He recalls: 'Kiltormer's efforts to win the club All-Ireland prior to 1991–1992 were chequered. In 1976 we lost to Tremane (Roscommon). Then in 1977, after beating Athenry, we ran into trouble with suspension and Athenry were nominated to go forward to represent Galway. In 1982 I was playing with Glen Rovers when Kiltormer won out again. That was the year St Rynagh's (Offaly) beat us when an incident occurred rather like the 1995 Football All-Ireland Final involving Charlie Redmond. A Rynagh's player who was sent off remained on and was involved in the play before withdrawing. We appealed and lost. Then in 1990 we lost to St Gabriel's (London) and even though most of the exiles were Galway lads, it didn't soften the blow.

'In 1991 after beating Athenry in the County Final we decided there would be no more slip-ups. Many of us were moving on in years; Tony Kilkenny, Seán Kelly and myself had been together a long time. I was quite amazed at the interest generated by the marathon series with Cashel King Cormacs. Winning that club All-Ireland was the perfect finale to my career. I had reached a burnout stage with Galway after contesting the four All-Irelands 1985–1988 in a row and the 1989 debacle against Tipperary soured it all for many of us. My appetite was now gone but I still felt I'd line out with the club for a while. Then we won two county titles in a row and were now facing Cashel of the Bonnars and Ramie Ryan trained by Justin McCarthy, a great hurling man, who specialised in nurturing a very flamboyant style of hurling. A supreme hurling artist himself, we travelled down to see Cashel in action against Clarecastle in Munster and were impressed. I had a few scores to settle with my former opponent Cormac Bonnar. The second game was the daddy of them all. Looking back now winning the club All-Ireland was probably better than the senior All-Ireland because here you were with your roots, the lads you had gone to school with from first class up, Seán McKeigue, Tony Kilkenny, Brendan and Pakie Dervan. You played against some of them in Primary School competitions and then lined out together for the club. The interest created in the community was immense. It was a mighty feeling to bring home the Cup to Kiltormer. I had written myself off and victory at the end was so sweet. I really enjoyed all those games, because it seemed there was less pressure. I remember togging out the last night before the final against Birr and saying to the lads "imagine this is the very last time I'll ever tog out for training again" and it was. Both Birr and Cashel were great sports. The hurling was pure. As I said before it was the perfect finale.'

The History of Kiltormer GAA Club by Paddy Goode was published in 1996.

Kiltormer, AIB Senior Hurling Champions 1992
*Back row: Justin Campbell, Seán Kelly, Tony Larkin, Seán McKeigue, Conor
Hayes, Martin Staunton and Brian McManus.*
*Front row: Dermot Cox, Fionán Curley, Damian Curley, Tony Kilkenny,
Aidan Staunton, Ger Kelly, Kevin Tierney and Pakie Dervan.*

5

St Martins' Centenary Title

St Martin's club represents a completely rural area in North Kilkenny bordering Carlow. The club covers three areas Coon, Muckalee and Ballyfoyle — a very big parish but thinly populated. Their success in winning the Kilkenny Senior Hurling Championship of 1984 marked their one and only title. Prior to that they were better known for their Gaelic football exploits, Muckalee always being known as a football stronghold. When the parish rule came in 1954, Coon formed their own team, eventually gaining senior status after winning junior and intermediate hurling titles, while Muckalee–Ballyfoyle formed their own team, which also graduated to senior status in the same way. Eventually the two senior teams from the same parish came together to form St Martin's in 1982.

In 1995 St Martin's were involved in a relegation play-off for senior status with Ballyhale Shamrocks. Martin's survived while Shamrocks, winners of three senior club All-Irelands, played intermediate in 1996. Their most famous player from the past is Éamonn Morrissey, who played for St Kieran's College in 1984 and usually came on as a substitute for St Martin's in their championship games despite his youth.

MAGNIFICENT MARTIN'S

That was the heading in the *Kilkenny People* of 5 October (Friday) for St Martins' county title win of 1984. The score was St Martin's 1-14 Ballyhale Shamrocks 1-7. John Knox led off his report: 'Hats off to the daring heroes of St Martin's (Coon–Ballyfoyle–Muckalee) the newly crowned Kilkenny

Senior Hurling champions. In a remarkable County Final at Nowlan Park they dethroned the super power of the last six years and reigning All-Ireland champions — Shamrocks (Ballyhale). In a number of ways this turned out to be an astonishing final, after a tense and close beginning. The success-starved winners were never led. They momentarily looked a bit doddery, when hauled back to level terms in the third quarter. But their finish was truly amazing.'

A goal 14 minutes from time by the strong Tom Moran dumped Shamrocks back just when they seemed poised to clinch the game. Then followed a quick point from the dazzling Johnny Brennan and Martin's were on their way. The 10,000 attendance rose to the newcomers as they surged to victory. Stars for the winners were the captain Johnny Brennan who shot 0-11 (seven from frees), Jim Moran in defence, Tom Moran, Tony Maher, Bobby Shore and Michael Maher. At the break Martin's led by 0-7 to 0-4. Seven of the famous Fennelly brothers hurled for the losers in this Shamrocks' first ever loss in a County Senior Hurling Final. There were great celebrations in the North Kilkenny area when the Tom Walsh Cup came home in triumph that night. 'I never experienced anything like it in all my days in hurling,' conceded a delighted St Martin's coach Tom Neville, the former Wexford star, who won All-Ireland Senior Hurling medals in 1960 and 1968 and Paul Kinsella, a fellow selector opined: 'It was the best ever day in sport that this parish has enjoyed. The first is always the sweetest and this being Centenary year made it doubly so.'

LEINSTER FINAL

In the Leinster Final, St Martin's defeated favourites Kinnitty (Offaly) by 2–11 to 0-12 in Athy on 2 December 1984. The atrocious fog conditions along with a 0-2 to 0-6 arrears, with two minutes remaining of the opening half, made the task even more difficult for St Martin's. But it all happened in those fateful two minutes. First Tom Moran goaled. Then his brother Jim along with Johnny Brennan, the captain, pointed to leave it 1-4 to 0-6 at half-time. Well-known hurling team-manager Diarmuid Healy takes up the story in the *Kilkenny People*. 'Another Tom Moran goal within five minutes of the re-start put the North Kilkenny club in command. And when Kinnitty narrowed the gap to a mere two points in the twenty-first minute St Martin's displayed real character and forged ahead once more.'

ALL THE WAY

Nobody had expected St Martin's to win in Kilkenny not to mind in Leinster but the club kept confounding the critics. Would they go all the way? Diarmuid Healy wrote that their display underlined the dictum: 'Where there is a will, there is a way.' He continued: 'The main ingredients of that lesson were a supreme determination, an arrogant confidence and a modest amount of skills. Those along with good marksmanship, well planned tactics and an ability to take the maximum advantage of almost every opportunity has made them a most formidable force.' Tom Moran finished with a personal tally of 2-4. This was another great feather in St Martins' cap. In the All-Ireland Semi-final the Kilkenny champions beat Ballycastle McQuillans in Callan by 3-15 to 2-7. Ballycastle posed a big problem at the start but gradually St Martin's got on top to lead at half-time by 2-7 to 1-3. In the other semi-final Castlegar defeated Sixmilebridge (Clare) by 3-5 to 1–5. And so the no-hopers had made it all the way to the All-Ireland Final on 17 March.

DRAWN GAME

Under a heading 'Brave Martin's Nearly Did It!' the *Kilkenny People* began: 'Great-hearted Kilkenny champions, St Martin's, went within a whisker of winning their first All-Ireland club senior hurling title when they were held to a thrilling draw by spirited Castlegar in the final at Croke Park. A smashing goal, nine minutes from time, by the uncontainable Tom Moran showed the mighty Martin's four points clear and within reach of their greatest success ever. But in a pulsating finish, the Galway champions battled back and Martin O'Shea, a Kilkenny man from Clara, grabbed the scores that forced the final to a replay.' The replay was fixed for Thurles on the following Sunday. Tom Moran once again was the star supreme with a personal tally of 2-3, helped strongly in attack by Jim Moran and Tom Walsh. Gerry McCarthy (*Irish Press*) described a piece of John Connolly magic which led to Martin O'Shea's late goal: 'Once more John Connolly rallied his forces. He came outfield seven minutes from time and wrong-footed the defence with an overhead palmed pass that put Martin O'Shea through. O'Shea carried the sliotar up to goalkeeper Shore before plugging it low with his hand to the net.' Earlier in his report he had paid tribute to goalkeeper Bobby Shore, who was in brilliant form for St Martin's.

REPLAY THRILLER

Michael Fortune in the *Irish Press* was captivated by it all: 'Mere words could not adequately describe this absorbing game which was a wonderful advertisement for the great sport of hurling. The hurling was fast and tough, every ball being contested with incredible fervour and making it a real classic. St Martin's won the replay by 1-13 to 1-10. Castlegar had a slight edge in the first half and led at the break by 1-7 to 1-5. Castlegar still held a two-point lead seven minutes into the second half but from here on in St Martin's started to turn the screw.

'Spurred on by the raking clearances from superb centre-half-back Jim Moran and the effective wing play of Tom Walsh and Michael Maher, the Kilkenny champions piled on the pressure in the second half. John Moran had the edge at mid-field and there were further aces in attack. With dynamic leader Tom Moran taking the attention of three defenders the space was created for Johnny Brennan, Patsy Moran and Danny Coonan to set about winning the Tommy Moore Cup. This they did admirably.'

The *Kilkenny People* used the same banner headline after this win as after the County Final. 'Magnificent Martin's' aptly described it all: 'With the firm conviction that come rain, hail or snow they were going to win this time, St Martin's motored to victory over Castlegar in an absolutely absorbing club Senior Hurling Final at Thurles.' Later on the writer came back to the opening paragraph: 'Indeed one would be left wondering about the conviction concerning the "hail" because it was during a hail shower entering the concluding quarter that St Martin's edged ahead with two points from frees by captain Johnny Brennan in the decisive break of the match.' John Moran received special plaudits – 'his second-half fielding was a joy to watch'. The writer described the scenes at the end: 'The delight of the Martin's players and their band of supporters knew no bounds. All had reason to be proud because from a "no hope" situation at the start of the campaign, the team progressed to make history.'

BONFIRES BLAZED

Bonfires blazed on the hills of Ballyfoyle, Coon and Muckalee to acclaim the heroes. The men in charge Billy Costigan (Chairman and Selector), Paul Kinsella (Secretary and Selector), Dick Nolan (Selector), Tom Neville (Coach), Billy Brett (Trainer) and Mick Behan (Masseur) all received plaudits. Tom Neville said it was 'all about hard work and dedication, with the emphasis on practising the skills of the game'. He revealed the players were very nervous in the dressing-room in Croke Park but the atmosphere in Thurles was more relaxed. This was the winning team:

Bobby Shore

Jimmy Kelly	Tony Maher	J. J. Dowling
Tom Walsh	Jim Moran	Michael Maher

Paddy Lalor   John Moran

John Morrissey	Patsy Moran	Johnny Brennan (capt.)
Danny Coonan	Tom Moran	Richard Maloney

Substitute: Éamonn Morrissey for Paddy Lalor in forty-third minute.

PAUL KINSELLA (SECRETARY–SELECTOR) LOOKS BACK

'Tom Neville came on board as coach and he brought a change of emphasis onto the coaching aspect of things and much more attention was paid to details. Our ambition was to win our first county senior title and everything else after that happened rather than being planned. We never saw anything further than the next game starting with the County Final. We won the County Final and the place went absolutely mad in a very joyful friendly scene of celebration. The team had matured and were prepared to do anything humanly possible to win, to follow any advice, take any instructions.

'They were firm favourites and we worried about how our fellows would handle Croke Park. They got a great start. We were following behind a lot of the time but they were lucky to draw with us. The replay was a brilliant game. The game hinged on Johnny Brennan's two points from frees in the middle of a hailstorm. To score in these conditions in tight circumstances was match-winning. Our mid-fielder Paddy Lalor got injured and we called in Éamonn Morrissey (then only a youngster) and he was only on the field a minute when he scored a point from 70 yards to put us two up.

'We didn't realise what we had achieved just then. In fact that feeling came long afterwards. On the day of the final the late Tom Moran, father of the four Morans, Tom, Jim, John and Patsy, the nucleus of the team, stayed at home to listen to the broadcast. That was the era before local radio and the only live broadcast was by Seán Bán Breathnach on Raidio na Gaeltachta. Well Tom Snr wasn't too good at the Gaeilge and knowing Seán Bán's love of Galway hurling he more than likely generated a sense of gloom. So Tom Moran Snr interpreted the result as a loss for Martin's and proceeded to set off for the local pub to drown his sorrows. When he got there the place was agog and it would be an understatement to say he got the surprise of his life.'

St Martin's, Centenary Champions (1984–1985)
Back row: Jim Moran, John Moran, Richard Moloney, Mikie Maher, Patsy
Moran, Jack Morrissey, Tony Maher, John Morrissey, Tom Moran.
Front row: Billy Brett (Trainer), John James Dowling, Tom Walsh, Bobby
Shore, Johnny Brennan (capt.) Paddy Lawlor, Danny Coonan,
Jimmy Kelly, Tom Neville (Coach).

6
Three Special Trains

The title of this book is evocative of Charles Kickham and '*Knocknagow*' and Tipperary. It is a modification of Matt the Thresher's famous line 'for the honour of the little village'. So it was entirely fitting that my first visit to Tipperary in connection with the book should be to such a rural village as Kilruane and to the home of its most famous hurling son, another 'Matt the Thresher', Len Gaynor the manager of the winning team. He had assembled in his house the club President and local historian, Canon Edward J. Whyte, the Chairman of the club in 1986 Jim Casey, the Principal of the Kilruane National School, and Gilbert Williams, one of four Williams brothers to win All-Ireland club medals.

THE HISTORY OF THE CLUB

Canon Whyte, retired now, took me through the history of the club. 'The club began roughly about 1900 which was called Lahorna De Wet's, a local townland Lahorna and De Wet a hero of the Boer War just ended. In their first year of 1901 they won the North Tipperary Hurling Championship. That team won out in North Tipperary from 1901 to 1909 winning one county title in 1902. Then over the years from 1910 to 1934 there were seven or eight junior teams in the area and when the parish rule came in 1934, meetings were held to unify all the junior teams. It took about three years altogether to get them together to form Kilruane MacDonaghs.'

Thomas MacDonagh

'The club was formed in 1936, called after Thomas MacDonagh, one of the signatories of 1916 and a native of Cloughjordan. The parish is really Cloughjordan made up of two outside areas Ardcroney and Kilruane (we have churches in all three places). There has never been any animosity about the name. I have been President of the club since I came here in the good times when we won three county senior titles on the trot — 1977–1979 and of course for All-Ireland year 1985–1986.

'On Easter Sunday 1966 on the occasion of the golden jubilee of the 1916 Rising, the Thomas MacDonagh GAA Park in Cloughjordan was officially opened by Mr Alf Murray of Armagh, then President of the GAA. In 1968 the pavilion incorporating four dressing-rooms was erected. Another field adjacent to the Park has been acquired and a New Stand was officially opened in 1995. The club is proud of its Park, its five County Senior Hurling titles 1902, 1977–1979, 1985, and a lone Senior Football Championship title in 1975. Len Gaynor is the club's most illustrious player added to the names Tom McLoughney, Gerry McCarthy and the Williams brothers who formed the nucleus of so many successes at club level.

'In the 1985 County Senior Hurling Final Kilruane MacDonaghs defeated their North Tipperary opponents Roscrea by 2-11 to 0-10. Bud Burke (*Midland Tribune*) under a heading "Magnificent Kilruane" praised the winners' splendid second half which saw them come from a 0-8 to 0-4 deficit to win convincingly in the end. Winning captain Tony Sheppard in goal was proud as punch to be presented with the Dan Breen Cup by the then County Chairman and former Minister for Transport Michael Lowry. Len Gaynor, the manager, was chaired shoulder high from Semple Stadium.'

THREE SELECTORS

Jim Casey, a County Councillor from Cloughjordan was Chairman of the club in 1985. 'We had three selectors, Len Gaynor (manager), Billy Shea and myself. Len is the present Chairman. In 1984 we had played Lorrha in the North Tipperary Championship and we hit a low ebb, scoring only three points, and were well beaten. Because things were so bad the club decided to hold a very early AGM — in November 1984. The three of us were appointed selectors and after a long chat, we put a panel together and decided we would call to each player and look for a commitment from them.

'It was an unusual procedure but we got that commitment from the panel we chose finally. We started training at the end of January in the Vocational School in Nenagh. And we started to win games — would you believe a total of 26 out of 28 games up to the time we won the All-Ireland crown.'

The critics had praised Kilruane's spirit after the County Final success. That spirit stood to them again in defeating Tallow (Waterford) in the Munster Semi-final at Tallow in a classic by 1-18 to 1-17. Gilbert Williams was *The Guardian* player-of-the-week, an honour richly deserved. With seconds ticking away and the scores poised at 1-17 each the ice-cool Gilbert scored the winning point from a free from mid-field in a tension-packed finale.

DRAW

The famed Rockies of Cork (Blackrock) were Kilruane's next opponents in the Munster Club Final. A draw of 1-8 each resulted and as Jim O'Sullivan (*Cork Examiner*) wrote: 'It was more a case of Kilruane MacDonaghs failing to win this drawn Munster Final than being held to a draw by a Blackrock side which displayed more courage than skill.' Kilruane led for almost the entire game but a Blackrock rally yielded an equalising point from Pat Moylan with just 20 seconds of normal time remaining. It seemed as if Kilruane MacDonaghs had shot their bolt. John Cahill was *The Guardian* player-of-the-week but in the replay a week later the Tipperary champions won by 0-12 to 0-6 to become Kings of Munster for the first time. John Dundon (*Tipperary Star*) paid tribute to Kilruane's 'steel, courage and fantastic commitment'. Once again jubilant Kilruane players carried team-manager Len Gaynor off the pitch 'a gesture of appreciation from his players for the immense part he played in their Phoenix-like rise from the ashes of indifference of a few years before'. He had sweet praise for wing-back Gilbert Williams 'who really stamped his authority on the game with a second-half display of wing-back play that had "class" written all over it'.

Gilbert Williams's greatest memory of that year was: 'Beating Blackrock gave us tremendous satisfaction. "Cork beaten and the hay saved" is a great saying here. Club rivalries die when Tipperary takes on Cork. It had great historical significance too. They had beaten us in 1978 and 1979 in the Munster Club Championship but more significantly still when Lahorna De Wet's won in 1902 it was Blackrock (representing Cork), who defeated them in the Munster Senior Hurling Championship. My grandfather was on that defeated De Wet's team.

Kilruane's next test was against Desmonds of London, whom they beat in Cloughjordan in Arctic mud-bath conditions by 2-9 to 0-4. Turloughmore (Galway) were next to fall in Nenagh on a bitterly cold February day by 3-9 to 0-9. Cúlbáire (*The Star*) described the win 'as another characteristically resolute exhibition by Kilruane'. The scene was set for the final in Croke Park on 16 March versus Buffer's Alley of Wexford, the club of folk hero Tony Doran.

GILBERT WILLIAMS

'Initially the idea of travelling by train was mooted and most people felt they would travel by car as there would be no traffic problems. As the day approached more and more decided they'd go by train once it was known the team was travelling on the train. Eventually three Specials were booked and the scene in Cloughjordan Station that morning was quite fantastic. The night before I drove down to Cloughjordan to sample the atmosphere which was quite unique. Every house had a black and white flag, bunting on the streets and this gave me and all the team a huge lift. We had a sense of history leaving our own small rural station for Dublin and hopefully victory. Like the exodus of local people to see the Pope in Limerick in 1979.'

Under a heading 'Williams Brothers Clinch It' Paddy Downey, doyen of sportswriters, wrote: 'An attendance of 10,176 spectators witnessed one of the recurrent heartbreaks of sport in Croke Park yesterday when one team had to lose an All-Ireland Inter-club Hurling Final that was balanced on a razor's edge for the greater part of an intensely exciting second half. At the finish it was Buffer's Alley who sipped the bitter cup after the Williams brothers, Gilbert and Jim, broke the deadlock to score a pair of winning points for Kilruane MacDonaghs in the last two minutes of the game.' Later on he gave star billing to Jim Williams for his splendid contribution of 'five great points in the second half. The middle score of those gave Kilruane the lead for the first time in the 41st minute.' The final score was Kilruane MacDonagh's 1-15 Buffer's Alley 2-10. Liz Howard (Tipperary PRO) in *The Guardian* wrote: 'The game was exciting, sporting, spirited and most enjoyable.' Liz selected her men-of-the-match as Jim Williams and Dinny Cahill and painted a lovely picture of the celebratory mood in the Clarence Hotel after the game.

PRIDE OF TIPPERARY

Bud Burke in *The Tribune* dubbed Kilruane 'The Pride of Tipperary'. In rather colourful prose he described the homecoming: 'History was made in the spring sunshine and the hurling heroes of the parish were given a splendid welcome home when they stepped from their special train in Cloughjordan on Sunday evening. Bonfires blazed in the night sky, old men wept with joy and young folk danced and sang the praises of their hurling heroes.' *Cúlbáire* (*The Star*) summed it up: 'They are a remarkable group of players, sharing a common quota of the right spirit. Quite a proportion of them have been together since the beginnings of senior success — and back beyond that to U-21, minor and various juvenile grades.' This was the winning Kilruane MacDonaghs team:

Tony Sheppard (capt.)

John Cahill	Denis O'Meara	Séamus Gibson
Joe Banaghan	Jim O'Meara	Gilbert Williams

Enda Hogan   Denis Cahill

Gerry Williams	Jim Williams	Éamonn O'Shea
Pat Quinlan	Paddy Williams	Philip Quinlan

Substitute: Séamus Hennessy for E. Hogan.

JUVENILE SUCCESSES

Gilbert Williams has these memories of the great effect the win had. 'It had a tremendous effect on hurling in the parish. Juvenile hurling had been traditionally very strong. We had gone through a valley period before 1985 but the All-Ireland provided the impetus for two juvenile county titles in 1989 and 1990. My own school won the North Tipperary National Schools' title in both Gaelic football and hurling in 1990. We had beaten Buffer's Alley in the All-Ireland seven-a-side in 1984 at Kilmacud and were quite confident our direct style of hurling would counteract their traditional Wexford approach of pick and carry. That was borne out on the day. They lifted and carried and we used a more direct style. Offaly to me are the classic example of the way to hurl. "You hit it when you see it," as Timmy Ryan of Ahane used to say. Len was a direct advocate of that. Early in March that year, before the All-Ireland, Father Bertie Troy of Cork came to us for a coaching session on a bleak cold day. He had one simple message for us, "direct hurling is effective hurling". He was preaching to the converted. Here in Tipperary we think it is a criminal offence for a wing-back to solo when he can hit the ball. We got it very close against Buffer's Alley, and we were thrilled when they went on to win the All-Ireland afterwards.'

LEN GAYNOR'S THOUGHTS NOW

Len Gaynor is a man who has given a lifetime to hurling. A very popular team-manager in 1985–1986. 'I grew up in this area and my elder brothers taught me the trade in our own backyard. There were eight of us, four boys, four girls and the girls could hurl too. We had a good yard and a good barndoor for goals. I was the youngest and left minding the goals while the others fought it out the field. I was skinny and small, still am I suppose, and they thought I was too small to make it. It used to sting me then.

'I was very proud of that 1985–1986 team. They were a very experienced bunch, many of them having won three-in-a-row with myself. We were lucky along the way now and again, never more so than against Tallow. To beat Blackrock was brilliant. Should have won the first day and we were written off. There was only a week in between. I brought them in to train on the Saturday. The weather was dry the first day but wet conditions were there the next weekend. So I got them ready in the wet on Saturday and they got used to the conditions and won well the next day. Frank Cummins was a very strong man and a great hurler. One of our guys hit him a shoulder and didn't knock him. A second one of ours hit him a shoulder and failed to stir him. But the significance of the two of our boys ramming into him wasn't lost.

'For the Desmonds' game the word went out we had to travel to London, a false rumour as it happened. At this stage we had got used to hiring a larger fleet of buses for every successive game. One of our greatest supporters got carried away with it all — one Jim Keogh — and said "we'll have to hire a boat to go to London". Croke Park... and with Buffer's Alley in the final. They were a mighty team. But we had great belief in ourselves. We had trained right through for a year without a break. Some people went to Croke Park who had never been there before (or indeed since). After getting to Dublin we had a puck around in the Na Fianna Grounds organised by my good friend Tommy Norton. We were dressed in our pullovers and slacks

47

and I remember when we arrived in Croke Park, the team looked a unit to be proud of.

'They were very officious in Croke Park. Kept us inside when we were ready to go. The fellows were fit to knock down the gates to get out. We didn't play that well in the first half but we didn't let them get too far ahead. They scored two goals early in the game and we had time to recover. In the second half we made our bid for glory and got our goal reasonably early. They didn't give up but fought back again and went a point or two up coming near the end. I was worried but the lads had come through a hard campaign. There was no panic. Eventually we went ahead and held on to win by two points. That was the crowning day of my hurling life. It was the local club. People I grew up with. People I saw growing up after me. Neighbours and friends and relations and everyone tied in together to a common cause.'

Kilruane MacDonaghs, 1986 All-Ireland Champions
Back row: *Jack Darcy, Tom Killackey, John Quinlan, Philip Quinlan, John Cahill, Enda Hogan, Joe Banaghan, Denis O'Meara, Éamon O'Shea, Jim Williams (Éamon Gaynor, supporter), Paddy Williams, Michael Hogan, Paul Mulcahy and Seán Williams.*
Front row: *Éamon Kirby, David Quinlan, Gilbert Williams, Jim O'Meara, Dinny Cahill, Tony Sheppard (capt.), Ger Williams, Séamus Gibson, Pat Quinlan, Séamus Hennessy, Ned Darcy and Ned Fogarty (Masseur).*

7

Sarsfields' Back-to-Backs

Although the Sarsfield's club itself is a comparatively new one, having been founded in 1966, hurling has always been played in the parish of New Inn–Bullaun since the early years of this century. The club was known as New Inn in the 1930s, St Enda's (a combination of Bullaun and Kilrickle) in the 1940s and St Killian's (a union of New Inn and Bullaun) in 1949 right up to the formation of the Sarsfield's club in 1966, after the Galway County Convention of 1966 ruled that there must be only one club in each parish. David McGann, later to become County Board Chairman, was appointed to a teaching post in New Inn in 1960. In 1964 Father McNamara, a Clareman, was appointed to a curacy in Bullaun. Both men with their undying love for the promotion of hurling had a profound effect on the development of Sarsfield's as a hurling power. Sarsfield's won the Galway Intermediate title in 1976 and since then have become the leading club in Galway, winning five County Senior Hurling Championship titles (1980, 1989, 1992, 1993, 1995) before going on to lift five Connacht and two All-Ireland crowns.

THIRD GALWAY TITLE

Sarsfield's won their third Galway Senior Hurling title in 1992. In the Galway Semi-final at Duggan Park, Ballinasloe on 25 October they lowered the colours of the 1992 All-Ireland champions Kiltormer by 0-11 to 0-7. They won the final after a replay with up and coming Carnmore. Noel Morrissey was back with Sarsfield's for the replay and in this game they pulled away to win deservedly. It was the first time I noticed the splendour of Pádhraic Kelly's hurling and the sheer artistry of Joe Cooney shone through. Sarsfield's defeated Oran (Roscommon) in the Connacht Final.

Buffer's Alley were easily defeated in the All-Ireland Semi-final at Wexford Park on 27 February by 4-13 to 1-10. Ronnie Bellew (*The Tuam Herald*): 'Youth and stylish hurling triumphed over experience and brawn at Wexford Park when Sarsfield's overwhelmed Buffer's Alley in a one-sided semi-final. The Galway team's test was made somewhat easier by the unfortunate Buffer's Alley goalkeeper Henry Butler, whose enforced errors were directly responsible for three of Sarsfields' goals.'

Super Sarsfield's

That was the heading of Francis Farragher's (*Connacht Tribune*) tribute to Sarsfields' All-Ireland Final success over Kilmallock in the final at Croke Park on 17 March 1993 on the score 1-17 to 2-7.

'Sarsfield's knocked on the door of greatness and it opened generously in front of them as they seized their chance to take their first All-Ireland with a composed and elegant display of controlled hurling. It was probably as comprehensive a display of hurling as we have ever seen from a Galway team at Croke Park in an All-Ireland Final.'

Sarsfield's conceded two major scores to Kilmallock at the beginning of each half. Helped by a stiffish breeze, the winners led at half-time by 0-11 to 1-1. In the sixth minute of the second half, Kilmallock had a goal from Paddy Kelly. Four minutes later an inspirational point from Mike Houlihan, their best player, left the score 0-12 to 2-2 in Sarsfields' favour. But then the Galwaymen surged again with points from 'Hopper', Joe Cooney and Peter Kelly to ease the situation. Kilmallock rallied with three fine points, Mike Houlihan getting a lovely sideline-cut point, a replica of one by Paddy Kelly in the first half. With five minutes to go the goal came to ease Sarsfields' worries. A long range Joe Cooney shot was fumbled by the Kilmallock goalkeeper Gerard Hanley before knocking it over his own line. That was it. A final magnificent Pádhraic Kelly point sealed Sarsfields' success.

On The Wings

Francis Farragher paid tribute to Michael 'Hopper' McGrath, Peter Kelly and Peter Cooney whose 'play on the wings' destroyed Kilmallock. Then you had the assured free-taking of Aidan Donohue. Of the man-of-the-match, Pádhraic Kelly, he wrote: 'Slow to settle he gave an exhibition of aggressive and compact wing-back play with a series of breathtaking clearances.'

It was a marvellous day for the people of the small 300-house parish of Bullaun and New Inn, summed up best by the words of David McGann, the local teacher who did so much to fashion many of them. 'I remember the junior days when we were glad to keep going — I remember the "Hopper" making a noble contribution with the National School.' Ronnie Bellew in the *Tuam Herald* paid tribute to 'the composed polished striking of Willie Earls and Pádhraic Kelly, Joe Cooney getting on top at mid-field, Noel Morrissey's fierce commitment and the accuracy of Peter Kelly and "Hopper" McGrath'. This was the Sarsfield's team:

Tommy Kenny

Pakie Cooney (capt.)	Brendan Cooney	Michael Cooney
Pádhraic Kelly	Donal Keane	Willie Earls

Noel Morrissey   Joe Cooney

Michael McGrath	Joe McGrath	Aidan Donohue
Peter Kelly	Michael Kenny	Peter Cooney

John McIntyre in a colour piece in the *Connacht Tribune* paid tribute to the Cooney family's contribution: 'It was certainly fitting that a Cooney (Pakie) should lead Sarsfield's to their greatest ever success — the family had made an incalculable contribution to the club's strength. Pakie, Brendan, Michael, Peter, the incomparable Joe, not forgetting the elder statesman Jimmy, a source of strength over the years.'

Pádhraic Kelly, the man-of-the-match, remembers: 'The winning of our two club All-Irelands have been the highlights of my career to date. The atmosphere in our parish during those two years was marvellous. I'd like to thank our three Michaels who were in charge of us — Michael Conneely (Trainer/Coach), Michael Mulkerrins and Michael Murray. Three of our own who had played together on our first ever County Senior Hurling Championship title winning team of 1980.'

GALWAY SENIOR HURLING CHAMPIONSHIP 1993

The big feature of the 1993 Galway Senior Hurling Championship was the return to power of the city-based side Liam Mellowes, who bowed out after a semi-final replay with Carnmore. So we had a repeat of the 1992 final, Sarsfield's winning comfortably by 1-10 to 0-4. Two weeks later Sarsfield's went on to win the Connacht title, defeating Four Roads (Roscommon) by 5-12 to 0-7 and then two weeks later defeated Seán Treacy's (London) in Ruislip (London) by 2-14 to 0-5. The Christmas holidays gave the Galway champions a badly needed rest.

Under a banner headline the *Connacht Tribune*'s Sports Editor John McIntyre, himself a former Sarsfields' team-manager featured, 'Kenny's Goal Turns Tide For Defiant Sarsfield's'. On the same day in Thurles Connacht defeated Leinster in the Railway Cup Hurling Final by 1-11 to 1-10. There had been much furore beforehand concerning the demeaning of this latter fixture but truth to tell the Club Semi-final lent great atmosphere to the Railway Cup occasion, now playing very much second fiddle to the club All-Ireland scene. The club game against St Rynagh's of Banagher was a clinker and Sarsfield's were lucky to carry the day.

John McIntyre led off his report of Sarsfields' win by 1-11 to 1-8 thus: 'It was a day when the team's superstars were consigned to almost background roles and their unsung heroes took central stage as Sarsfield's survived the toughest examination yet of their champion pedigree in a rousing game at Thurles.' All was now set for the final on 17 March against the Munster champions Toomevara, coached by Seán Stack of Clare.

THE FINAL

Peadar O'Brien waxed eloquent in his *Irish Press* tribute to Sarsfields' historic two-in-a-row success by 1-14 to 3-6. 'It was entirely fitting that Sarsfield's from Galway should write their name into the history books of hurling when they became the first club team to win two All-Ireland titles in a row at Croke Park. In the process they overcame a Toomevara team which was reduced to fourteen men for the last 35 minutes and a team whose first-half tactics were, to say the least, debatable. Sarsfields' victory was a tribute to their splendid striking, a great second-half performance particularly from the half-back line and mid-field and some superbly accurate free-taking from man-of-the-match Aidan Donohue.'

Francis Farragher's (*Connacht Tribune*) under a huge headline 'Super Sarsfield's Triumph' led off: 'The record books will show a history-making two-in-a-row of All-Ireland club hurling titles for Sarsfield's but what they will not reveal is the enthralling mix of drama, trauma and tension which marked this heart-stopping final at Croke Park. In the end it was all about resolve, experience and the absolutely crucial quality of never panicking under the most extreme pressure, which was most acute in the concluding seven minutes when Toomevara looked set to hold on for their first ever All-Ireland club hurling title.'

Three goals in the 13th, 29th and 44th minutes rocked Sarsfield's to their roots, the third coming when Sarsfield's were on their way back. 'As the minutes of the final quarter ticked away it became increasingly obvious that it would take a Sarsfield's goal to get them back on course.... and only one man could provide that inspiration. Joe Cooney took on the mantle of responsibility to move up front and try and set up the life-saving goal and what a spectacular effort it was when it came five minutes from time when Toomevara were defending a 3-6 to 0-12 lead. A Pádhraic Kelly sideline cut from the right wing drew an Olympian leap and catch from Cooney, who, almost in the one movement, slipped a short pass to Michael Kenny and from a seemingly impossible angle, "Bottler" crashed the sliotar to the net.' Man-of-the-match billing was given to Joe Cooney 'although he was hard pressed by that most compact package of hurling purée in Pádhraic Kelly'. The winning team was exactly the same as fielded in the previous final, with John Keane coming on for the injured Noel Morrissey.

TEAM-MANAGER'S THOUGHTS

Michael Conneely: 'I never really intended to get into management though I had my own ideas about the job. Then the players put pressure on me and I took it for one year only, with a Galway Senior Hurling title in my sights. And it took off from there. Of the two All-Ireland successes, the first one has to be the most memorable... then to win it for the second successive year and make history when everyone was telling us we couldn't do it!

'Managing is so different from playing. As a goalkeeper I was very much on my own. You tended to think only about your own game and how to perfect it. Minding your own patch. I prefer the managerial end now as I have a great bunch of lads with me. Now I have to think more about the game as a whole, to worry about 15 positions, not just one.'

JOE COONEY'S THOUGHTS

In years to come we will be wondering if Joe Cooney was the greatest Galway hurler of them all. He lives in a lovely pastoral setting in rural Bullaun. 'Here in Bullaun we started our hurling at a young age. We had a very small school and just a seven-a-side team which Frank Corcoran, our present Chairman, used to help organise although he wasn't a teacher in the school. Over in New Inn David McGann was a huge influence in his own school and in our juvenile years later. The whole family of Cooneys were slow developers at hurling really. We seemed to improve after we left National School. Jimmy was the eldest of us. He was the one we all looked up to as he began to play for Galway in 1978. I started playing for the county at U-16 and after that in minor. Believe it or not I started at U-16 level in goal for Galway but was soon moved to the forwards. I was fortunate to be on Galway's first ever All-Ireland winning minor team of 1983. Then followed U-21 and senior successes under Cyril Farrell. We had a great blend of the likes of Conor Hayes, Sylvie Linnane and Steve Mahon, all seasoned strong fellows mixed up with the younger brigade which included myself. I suppose I've jumped into the other category myself now!

'With the club Sarsfield's we were there or thereabouts for five or six years in search of a county senior title after our first in 1980. Then we started to put it together and in 1989 we beat Athenry in the County Final only to lose to Ballyhale Shamrocks in Ballinasloe in the All-Ireland Semi-final. That is a sore memory for me. At the time I was going out with Catherine Mannion (my wife now) and the weather was very wet with huge floods on many roads. I borrowed Brendan's car to collect Catherine but it stalled with the floods and I was late for the game and didn't get into the game for ten minutes. Of course, I was blamed when we were beaten but my delay was due to a series of accidents. Then came the 1992 and 1993 successes in Galway.

'At the final most of our team had never been in a Croke Park dressing-room. To walk in there and leave down your stuff and imagine all the great men who togged out there was a bit unnerving for some. One of our lads Dermot Hynes, sat down beside me and said, "Aren't the dressing-rooms small enough after all", and that about summed it up. It was a big day for a small club. The first final against Kilmallock was one we felt we'd win after about ten minutes. I was on Mike Houlihan, a good tough hurler and I had my hands full all day. Of all the awards I've got, that first one in 1992 tops them all. Better than the senior county All-Irelands. You were there with your own local lads whom you knew all your life which made it special. There were six of us involved (Jimmy was a substitute the first year). Bringing six All-Ireland medals back home felt good. Michael McGrath was very close to me always. We travelled many miles together and being on the senior team a year before me he paved the way for me a fair bit. He is one of my closest friends. Having so many Cooneys playing was a great help. We knew exactly what to expect from each other.

'Winning it for the second time was a great bonus. We were lucky to have Mike Conneely in charge because he never really pushed us too hard. In the second year it was much tougher. It was touch and go in both the semi-final and final. The final against Toomevara was ding-dong all through. This game was the greatest club game I ever played in.

'I was delighted to be honoured with selection on the AIB Silver Jubilee team announced last year. It's an award I'll cherish, probably the greatest I've ever got.'

Sarsfield's AIB All-Ireland Club Hurling Champions 1993
Back row: Michael Cooney, Joe McGrath, Peter Cooney, Tommy Kenny, Joe
Cooney, Brendan Cooney, Noel Morrissey.
Front row: Donal Keane, Aidan Donohue, Pakie Cooney, Peter Kelly,
Pádraic Kelly, Michael McGrath, Willie Earls, Michael Kenny.

8
Keep Right On...

You can't help noticing the fine playing fields, GAA Clubrooms and Social Centre of the enterprising Clann na nGael GAA club just beside the main Galway–Dublin Road, roughly half way between Ballinasloe and Athlone. The night in March 1996 when I visited the club, the senior team was training under a very impressive operation and you could see the floodlit scene from miles away. In the very rural setting of Johnstown I wondered how this place spawned one of the greatest club football teams to come out of the West of Ireland. After meeting Donal Shine, the current Roscommon senior football team-manager, former player and manager of Clann, Vincent Harney, former player and one of the youngest Chairmen ever elected in a GAA club and another former player Liam Dunne, who is one of the club's PR men, I knew why this club ticks.

THE HISTORY OF THE CLUB

In 1936 the two curacies of Drum and Clonown were amalgamated to form Clann na nGael. Just two rural townlands of the Athlone parish of St Peter and Paul. The big breakthrough for the club came in 1961, when the first ever Roscommon Senior Football title was annexed with the defeat of Elphin by 2-8 to 1-10, many of the team coming from the successful county minor title winning teams of the late '50s. Lads like Johnny O'Neill, Tom Cunniffe, P. J. Shine, Tony Whyte, Peter and P. J. Watson, Tony Kenny, Paul Lennon and Seán Dempsey. That was the beginning of a fairytale story of success which has seen the club break and set all records in Connacht club football. In all the club has won 19 Roscommon Senior Football titles (including an eight-in-a-row 1984–1991), and has won six Connacht Senior Football club titles in a row 1984–1989 (they lead the list of title winners with seven) only to lose five All-Ireland finals in the '80s, which included one four-in-a-row of final losses 1987–1990. Such a sequence of losses might have devastated another team, but they never threw in the towel and they continue to hope and pray that their day will come yet.

DONAL SHINE

Donal Shine, who was team-manager during the four-in-a-row All-Ireland sequence, never gave up the fight. I reminded him of my last visit to Johnstown to see the 1985 replay with Castleisland Desmonds. Was he playing then? 'I was indeed. A very wet day. It was my very last game for the club, having played first in 1968 at the age of 17. I took over as team-manager the day I retired. Just 33, I had no problems moving into a new scene, having worked together with the group for so long. In all I won seven Roscommon Senior Football titles and as manager of the club won eight more. Some people say to me that it was a great pity we never won an All-Ireland club title but it was so enjoyable at the time that we hardly missed it. I remember distinctly when we won our first Connacht title in 1982. After winning the county title that year we decided to have a real shot at the Connacht title and won it. We lost out in Roscommon in 1983 but we came back with a vengeance in 1984. The Connacht title became very big for us because to get at the All-Ireland we had to triumph in the West first. Castleisland Desmonds beat us in two All-Ireland Semi-final replays in successive years 1985 and 1986. We were very unlucky not to win the first drawn game in Castleisland in 1985. We learnt to take the rough with the smooth and that attitude helped us to bounce back year after year.

'I also remember chartering trains to Ballina and Castlebar and when we crossed the Border to play Burren (Down) in their home ground in 1989, an amazing number travelled to the North of Ireland for the first time ever.'

Greatest thrill

The greatest thrill in that long sequence? 'Anytime you reached a particular milestone like three County or Connacht titles in a row were major thrills. Because the only other club to do that were Burren, who had been after three-in-a-row of Ulster titles and didn't manage it. Then we went on to record six-in-a-row of Connacht titles. Each year the feeling got better. In 1988 we played Portlaoise in Portlaoise and we were certainly wary of them as they had beaten us well in the 1983 final. It was put down as one of the best club games ever played and we won it by a point. I felt after the semi-finals that we were really on song. Just something didn't go right for us in the finals. The dressing-room scene wasn't that bad really. I always said: "It's a short year since we were here last year lads. We had a great year up to today. One bad day in the year isn't too bad.".'

The legacy was taken by Clann na nGael from the club's involvement on such a high All-Ireland plateau. 'We never treasured it at the time but our name was known throughout the land and we have built up great relationships with clubs and GAA people throughout Ireland. A friend of mine from Athlone named Éamonn Mahon once told me he was hoping we'd get beaten soon we were winning so much, until one night he had to visit his wife in Portiuncula Hospital in Ballinasloe. It was snowing heavily as he passed the Johnstown pitch and he was amazed to see a full field out training. On returning home an hour and a half later he ventured into Johnstown again. Still at it, the twenty-five or more players were doing sit-ups, with me in front of them doing the same thing. Éamonn just didn't want to see us beaten after that! Great relationships were born out there. We really had a great social life and involved all our wives, girlfriends and families in it all.'

Club structure

'There was a lot of passion in the club. There was always someone willing to step in and do the job that needed to be done. Nothing was put in my way in the organisation of challenge games. Finance was always provided. We paid all our bills. We always seemed to have a forward thinking Committee which we kept fresh by introducing young faces every so often. We tried to recycle our players into management especially at under-age level. Before I took over senior management I served my time as juvenile team-manager while I was a player. Now I've taken over as Roscommon team-manager and Tony McManus, our greatest ever player, then took over Clann. It certainly is possible to win the All-Ireland because we have held on to the know-how to win. Finally, my happiest memory of all was the day we won in Burren, seeing the unbridled joy of our supporters as they carried off their heroes in the pelting snow.'

HISTORY AND SEVENS TITLE

The club is rightly proud of its many achievements in titles won at all levels. In latter times a very thriving Ladies' Football club is making its mark. In 1984 Tony Whyte, one of the clubs most respected men, player, manager, wrote the official club history which was launched by Michael O'Hehir. That was published for centenary year 1984. Tony was a superb footballer, being selected for the Ireland team of 1962 for the annual game against the Combined Universities. P. J. Shine was another outstanding Clann man and Tony Kenny, now living in Dublin, is still as keen on the game to-day as when he brought that youthful enthusiasm for the game to UCG in the '60s.

In September 1989 they received some consolation as a club by winning the All-Ireland 'Sevens' title so brilliantly organised by the Kilmacud Crokes club in Glenalbyn on the eve of the All-Ireland Senior Football Final annually. Clann had won an All-Ireland at last, beating the host club in the final by 3-8 to 2-10. It is a tough competition. The winning panel was Paul Naughton, Mike Keegan, Fran Nicholson, Anthony McManus, Joey Connaughton, Paul McManus (capt.), Éamonn McManus Jnr, Éamonn McManus (Snr) and Tony McManus (Manager:Donal Shine). There was a huge reception for the winning Clann na nGael team at St Peter's Church after they crossed the Shannon with an All-Ireland Cup at last.

TONY MCMANUS

In the club's successful run many footballers won many medals and quite a number won representative honours. The pride of them all was Tony McManus who, in a long career, won 14 Roscommon Senior Football Championship medals and became the club's first All-Star in 1989, a feat achieved later by Enon Gavin in 1991. McManus was one of the greatest forwards I have ever seen. But Clann was not a one-man-show by any means. Quality players like Éamonn McManus Snr and Éamonn Jnr, Joey Connaughton, Fran Nicholson, Mike Keegan, Emmett Durney and Enon Gavin starred often for Roscommon as well as Clann.

VINCENT HARNEY

Vincent served as Chairman of the club on three occasions starting in the position as a very young man: 'I became Chairman in 1973 at the age of twenty while still a player (I played on until I was thirty-nine). My second term began in 1983 for four years and my third term began in 1990. In all I won 11 county senior medals, some of them while on the bench and at the end of my playing days a county junior medal which I cherish too. A Treasurer of the club is very important. Martin McManus grew up with me too and for a long period was Treasurer. We were pretty unique in that the main officers were usually active players. Martin, God rest him, died suddenly in 1995 and he is missed a lot.

'Meeting other clubs and visiting their grounds gave us ideas of course. I remember when we first went to Castleisland in 1985 our eyes were opened to the social aspect of a GAA club. We were fortunate to come in contact with this type of hospitality in our formative years. It took some time for us to provide the facilities we now enjoy. Johnstown has always been our home. We had a dressing-room structure which we built in the '70s which served us socially as well but while we loved the place, the facilities were inadequate. We needed more sophistication both in the design of our GAA complex and the provision of extra playing facilities. Our area is one of the few rural areas in the West with a growing population, which in itself is a treasure. Our first priority was a second playing pitch to be floodlit if possible. We acquired the necessary land eventually after a delay of a few years. The GAA centre came next and we incorporated our old dressing-room structure into the design (it is now our weights room and means a lot to many of us). The old structure was opened in 1970 by the late Brian Lenihan and was designed by Paddy Nicholson, one of our greatest club workers ever. We have a bar facility for special occasions, using our local publican to operate it on a lease basis. We have a catering facility too. The official opening of our new Grounds, Clubrooms and Social Centre was performed by GAA President Jack Boothman on 27 August 1994, when the Artane Boys Band was in attendance. I'm very proud of it all and we use the facilities on a regular basis.'

A PRIEST REMEMBERS

Father Ciaran Whitney became curate in Drum in 1989 and even though Father Whitney wasn't much of an enthusiast he quickly became absorbed in the scene. 'On my first Sunday there many people came to welcome me after Mass. Among them were two old women. They asked me was I very involved in the GAA. I confessed that while I was interested, I hadn't been involved very much in the past. One of the women replied, "Ah Father you'd better get involved in Clann because it's the first religion around here."' So Father Whitney got involved and became a member of the club.

'Clann na nGael is not just a football club — it is a massive social movement in the Parish. One has only to socialise after a game with the team and supporters to see that it involves not only the fellows but also their girl-friends, wives, mothers and grannies. It is no surprise then that there are parents available to drive 80–90 youngsters to Johnstown on a Saturday or Sunday morning for training and Parish Leagues. During such a session the priest can drop in and wander around and meet more parishioners than he would meet in two weeks of house to house visitation.'

The Clann na nGael team defeated by Burren in 1988
Back row: Donal Shine (Trainer), Vincent Harney, Paul McManus, Jimmy McManus, Padraig Naughton, Thomas Seery, Michael Keegan, John Dowling, Gerry Lennon.
Front row: Joe Connaughton, Anthony McManus, Tom Lennon, Owen McManus (capt.), Éamon (Jnr) McManus, Tony McManus, Fran Nicholson.

9

From Rags To Riches

My visit to the Kilmacud Crokes GAA club took place on 16 March, the eve of the 1996 AIB All-Ireland Club Finals in Croke Park. A modern addition to the Club Complex at Glenalbyn was nearing completion. A team of hurlers had just togged in after a training session. A packed TV room watched the post mortems of the Ireland against England Rugby International on the big screen. Mattie Glynn, a co-student of mine at St Jarlath's College, Tuam, County Galway, was my host for the evening. The place hummed with life. A focal point in a large community.

The club is undoubtedly the 'youngest' ever to win a club title. Founded in 1966 and based in the Stillorgan–Kilmacud–Mount Merrion area of Dublin City, the club developed from an amalgamation of the long established Crokes hurling club and Kilmacud, a more localised football unit founded in 1959. The Benburbs GAA club from neighbouring Clonskeagh joined up with Kilmacud Crokes in 1972. Both Kilmacud and Crokes had purple and gold as their colours. These colours remained and the Red Hand of Ulster in the club's crest recognises Benburb's connection.

Success at club level wasn't long in coming, especially in the hurling scene. In 1964 the lands of Glenalbyn House and the house itself — one of the stately homes of Stillorgan — were acquired by the club. The Glenalbyn Community Centre was founded in 1968 under the aegis of the club to cater for a wide range of activities. In 1974 a Camogie club was formed. The name of the club has become known nationwide since it began to host the All-Ireland seven-a-side titles in 1973. The big achievements in terms of titles won are two Dublin Senior Football (1992 and 1994), one Leinster Football (1994), one All-Ireland Football (1995), three All-Ireland Sevens Football

(1983, 1988, and 1990), four Dublin Senior Hurling (1966, 1974, 1976, 1985) and two Dublin Senior (B) Camogie titles (1988, 1989). The winning of the AIB club football title of 1995 was the culmination of the dreams of many club members, living and dead, who strove to bring a rural club spirit into the heart of the metropolis.

TOM ROCK

The Chairman of the club, Tom Rock, took me through the club's activities 'The buying of Glenalbyn House and its grounds in 1963 was the brainchild of our then Chairman, the late Micheál De Búrca, the local schoolteacher and a man of great vision, after whom our football pitch is named. The club to-day is still based at Glenalbyn House. At the moment we have fifty teams competing from U-10s to senior in Hurling, Gaelic Football and Camogie. In some age groups we have up to three teams competing. Hurling successes came easier at the start but we eventually won the Dublin Senior Football Championship in 1992, lost in a replayed final in 1993 and won the title again in a replay in 1994. To win the 1995 All-Ireland was the achievement of a life-long ambition of so many of our loyal and industrious workers. The benefits to the club from that success in years to come will be fantastic.'

LARRY RYAN, SECRETARY

'We started the seven-a-side competitions in 1973 for both Gaelic Football and Hurling and Camogie began a year later. The growth of our All-Ireland sevens has made our club known throughout the land. As well as being competitive, the whole occasion is very social. Being Secretary of the club is a huge job but I retired from Telecom last Monday and can give it more time now! Any weekend we could be involved in twenty-four games. Sometimes I'd see ten games a week. We are proud of the fact that our club supplied Dublin's first ever All-Star in hurling, corner forward Mick Birmingham, in 1971 and a second hurling All-Star in our clubman Pat Cleary (Offaly).'

THE MARCH TO VICTORY

After beating St Vincent's by 0-11 to 0-9 in the semi-final with captain Mick Dillon outstanding, Kilmacud Crokes qualified to meet old rivals Erin's Isle in the County Final. Erin's Isle had the Barrs, Keith and Johnny,

Mick Deegan and Charlie Redmond on board and had won their first ever Dublin Senior Football title in 1993 defeating Kilmacud Crokes in a replay. A battle royal ensued, ending in a draw in a thriller on the score 0-12 to Erin's Isles 1-9 at Parnell Park on Saturday 15 October 1994. J. J. Barrett of Tralee, who covers the Dublin GAA scene so comprehensively in the *Evening Herald* wrote that Dublin football 'had one of those pet days when the weather, the huge crowd, the referee Joe Woods and the competition between two fine sides all excelled together'.

In the replay at the same venue a week later the Crokes won after extra time by 1-14 to 2-10. J. J. Barrett paid tribute to the spirit of Erin's Isles who came back from a deficit of 1-8 to 0-4 to be level at full-time 2-6 to 1-9. His man-of-the-match was Mick Dillon. The passage through Leinster was tough. First former All-Ireland champions Baltinglass were beaten at home in Aughrim by 0-12 to 0-11 with John O'Callaghan outstanding at centre-half-back. Next it was a victory over Ferbane at Portlaoise by 4-13 to 1-6 with the three Leahys (not related) Mick, Maurice and Robby in top form.

In the Leinster Final at Newbridge, Seneschalstown (Meath) were beaten by 0-12 to 1-8. Eugene McGee (*Evening Herald*) wrote 'the game matched anything seen at inter-county level this year for effort, hard grafting and dedication'. J.J. Barrett (*Evening Herald*) wrote: 'It was only fitting that the great-hearted warrior of Mike Sweeney's Galway blood — son John — should run onto Paddy O'Donoghue's defence — splitting pass and with a vengeance the Crokes defender lashed over the winning point.'

In the All-Ireland Semi-final on 26 February in Thurles, Crokes against the odds beat Castlehaven by 1-11 to 1-7. Even the West Cork paper the *Southern Star* wrote that the losers got away lightly. Seán Moran in *The Irish Times* praised the winners who were, as he put it 'more of a unit and less dependent on individuals' than the opposition. He lauded 'the overwhelming contributions from the venerable Mick Leahy and Niall Clancy'.

THE FINAL

The club published a special issue of the club's magazine Macalla for the occasion. A full programme for the day was organised starting with Brunch at Glenalbyn House at 10 a.m. on Lá le Pádhraic 1995. A special fleet of buses bedecked in the club colours departed Glenalbyn at 11.45 a.m. Banquet in Marquee at 6.00 p.m. followed by Music and Dance at 8 p.m. To start with, the game with Bellaghy Wolfe Tones, whom I had seen deservedly beat Tuam Stars in Enniskillen. The day was bitterly cold, worsened by the prevalence of a gale force wind. In the end Kilmacud Crokes won their first All-Ireland AIB Club Final by 0-8 to 0-5.

Peadar O'Brien (*Irish Press*) led off: 'Mick Pender, the Dublin reserve goalkeeper, was just one of the heroes of an almost incredible hour's football in Kilmacud Crokes' first All-Ireland success. Pender moved superbly to his right to deflect for a "45" a last gasp penalty from Bellaghy full-forward Damian Cassidy. And immediately after that "45" was kicked wide and the ball kicked out, referee Paddy Russell from Tipperary signalled the end.' It was a fitting result to a splendid game in the prevailing conditions. The winners, aided by the wind, led at half-time by 0-6 to 0-1. Was it enough against Bellaghy, who fought like terriers into the wind? The winners surprised everybody by taking the game to Bellaghy at the start of the second half and they scored two precious points into the hurricane to lead 0-8 to 0-1 with twelve minutes remaining. Now Bellaghy found the range, inspired by Karl Diamond, with four points in a row before the dramatic finish already described. Tom O'Riordan (*Irish Independent*) praised the tenacity, fitness and unshakeable resolve of the winners. Vincent Hogan (also of the *Irish Independent*) in a colour piece, which is his forte, lauded the winners' big men 'John O'Callaghan, John Sweeney, Pat Burke, Mick Leahy and Mick Dillon'. J. J. Barrett (*Evening Herald*) paid tribute to a magnificent triumvirate 'the back-room men, the fans and the players who defied the odds to bring such glory to South Dublin'. In over 40 years of viewing games at Croke Park it was the coldest and windiest I ever remember.

The winning team was:

	Mick Pender	
Rory Ward	Con Cleary	Robbie Leahy
John O'Callaghan	John Sweeney	Pat Burke
Mick Dillon (capt.)	Mick Leahy	
Padraig Dalton	Séamus Morris	Peter Ward
Niall Clancy	Maurice Leahy	Pádraig O'Donoghue

Substitute: Tommy Gunning for Maurice Leahy.

MEET THE MANAGER

Tommy Lyons, the successful team-manager is of Mayo stock, whose father Tommy 'Tansey' Lyons played alongside Seán Purcell in St Jarlath's College, Tuam's first ever Hogan Cup success in 1947. Tommy Junior was reared in Castlebar before going to live in Dublin at the age of 10. 'The seeds of the love of football were sown in me by my Dad. Ours was a football-mad house. The Lyons brothers of Meath are our second cousins and so is John Gibbons of Mayo and Meath fame. I played for Kilmacud Crokes but a bad knee injury at the age of 19 curtailed me somewhat. Kilmacud Crokes has been everything to me since. Dom Twomey, nicknamed "The Fish", taught me in Clonkeen College and had a big influence on me. I was a surprise choice as team-manager, having retired from senior football two years before in 1989. I wouldn't have challenged Martin Glynn, who was the team-manager. But Martin agreed to join my selectorial team. We went on to win our first county senior title in 1992, rare for a South Dublin club, the power base of Dublin football being in North Dublin for so long. We won our first All-Ireland Sevens title in 1983 — I was on that team. What I tried to do was mould a group of guys together and put a bit of passion and heart into them. We tried to create the village concept in a city club. We insisted on the senior players getting involved with our juveniles. We made an inspired choice at the time of Mick Dillon as senior captain.'

1992 county title

'Winning the 1992 County Senior Football Championship title was very big — our first. The Dublin Club Championship is by far the hardest one to win in this country. We beat Thomas Davis in a replay in the semi-final, a club which had won three county senior titles in a row and were just pipped that year in the All-Ireland Final by Dr Crokes of Killarney. Bringing the Cup across the Liffey to the Southside was a great thrill. In fact six of the last eight Dublin Senior Football Championship titles have come Southside. My greatest memory of this team was beating Erin's Isle in extra time in the replay of the 1994 final. That was my greatest thrill in management.

'I've had two dreams in my life. One was to win the club All-Ireland. In 1992 we didn't put our heart really into it. 1994 was different. First we beat Baltinglass in Aughrim who had never been beaten in Aughrim in Leinster club football. An easy win over Ferbane followed. Between Erin's Isle,

Baltinglass and Ferbane all of our scores were from play, save one point. Football played on the move. Then followed our first Leinster title win and then the win over Castlehaven. We played our purest football ever that day and won well. My football philosophy revolves around positivity. Too many GAA teams go in for spoiling tactics. My defenders were instructed never to foul. It was an incredible moment to win the All-Ireland, my best ever. My second dream is to manage an All-Ireland winning senior county team.'

SEÁN DONNELLY

Chairman for fourteen years in its formative times, Seán can look back on the growth with pride. 'In 1970 our highest adult football team was playing the lowest junior football grade — Division III. So when you put our All-Ireland victory of 1995 into that context, it is an incredible rags to riches story. My link with both ends of that is, that I was captain of the junior team of 1970, our first football team to win a county football trophy and a selector on the All-Ireland team of 1995.

'In our complex here we have one full pitch, two full pitches in Silver Park beside Leopardstown Racecourse, land we acquired in 1980, two more leased from the County Council in Mount Merrion and we have pitches available to use from both Benildus and Oatlands Colleges. At any one time we can call on seven pitches.'

DILLON AND LEAHY

Mick Dillon came to Dublin from Wexford in 1985 and joined Kilmacud Crokes. 'Declan Clancy, Niall's elder brother, who worked with me, was the man who first introduced me to the club. My major commitment to the club began when Tommy Lyons took over. He asked me to become captain for the Sevens of 1991 and it began from there. I've been captain ever since — for the 1992 title and all that happened in 1994–1995 including our first ever Division I Senior Football League title in 1994. A great relationship developed between the manager and myself. Anything coming from the players came through me. We communicated a lot, daily almost and got on very well together. As to the team there is a great bond between all of us. We socialize together as well as playing together.

'It was a tremendous honour to captain the team and to receive the Andy Merrigan Cup. Going to the schools with the Cup is another great memory. I was lucky to be the one in charge of a great bunch of fellows. My greatest memories of it all would include the scenes in Thurles after beating Castlehaven.'

The charismatic figure of the Kilmacud Crokes team which won the All-Ireland has to be mid-fielder Mick Leahy. 'I'm playing with the Crokes since 1980–1981. I had my ups and downs in 1992. Was dropped by Tommy in 1992 and that kick in the pants helped shake me up. I was thirty-three then but when I was introduced as a substitute late in the first half of the 1992 final against Civil Service there was plenty of fire in my belly. Dropping me had really fired me and I think it was one of my better games.

'Winning the All-Ireland provided me with a numb feeling on the day. I was so delighted for so many guys who served our club for so long.'

Kilmacud Crokes, All-Ireland Club Football Champions 1995
Back row: Mick Jones, Séamus Morris, Frank Rutledge, Ken Lenihan,
Mick Leahy, Tomás Ó Flatharta, Gavin Gray, Mark Duncan,
Mick Pender
Middle Row:Niall Clancy, Rory Ward, Paul Walsh, Charlie Mitchell, John
Sweeney, Maurice Leahy, John O'Callaghan, Colin Redmond,
Paddy O'Donoghue, Con Cleary.
Front row: Seán Donnelly (Selector), Tom Lyons (Manager), Robbie Leahy,
Tommy Gunning, Pat Burke (Vice-capt.), Mick Dillon (capt.),
Pádraig Forde, Pádraig Dalton, Peter Ward, Dom Twomey
(Selector), Martin Glynn (Selector).

10
Sixmilebridge

It was inevitable after Clare's All-Ireland Senior Hurling Championship win of 1995 and the subsequent emotional scenes in Croke Park and elsewhere that the Clare Senior Hurling Championship of 1995, which had still to be concluded, would be a cherished and hard-won title. I saw Down break the barrier in 1960. I was there when Galway broke all the hoodoos in 1980. It was the end of a fifty-seven-year drought. I saw Offaly win their first in hurling and football and the recent Donegal and Derry triumphs. But nothing compared to the scenes after Clare succeeded in 1995. It was their first ever Senior Hurling Championship success in Croke Park — their second in all — and their first success since 1914, 81 years before.

The Canon Hamilton Cup, which commemorates a former legendary Clare GAA official, is the prize for the Clare Senior Hurling Championship. Sixmilebridge had a good win over Newmarket-on-Fergus by 2-8 to 0-9 but in the quarter final they survived by the skin of their teeth against a fast finishing Tulla team by 3-13 to 4-9. Then followed an easy win over Cratloe by 1-23 to 0-4 and all was set for the County Final against Scariff in Cusack Park, Ennis on 29 October. Sixmilebridge were the firm favourites, seeking their 8th County Final success. Their's was the great success story of club hurling in Clare for the past two decades — 1977, 1979, 1983, 1984, 1989, 1992 and 1993. Some players had seen success in many of those finals.

It was entirely fitting that the Clare hurling showpiece of 1995 should do justice to the year. Séamus Hayes, who has covered Clare hurling for so long in the *Clare Champion*, described it as 'one of the best Clare Senior Hurling Championship finals for many years. The East-Clare-side produced a marvellous display which saw them lead the hot favourites from the second minute until a last minute goal gave Sixmilebridge victory. For Sixmilebridge substitute, David Chaplin, it was indeed a special occasion. Sent in to replace elder brother Danny with just over five minutes remaining, he got the vital goal after a Gerry McInerney effort from 50 metres had rebounded off the post into his path.' The game will long be remembered for David Fitzgerald's outstanding double save midway through the second half; the great impact made by Sixmilebridge substitute Pat Hayes and the vital contribution of the very experienced Gerry McInerney, whose entire Championship total of 3-13 won for him the Top Scorer Award.

FLAN QUILLIGAN

For Flan Quilligan it was a special occasion. He alone of the squad was winning a unique eighth county medal having been part of every 'Bridge success. A great day too for the Chaplin family, four of whom, Christy, John, David and Danny, won medals, bringing the family collection to a huge 17. Top scorer Gerry McInerney won his seventh medal. It was a special day too for the men in charge: selectors Mick O'Shea, John Nihill, Jim Fawl (Trainer) and Pat Morey (Coach). The latter, together with Sixmilebridge's most famous star Seán Stack, had been part of all previous seven triumphs.

Munster success came quickly and more easily than anticipated. First Ballygunner of Waterford were beaten in their own Walsh Park by 5-11 to 2-10. Long-serving Flan Quilligan was quite outstanding, getting inspired assistance from the Chaplin brothers John and Christy and Noel Earley. In the final proper at Páirc na nGael, Limerick, before 7,125 spectators, Séamus Hayes (*Clare Champion*) described Sixmilebridge's easy win by 2-18 to 1-7 over Éire Óg, Nenagh as 'arguably Sixmilebridge's greatest ever performance'.

It was a particularly special occasion for county men David Fitzgerald, Michael O'Halloran, John and Christy Chaplin, who were part of the great Clare team of 1995 and a fitting finale to a fine year for Clare.

SARSFIELD'S

Sarsfield's of Galway were the next big obstacle, the only club to win two All-Ireland hurling club titles back-to-back. Sarsfield's were forced to line out without star half-back Pádraig Kelly and regular goalkeeper Tommy

Kenny, who was replaced by Francis Madden, playing his first ever Senior Hurling Championship game. Although the injured Kelly did come on as a substitute, the absence of goalkeeper Tommy Kenny proved too much and Sixmilebridge powered to a 5-11 to 1-12 victory, with veterans Gerry McInerney and Flan Quilligan contributing 3-6 of the winners' total. Played in a downpour at Semple Stadium, Thurles, the winners started superbly and were 1-3 to 0-1 ahead after eight minutes. Inaccuracy frequently proved their undoing and they should have been further ahead than 2-5 to 1-5 at half-time. Sarsfield's took the initiative in the third quarter, when they went into a one-point lead. A late tackle on Sarsfields' Joe Cooney in the 44th minute completely curbed his contribution and the advent of Gerry McInerney to centre-half-forward from the corner at the same time had a significant bearing on Sixmilebridge's last quarter dominance. As Liam Horan (*Irish Independent*) reported 'McInerney took the baton'. The winners were very well served by John Chaplin at mid-field and in defence by Kevin McInerney and John O'Connell. In Sixmilebridge's late flourish, goals by David Chaplin, Quilligan and Danny Chaplin presented a final scoreline which did not reflect Sarsfields' great efforts in the first three quarters of the game. It was a well deserved win for Sixmilebridge, who now faced Dunloy Cuchulainns (Antrim), who surprisingly beat Glenmore (Kilkenny) by 2-13 to 0-7 in the other semi-final at Croke Park. Dunloy were appearing in their second successive final having drawn with Birr on the previous St Patrick's Day.

Momentous Week

It had been a momentous week for me. I flew to Dublin on the Saturday from Stanstead Airport after a very satisfying Cheltenham Racing Festival featuring so many Irish victories. A visit to the Kilmacud Crokes GAA club on the Saturday night (16 March) whetted my appetite for the morrow, which also featured the football final of Éire Óg of Carlow and Laune Rangers of Kerry. St Patrick's Day dawned sunny but cold. The St Patrick's Day Parade made it difficult to get to Croke Park in time for the first game at 2 p.m. between Dunloy and The 'Bridge. Gerry McInerney deputised as captain for the injured Ian Mulready. Each club was very well supported in an attendance of over 20,000.

Tom O'Riordan (*Irish Independent*) led off his report of Sixmilebridge's All-Ireland triumph by 5-10 to 2-6 thus: 'Another unforgettable day in an extraordinary few months for Clare hurling came with Sixmilebridge's victory over Dunloy in the AIB Club Final at Croke Park. In the end the pure strength and fitness of the Clare champions not alone overwhelmed Dunloy but left them drained, exhausted and almost without spirit during the closing 16 minutes. In that spell Dunloy failed to raise a flag as the well-balanced Clare side exposed their limitations with some superb scores, turning a two-point lead (3-5 to 2-6) into a rout as they raced through with points from all angles near the finish.' Séamus Hayes in a special supplement of the *Clare Champion* paid tribute to 'the brilliant performances of central defenders Kevin "Socks" McInerney and John O'Connell together with two excellent goals from David Chaplin as the inspirations of their success'.

The margin, as in the semi-final, may have been flattering but again there was no denying the fact that Sixmilebridge were utterly deserving champions and there were many great scenes of joy and emotion before Ian Mulready went to the podium to receive the Tommy Moore Cup from GAA President Jack Boothman.

BONFIRES BLAZED

Bonfires blazed across the parish of Sixmilebridge on the Monday night of the 18 March and thousands turned up to greet the champions home atop an open double decker Bus Éireann bus with the Tommy Moore Cup held aloft. It had been a great honour for the 'Bridge to march behind the Artane Boys Band on final day but to bring home the Cup was the ultimate. Jim Fawl, the trainer said: 'I never doubted the team's ability to win but was a little concerned in the second half when just two points separated the sides.' Flan Quilligan of the eight medals said: 'It's really a great day for the club'. This was the winning team:

David Fitzgerald

Michael O'Halloran   Kevin McInerney   Michael Twomey

Christy Chaplin   John O'Connell   Pat Hayes

John Chaplin   Noel Earley

David Chaplin   Flan Quilligan   Martin Conlan

Declan McInerney   Danny Chaplin   Gerry McInerney

Substitutes: Ian Mulready, who came on for Danny Chaplin (57 minutes), Niall Gilligan (0-3) for Quilligan (43 minutes) Noel O'Gorman for Hayes (40 minutes), Brendan Flynn, Alan Mulready, Alan White, Séamus Cusack, Keith Walker and Carey Downes.

DAVID FITZGERALD

Davy Fitzgerald, son of Clare County GAA Secretary, Pat, is the impish teenage-looking goalkeeper of Clare, Sixmilebridge and Munster hurlers. When he walked into the foyer of the West County Hotel, next door almost to his *alma mater* St Flannan's College, Ennis, I was amazed at his humility, for his goal-keeping has the flamboyant touch of the late Ollie Walsh. It was the end of a glorious two or three weeks for the 24-year-old Powerscreen All-Star goalkeeper of 1995. First it was the historic victory of Sixmilebridge on St Patrick's Day. On the following day in Cusack Park, Ennis he shone in goal for Munster hurlers in the Railway Cup Final, getting a huge lift from the crowd. Then followed a good National Hurling League win over Cork, in Cork. Finally he joined the Sixmilebridge squad belatedly for a Continental holiday. 'It has been a year I'll never forget. Anything I played in I seemed to win, bar our National Hurling League Final loss to Kilkenny in 1995.'

How does the jovial Sixmilebridge lad compare the two All-Ireland wins? 'Winning the All-Ireland with Clare was very special. But winning the AIB Club All-Ireland with Sixmilebridge — where I started hurling along with the lads I knew and grew up with — made it a bit more special in that sense. To have so many clubs in Ireland competing for that honour and to come out on top after it all gives you a very special feeling. Bringing the Cup back to the 'Bridge was unbelievable. I got very emotional as I never anticipated the huge crowds that came on that Monday night from all over Clare. The square was packed to capacity — the biggest crowd ever assembled in Sixmilebridge.

'Christy Chaplin was a classmate of mine in both the National School and later for a few years in St Flannan's. Alan White, one of our panel, was with us too. John Chaplin was a year or two ahead of us. Martin Conlan was a few years behind. The first man to start me playing hurling was my uncle John Fitzgerald, an O'Callaghan Mills man. But my great playing idol always was Gerry McInerney. He was always in our house and whether with Clare or

73

the club his style of play was exceptional. In all I've won four County titles but this year's one is the most precious. Over a period of a few years our club had a lot of hardship. We lost three Munster club finals and that was sore. 1992 was probably the worst year. We lost the Munster Club Final to Kilmallock. A day or two after that we lost one of our players Pádhraic McNamara, same age as myself, just about to play for the county and that was a dreadful shock. I'd have to say we were fortunate to beat Scariff in the final.

'Another man who did a lot for my hurling was John Lynch, who captained the Clare minor team in 1981 to win the Munster title. I lived right beside him on Thomond Terrace. There was a factory nearby and every night he pummelled me with shots at goal, left, right and centre, hour after hour. Flan Quilligan and Pat Morey have been the backbone of our team, not the county fellows like myself; add on Danny Chaplin and Gerry McInerney. The four county players on the team are just ordinary lads. Those fellows had made the club tick and the respect we all have for them is immense. They are very down to earth, make everything simple and they push us all hard. Seán Stack wasn't on the panel this year but was a pillar in the past. He still keeps tipping around. Noel Casey is another former star. We also had Paddy Meehan and Kieran O'Shea, son of present selector Mick.'

Greatest memory

'The County Final is a special memory. Down a couple of points and the time up. I pulled down a ball going over the bar, hit it out, caught by Gerry McInerney. He hit the post and we stuck it in the net. One single minute turned our whole year. It has been a great year but we still have our feet close to the ground. We know what it is like to be down and winning nothing.'

Davy is remembered for his penalty goal against Limerick in 1995. 'I'll not forget it. A lot of people will remember my joy at scoring it and the race back to goal. I love doing things that I shouldn't be doing. Compare it to the goal I let in in the All-Ireland Final. I felt badly after that but recovered.'

Non-drinker and non-smoker

Has he any message on life for the youth of Ireland? 'You're young for a certain length of time and there are better things to be doing than drinking and smoking. I never drank alcohol or smoked. You should get out there and get involved in sport. When you come to 18 or 19, that's the time to make up your mind whether you want to drink or smoke.'

When asked if he modelled himself on anybody he said: 'I was glued to one position whenever Clare played and that was behind Séamus Durack's goal. I watched every move he made and modelled myself on him. He was flamboyant too. He liked to come off his line as I do. I was at Ollie Walsh's funeral and have great respect for his son Michael's goalkeeping. Goalkeepers are a breed unto themselves. It's a tough position. Lonely enough. You have to be totally focused all the time in a game even if you never have to save a ball.'

Sixmilebridge, All-Ireland Champions Sixmilebridge 1996
Back row: Danny Chaplin, Michael O'Halloran, Kevin McInerney, John
Chaplin, David Fitzgerald, David Chaplin, Pat Hayes, Mike
Twomey
Front row: Christy Chaplin, Martin Conlon, Gerry McInerney, John
O'Connell, Declan McInerney, Flan Quilligan, Noel Earley.

11

Laune Rangers

Laune Rangers of Killorglin have a proud place in Kerry's football history. According to club historian Pat O'Shea the club was founded as a result of a meeting at the door of Jimmy Coffey's pub in 1887. They won the Kerry Senior Football title in 1889, 1890, 1892, 1893, 1900 and 1911. In 1892 representing Kerry, Laune Rangers won their first Munster title accounting for Dungarvan (Waterford) in Fermoy before losing to Young Irelands of Dublin in the All-Ireland Final at Clonturk Park. They could hardly have imagined in those far-off days that it would take over 100 years for another Laune Rangers team to reach an All-Ireland Final. Only this time it was to be a successful one. Then followed the lean years, when the football star almost disappeared. Present Joint Club Treasurer Jimmy Coffey remembers the lean years of the 1950s and the joy of winning the first of many Mid-Kerry titles in 1958.

The club took the momentous decision to re-enter the County Championship in 1970 after an absence of 51 years. Bleak years followed, but a youth policy was embarked upon with Pat O'Shea as the chief architect aided by Liam Shannon, Noel O'Mahony and present Club Chairman, Jerome Conway. In the intervening 25 years the club has won 23 county juvenile and five county minor titles. Eventually the Kerry Senior Football Championship title was lifted in 1989 under the guidance of Noel O'Mahony. John Evans took over in 1991 and led the team to further County Senior Football Championship successes in 1993, 1995, and 1996.

KERRY FINALS

The County Final of 1995 saw Laune Rangers defeat East Kerry by 1-7 to 0–6. It was a poor game, described by Mikey Sheehy as 'the worst County Final seen by me'. East Kerry failed to convert a penalty in the 17th minute and this save, coupled with an opportunist goal by ace striker Gerard Murphy, the captain, early in the second quarter set the winners on the high road to success. The winners may thank the mid-field supremacy of Timmy Fleming and Pierce Prendiville over Séamus Moynihan and Donal Daly. *The Kerryman* newspaper devoted five pages to the triumph with a half page colour photo of Mike Hassett powering through. Typical of the spirit of Kerry club football was the remark of county star Séamus Moynihan when he visited the winning dressing-room: 'Don't stop now lads and keep the Kerry flag flying.' Solid centre-half-back Tommy Byrne won the AIB man-of-the-match award and both Seán Moran (*The Irish Times*) and Mikey Sheehy, paid tribute to 'the brilliance of Billy O Sé'. There was a huge reception in Killorglin that night for the arrival of the team with the Bishop Moynihan Cup. Pat Costelloe, a Killorglin man based in London for 30 years, came home for the game and the celebrations. 'I did the same in 1989,' he said with joy as he inhaled the happiness and joy and recalled happy days of yore. The Munster title loomed ahead. The first game was a daunting task against the Cork champions Bantry Blues in their own Wolfe Tone Park.

In a very close game Laune Rangers triumphed in the end by 2-8 to 1-10. Éamon Horan of *The Kerryman* was ecstatic: 'In recent years Laune Rangers have had several notable triumphs including their successes in the County Senior Football Championship. But I doubt if any of these triumphs would quite match the magnificent victory over a stout-hearted Bantry Blues team last Sunday. Before 5,000 spectators Laune Rangers in a titanic finish held out for the narrowest of wins after a tremendous fightback by the losers in the final eight minutes which had the big attendance spellbound in a welter of drama and excitement.' It was a marvellous team performance and Gerard Murphy was the star of the day. He finished with a personal tally of 2-4 and 'dazed and dazzled the opposition with the sheer skill of his football from start to finish'. The Munster Final win by 3-19 to 2-4 over Moyle Rovers (Tipperary) at Páirc Uí Rinn, Cork was an anti-climax by comparison.

Semi-final Against Corofin

Semi-final day, 18 February 1996, was one of the coldest, windiest and wettest days of a bad winter. Yet a huge crowd came to Cusack Park, Ennis, to see Clare hurlers beaten by Kilkenny and the weather conditions tended to worsen for the Football Semi-final between Laune Rangers and Corofin (Galway) later in the programme. I'm oftentimes amazed at how the club championships have come to develop and prosper despite their timing, which very often clashes with inclement weather of all kinds. Hail or shine the competitions grow in esteem with the passing years. In a close encounter Laune Rangers were lucky enough to survive a late burst by Corofin to win by 0-8 to 0-6.

Corofin, aided by a gale, led at half-time by 0-3 to 0-2 and that lead didn't seem adequate. Rangers had battled heroically to contain the Galwaymen all through the first half, none more than strong centre-half-back Tommy Byrne, a tower of strength ably supported by the Hassetts, Mike and Adrian, and Mark O'Connor. The winners were forced to field without Gerard Murphy for whom Billy O'Sullivan, former Kerry U-21 star, deputised so ably. The rain continued to spill down in the second half and Timmy Fleming pointed to level. The expected avalanche of Kerry scores never came. Billy O'Shea got the lead point and Conor Kearney, who had a star game second half, kicked a brilliant point. Fleming and Prendiville were lording it at mid-field and when Fleming pointed in the 45th minute to leave it 0-6 to 0-3 the game seemed over. Corofin showed a brave heart and hugged it back 0-6 to 0-5 with 10 minutes remaining. The winners held on for a deserved triumph by 0-8 to 0-6. Tommy Byrne was my star of the day.

The Kerryman

St Patrick's Day 1996 dawned well but a cold rain engulfed Croke Park in the afternoon. Nothing to compare with the dreadful conditions of the year before. *The Kerryman* supplement brilliantly portrayed the story of Laune Rangers, 12 pages in full colour, pen-pictures and absorbing articles from Jimmy Coffey and Jerome Conway. Kerry people glory in little hype, in being taken for granted. The perfect scenario for a Kerry win.

It was a rattling great game. The Rangers got the goals that mattered at the best times — the start, two before half-time and the killer fourth nearing the finish to copper-fasten victory. Right from the word go the Kerry team played with purpose and discipline. My star of the day, Michael Hassett, set a high standard and kept a cool head though opposed by Willie Quinlan, small in physique but big in heart, and gifted with marvellous acceleration which is so rare nowadays. Éire Óg recovered from Gerard Murphy's goal in the third minute after a combined move involving Mike Hassett and Paul Griffin. The Carlow men had won the toss and elected to face the wind. By the seventh minute Éire Óg had drawn level with a succession of great points, one in particular from Joe Hayden after a flowing movement involving many Éire Óg players. 'This was a final that throbbed with excitement and passion.' (Éamon Horan, *The Kerryman*). It was nip and tuck all the way, Éire Óg favouring the short passing game, Rangers varying the possession game with some direct play. Mid-field honours were flowing Éire Óg's way with Jody Morrissey and Hugh Brennan on top of Timmy Fleming and Pierce Prendiville. Approaching half-time Laune Rangers were just staying with Éire Óg when, being led by 0-6 to 1–2, they shot back with as good a goal as I've ever seen in Croke Park in a final. The game was 27 minutes old when Timmy Fleming directed a free to Liam Hassett, who in turn passed to Billy O'Shea on the burst, who raced goalwards and shot to the net in a brilliant example of the move orchestrated by Mick O'Dwyer in the 1970s. Éire Óg were now in tatters. Gerard Murphy first timed a shot over the bar in the 28th minute and then came the doubtful penalty award against Éire Óg goalkeeper John Kearns, who upended Gerard Murphy in the area of the square. The penalty decision was disputed both on the field and in the press box. But with no frills Laune Rangers' dependable centre-half-back Tommy Byrne came up and drilled it home. There was no sympathy or indecision. The half-time whistle sounded 3-3 to 0-6 in Laune Rangers' favour. Éire Óg's first-half dominance didn't deserve this.

FIGHT BACK

Would Éire Óg fight back? Fight back they did, with Garvan Ware now switching with Jody Morrissey and with ten minutes to go the score read 3-4 to 0-11, just two points in it and all to play for. Laune Rangers' defence was now magnificent under pressure. In the 53rd minute Timmy Fleming pointed a free to leave three points between the teams. And then it happened. Billy O'Sullivan, who had come on for Paul Griffin, struck the killer blow. Billy O'Shea set the attack in motion, Conor Kearney flicked the ball beautifully ahead of O'Sullivan, who steadied and shot for goal. The ball was partially blocked but spun in the air and rolled into the net to wrap up the All-Ireland title for Killorglin's Laune Rangers. Éire Óg were now frustrated and deflated. They had given their all in a brilliant display and felt the gods weren't on their side. You make your own luck in games, accept any gifts that come and never carry decisions on your back. It's a lesson Éire Óg will have learnt. The final whistle saw the score Laune Rangers 4-5 Éire Óg 0-11. The best Club Final since Éire Óg against O'Donovan Rossa (draw). At the final whistle the fans from Killorglin took the field and great were the celebrations as Jack Boothman presented the Andy Merrigan Cup to winning captain Gerard Murphy. The club team which failed in Clonturk Park in 1893 was successful at last. Billy O'Shea won the AIB man-of-the-match award. The photograph of John Evans, hand aloft and cheering wildly, as he mounted the steps of the Hogan Stand to clap the backs of his charges told the story. The hardship, the pain, the wet nights had not been in vain.

I happened to be in the Ashling Hotel in Parkgate Street when the winning Laune Rangers team alighted from the team bus and carried the Cup into the hotel. No shouting or prancing or crowing, this victory was taken with calmness and dignity that was a joy to behold. Yes there was joy in every face, hugs from mothers, sisters, girlfriends and friends. One felt the celebrations on home soil would not be quite so subdued. It was a great example to those watching on how to win with grace. Owen McCrohan, of *The Kerryman*, ended his piece: 'It was a tremendous achievement by the Killorglin men and their trainer John Evans and they deserved the ecstatic welcome that awaited them on Sunday night when they brought the All-Ireland Cup over the Laune Bridge into the warm embrace of their own people.'

JOHN EVANS

John Evans, trainer of the Laune Rangers team is Killorglin born and bred. He played club football for years with the club soldiering in the mid-Kerry division with little success. He lives in a spacious house atop the town he loves with a great view of the river Laune and the town itself. Built on the family farm, John lives close to the town graveyard a few hundred yards away also on hilly ground. He started his juvenile playing career in 1967 under Pat Shea, 'our guiding light at the time'. He played for the Kerry minors in 1973 with lads like Paudie Ó Sé, Ogie Moran, Pat Spillane and Seán Walsh. He won an U-21 All-Ireland medal with Kerry as a substitute in 1975. He played for The Kingdom team in London in 1976, winning the All-Ireland seven-a-side title, then organised by UCD and sponsored by Carrolls. This win had a great lesson for John. 'Those ten lads trained together, ate together, and worked together providing a unity necessary for success.' He joined the Gardaí in 1977 after returning home and played a few times for Kerry. While stationed in Dublin, he captained the Garda team for a year. He moved back home and started to train the minor team of the club in 1988.

John returned from Kevin Street Station in Dublin to take up duty in Knocknagoshel. 'I was on my own as a Garda there and I wanted to get involved in the community and there is one door in Kerry always open to you — Gaelic football. It opened up everything for me. This village which is steeped in history, is the home of Eddie Walsh. I took over the team in 1981 and helped steer them from Division IV to Division II and in that six years I learnt a lot about handling players and training teams. The heart and pride and determination in a country team is unbeatable.

'Laune Rangers won the Kerry Senior Football Championship in 1989 after a lapse of 78 years. Fitting too as a reward for the under-age policy of the club embarked on in 1972 because we had been winning everything in the county at under-age level for years. Men like Jerome Conway, Liam Shannon (Joe's Dad) Pat O'Shea, Patsy Joy, Jimmy Coffey made it all hum. Noel O'Mahony was in charge of the great achievement. I trained under him and learnt a lot from him. It was he who blazed the trail.'

John took over the senior team in 1991, a time of many retirements and serious injury. 'A good time to blood many of the former minors. The team wasn't gelling. Then it started to happen at the end of 1992. In 1993 we won the Kerry Senior Football Championship. The 1993 County title couldn't compare with 1989 but the team had bonded together greatly. In 1994 we were flying, but we lost out to Dr Crokes — five points up cruising in the second half. Roland Neher shot the winning goal for them in injury time. Game over. My father died two days after that, so it was a bad time.'

1995

'The first thing we did was select our captain. Next oldest up is my system. Gerard Murphy was the choice of John Griffin, Patsy Joy and myself. We

12
Buffer's Alley

The Buffer's Alley GAA field and Sports Complex lies on the main Wexford–Dublin road close to Kilmuckridge and Monamolin, the two rural townlands served by the club. Such is the massive success enjoyed by the Buffer's Alley club in the recent past they won 12 Wexford Senior Hurling titles including their first ever in 1968) that one would think that success came their way automatically, but in fact it took a long time and tons of hard work before this very rural GAA club scaled the heights. The club was founded in 1900 and experienced fluctuating fortunes, winning its first county title (junior) in 1905. The Wexford intermediate title was won in 1965. During my visit to the club, I called to see the very impressive clubhouse and GAA grounds at Ballinastraw, Monamolin. It is a place worthy of one of Wexford's top GAA clubs. The club in its recent years of hurling success has also annexed a number of football titles, and has had an incredible influence on camogie in Wexford, has played its part in the promotion of Scór and is involved at every level from U-12 upwards.

1988–1989

Winning the Tommy Moore Cup in 1989 is the club's top achievement and Wexford's one and only club All-Ireland to date. After a pulsating second-half fight-back Buffer's Alley drew with bogey team Rathnure, the champions, on 16 October 1988 at Wexford Park before a record attendance. Rathnure coasted to an easy 0-13 to 0-4 lead at half-time after a drab first half. The Alley's switches at half time worked wonders especially the placing of Martin Casey at centre-half-forward. All-Star half-back John Conran had to fling himself headlong to block a Mick Butler shot for the winning point in the end of what the *Wexford People* described as 'a second-half showpiece of free flowing, fast and furious hurling'. The final score Rathnure 2-14 Buffer's Alley 3-11. It was back again to the same venue and same referee, Dickie Murphy, the following Sunday. This time the Rathnure bogey was finally laid to rest and Buffer's Alley won by 2-10 to 1-5.

DAMP SQUIB

This was a damp squib of an affair compared to the drama of the first day but for Buffer's Alley it was their first final win in six over their old rivals. Vintage hurling was out of the question on a rain soaked pitch. The never-say-die pulling power and lion hearts of Paul Gahan, who won the man-of-the-match award, Seán Whelan and Paddy Donohoe were the work-horse heroes for the winners. Phil Murphy in his 'Comment Corner' in the *Wexford People* wrote: 'Compliments are due to both teams for providing such a sporting contest in conditions that were really appalling — there were times in the second half when I wondered if the game would be finished as the players sloshed through ankle-deep water.' Tony and Colm Doran (substitute), Fr Martin Casey, Henry and Mick Butler all collected a ninth Wexford Senior Hurling Championship medal. Pat Kenny, the captain, was chaired off the field and much was the celebration that night in the GAA complex as the Gain Cup came home to familiar surroundings.

BEATING SHAMROCKS

On through Leinster to the Leinster Final against Ballyhale Shamrocks on 4 December in Dr Cullen Park, Carlow. Buffer's Alley led at half-time by 1-10 to 0-2 due mainly to the veteran double act in attack, Mick Butler, who was deadly accurate from placed balls and a Tony Doran 'special' goal scored after ten minutes. Phil Murphy, *Wexford People*: 'One out of Tony's top drawer, a replica of so many wonderful goals for club and county in the past two decades or more.' Would they hold out? The Shamrocks and the Fennellys fought tooth and nail for victory and the score stood 1-11 to 1-9 with three minutes remaining. Then Mick Butler clinched the title with a marvellous point from out on the right sideline after he had beaten off a series of tackles in a wonderful personal scoring display of 0-10. In the semi-final at Wexford Park, Buffer's Alley defeated Four Roads (Roscommon) by

2-19 to 0-9 while O'Donovan Rossa of Antrim surprisingly beat Patrickswell in the other semi-final by a point. All was now set for the Alley's second All-Ireland appearance on St Patrick's Day. The score Buffer's Alley 2-12 O'Donovan Rossa 0-12.

WHIRLWIND START

The Belfast team started well and led by 0-6 to 0-1 after ten minutes. This deficit would have been more but for Henry Butler's brilliance in goal. Two switches of Paul Gahan to centre-half-back and Tom Dempsey to mid-field worked wonders. Gahan contained the Ciarán Barr threat and Dempsey helped swing the balance at mid-field. The sides were level 0-6 to 1-3 after 18 minutes, Séamus O'Leary goaling from a Mick Butler flick on. Buffer's Alley led at the break by 1-5 to 0-7. The Wexford team dominated the second half and won comfortably in the end by 2-12 to 0-12. The Alley team were a team of heroes, some standing out above the others, like Henry Butler in goal early on, Pat Kenny at full-back, Paul Gahan after switching to centre-back, Tom Dempsey at mid-field, Tony Doran, inspiring as always in attack, Fr Martin Casey, who ran himself into the ground, Séamus O'Leary and Mick Butler. The final was the Alley's 14th game in a long hard campaign which began in Enniscorthy on 17 April 1988.

The winning team was:

Henry Butler

Barry Murphy	Pat Kenny (capt.)	John O'Leary
Paul Gahan	Mattie Foley	Colin Whelan

Éamonn Sinnott   Seán Whelan

Tom Dempsey	Fr Martin Casey	Paddy Donohoe
Mick Butler	Tony Doran	Séamus O'Leary

There were great scenes of jubilation in Croke Park, best described by Phil Murphy in an emotive colour piece on the victory. 'I stood on the Croke Park pitch on St Patrick's Day and watched a Wexford man being presented with the cup of victory. A whole generation of Wexford people have grown up without knowing a moment like this. These were my thoughts as the presentation ceremony was held up while Tony Doran was shouldered through the throngs to the victory rostrum. A special moment for the red-haired leader because he was the link through all those twenty-one years of hurling heartbreak. He had been there as one of the young stars of that 1968 win over Tipperary. And there were two more links with that great day in 1968 — Fr Martin Casey and Mick Butler were part of the Wexford minor team that made it a Wexford double All-Ireland win.'

TONY DORAN LOOKS BACK

Tony Doran, the man from Boolavogue, was just three weeks short of his 43rd birthday when he won his club All-Ireland medal. When I visited him at his farm in Mónagréine, Monamolin in April he recalled the time and what it meant. 'Winning the All-Ireland title with Buffer's Alley was my greatest thrill. You'd have to go back to 30 years ago before the club championships ever started, it was something we didn't even dream of as a struggling junior club. To win the All-Ireland was the icing on the cake.

'Four of the team had been there from the start — goalkeeper Henry Butler, his brother Mick, Fr Martin Casey and myself. Fr Martin had a great influence on the club and was very loyal to us, maintaining the link no matter where he was stationed as a priest. Buffer's Alley encompasses Kilmuckridge and Monamolin. The Butlers are from Kilmuckridge. Another person involved from the start was my brother Colm but though he played in an earlier round in our All-Ireland year, he was hospitalised with a back operation before the final. He still got out to see us win. In all we have won 12 county Senior Hurling titles including our first in 1968 and I was associated with 11 of those wins, playing in 10 and coming on as a substitute in the 11th. Fr Martin Casey has all 12 medals, missing just two finals.

'We didn't go out at the start with the intention of winning the All-Ireland. We went out at first to win the Wexford title and beat Rathnure at last. To beat Rathnure eventually in a replay was our biggest club achievement up to that date. At the time we thought nothing could surpass that achievement. After that we beat Carlow Town, none too impressively, then Seir Kieran of Offaly in a very close shave. Another close game with Ballyhale Shamrocks on a windy day and we had won Leinster. O'Donovan Rossa (Belfast) were a very good team. Early on they had the run of us and we were very slow to settle.'

Comparison with 1968

'To be quite honest I can hardly remember anything about the All-Ireland win of 1968. But I'll always remember 1988-1989. I never felt too old with the younger lads but used to wonder should I make way in the team for a younger player.

'There was great joy after we won. We dined *en route* home with the Moore Cup in the Grand Hotel in Wicklow Town and it seemed all the parish was there before us. Eventually we arrived back to our own Clubhouse in Monamolin, where we all celebrated together until the small hours. We have our own bar facilities and it was the ideal place to celebrate our success. We had a great reception in Gorey on the following night and returned to our local pub in Monamolin, Tom Lawless's, later. Before we got our own Headquarters, Lawless's had always been our celebration spot on nights after County Final successes. I never drank alcohol in my life but still partook in and enjoyed all the celebrations. We also celebrated, after a few nights' rest, in Robbie Hammell's of Kilmuckridge and about a week after that another night out was had in Boggan's of Kilmuckridge.

'We bought our club grounds in 1971, developed it by degrees and opened it officially in 1975. We opened our Clubhouse in 1978 and it has become the focal point of the whole area. It is a second home for me and all my family. I was honoured to be selected on the AIB Jubilee team especially when I saw many of the great names that were not lucky enough to be selected. At the time we won the All-Ireland, Mick Butler was Chairman of the club, I was vice-Chairman (both of us players) and Joe Doran my brother, who was another player from the 1968 era, was Club Secretary.'

ALAN AHERNE

Alan Aherne is a young journalist with the *Wexford People*. An outstanding communicator, he is GAA through and through. He had this to say of Buffer's Alley's success: 'Buffer's Alley proved Wexford can still produce winners. Anyone from Wexford in Croke Park in 1989 saw a Wexford team win and a Wexford man, Pat Kenny, getting the Cup. You cannot think of Buffer's Alley without thinking of Tony Doran. My particular memory of that final is of Tony going up for and grabbing the ball and immediately being surrounded by four or five O'Donovan Rossa defenders, yet despite all their attention he still got a score for Buffer's Alley. I'll never forget the cheer that went up when he got that score. Regarding the club they came from nowhere in the 1960s mainly inspired by the Dorans and the Butlers and went on to win 12 county titles. Then they won the All-Ireland title and became worthy All-Ireland champions. They were great ambassadors for Wexford.'

Buffer's Alley, 1988–1989 Senior Hurling Club Champions
Back row: Tony Doran, Barry Murphy, Marney Burke, Mattie Foley, Paul Gahan, Henry Butler, Bernard Martin, Matt Furlong, John Gahan, John Donohoe, Ger Sweeney, Colin Whelan, Seán Whelan.
Front row: Fr Martin Casey, Mick Butler, Tom Dempsey, Pat Kenny (capt.), John O'Leary, Séamus O'Leary, Paddy Donohoe, Éamonn Sinnott, Harry Lee, Fintan O'Leary.

13
Birr's First For Offaly

1994 was a vintage year for Offaly hurling. The manner in which they won the senior All-Ireland hurling title in the last few minutes, after Limerick seemed secure, had the county agog. The three minor All-Ireland successes of the 1980s were bearing fruit. It was going to be difficult to win the Offaly Senior Hurling Championship title in such a brilliant year for the county.

The old rivals St Rynagh's were beaten in the semi-final on 16 October by 2-14 to 3-8. Then in the final in their own St Brendan's Park, Birr won their 12th Offaly Senior Hurling Championship title defeating Seir Kieran of the Dooleys by 0-8 to 0-6 on a badly cut up pitch softened by heavy rain. Both sides deserved credit for providing such a fine quality of game in the circumstances. Seir Kieran led at half-time by 0-4 to 0-3. Good work by Daithí Regan at mid-field in the second half and two vital points three minutes from time by Declan Pilkington and Oisín O'Neill saw Birr home. Now it was a chase for their second Leinster title (their first was in 1992).

HISTORY OF THE CLUB

Birr enjoyed considerable success on home fields in the early days winning the Offaly crown for the first time in 1912. Birr's golden era of success came between 1938 and 1948, when they won six county senior titles in the era of Des Dooley (their first player to play for Leinster), Billie Nevin, the Grogans, Phil Purcell and Jack Cloonan. Then a bleak era followed broken by a county title win in 1971. Then another era of frustration before the 1991 title. There was always a deep hurling interest in the town fuelled in no small way by the Presentation Brothers both at primary and secondary school level.

Two easy wins over Kiltegan at Birr by 1-9 to 1-4 and over Raharney at Tullamore by 1-15 to 1-4, within six days of each other, paved the way for a Leinster Final meeting with Oulart–The–Ballagh of Wexford for 4 December at Nowlan Park, Kilkenny. A late Oulart goal from a deflection earned them a lucky enough draw on the score 1-7 to 0-10 in a bitterly contested game played before 6,000 spectators. Birr led at the break by 0-6 to 0-5. In the replay a week later, at the same venue before 10,000 spectators, Birr carried the day by 3-7 to 2-5. Tom Humphries (*The Irish Times*) in a colourful introduction, wrote: 'Replays carry their own baggage. Late in the game the white winter sun began casting long shadows. The wholehearted exchanges which had marked and blighted the drawn game began casting shadows too. Birr had a man sent to the line but the economy of their hurling was such that a deficiency in personnel was never going to hinder them significantly. Here was a splendid game, an hour of raw and fierce hurling. If it had imperfections, these served to add to the game's beauty. Joe Erritty at full-back had an outstanding game. In the Pilkingtons, Declan and Johnny and Brian Whelahan, Birr had star players around whom the rest of the team revolved comfortably, while towering Daithí Regan proved a major handful at full-forward. Birr led at half-time by 3-3 to 1-3.'

On 19 February at Semple Stadium, Thurles before 9,094 spectators Birr defeated Kilmallock by 2-8 to 0-9 in what Seán Moran (*The Irish Times*) described as 'a tightly contested thriller'. Birr trailed by three points 0-5 to 0-8 entering the last ten minutes of the game but 'with a late surge that will have been depressingly familiar to the Limerick contingent in the crowd, the Birr lads scored 2-3 to 0-1 in that vital last period, the second goal coming in added time'. In a day which started damp and ended in monsoon-like rain conditions with the attendance cowering in the stands, the standard of play tended to deteriorate. Still all of Birr's scores came from play.

THE FINAL

I flew home from the Cheltenham Racing Festival for the club finals in Croke Park on St Patrick's Day, yet another National Feast day of cold windy and showery weather. As the day wore on the weather deteriorated badly. Peadar O'Brien (*Irish Press*) writing on the conditions: 'Surely the GAA must move now and re-schedule these tests for a better time in the year. At the end of the hurling game especially, black clouds reduced visibility and hailstones marred a splendid day.' But the conditions didn't deter Birr and Dunloy Cuchulainns of Antrim from serving up a thriller, which ended 0-9 apiece before 18,544 spectators. There were times towards the end of this game when I feared for the New Stand as advertising hoardings were uprooted by sudden gales and created all sorts of perils for the players who soldiered on relentlessly in wind and hail. This was our ancient game played at its passionate best. Birr, who produced a fine second half, were fortunate to get away with a draw.

Sean McGoldrick (*Irish Press*) wrote: 'Once again the All-Ireland Club Hurling Final has produced a match, which was almost as skilful as it was exciting. And it climaxed in the kind of epic finish that would look impossible in a film script. The contest was eight seconds into lost time when Dunloy mid-fielder Tony McGrath stroked over the equaliser from near halfway. Birr had few complaints. They were behind for 53 minutes and although a storming second-half performance all but wiped out the memory of their first-half eclipse, both teams deserved another chance. Just as the Hurling Final entered its most exciting phase, the thunder pealed, the gale howled and the hailstones left the sticky surface covered in a carpet of white.'

THE REPLAY

The replay at Croke Park saw Birr win easily by 3-13 to 2-3. Tom Humphries (*The Irish Times*): 'Dunloy came to Croke Park knowing they had let Birr off the hook on St Patrick's Day. Nothing could have prepared them for conceding two goals in the opening four minutes. That wasn't the worst of it — Dunloy never scored in the first half, being 2-7 to 0-0 behind at the break.

'Declan Pilkington lobbed a ball into the heart of the Dunloy defence in the first minute. Paul Murphy materialised. Bang! Minutes later still reeling Dunloy conceded a "65" to Brian Whelahan and followed the arc of its flight past the flashing hurleys of Paul Murphy and Oisín O'Neill. Bang! Bang! Two body blows which knocked the wind and the spirit out of Dunloy.'

This was the Birr team:

Robert Shields

Michael Hogan	Joe Erritty	Brian Hennessy
Brian Whelahan	Gary Cahill	Noel Hogan

Johnny Pilkington (capt.) Conor McGlone

Oisín O'Neill	Paul Murphy	Declan Pilkington
Adrian Cahill	Daithí Regan	Simon Whelahan

Substitutes: Ray Landy for M. Hogan, Louis Vaughan for C. McGlone, Matt Finnane for O. O'Neill, Liam Power, Tony Murphy, Declan Brady, Conor Hanniffy, Frankie Pilkington, Gareth Doorley.

BRIAN WHELAHAN'S THOUGHTS

Brian Whelahan captained the Offaly minors to All-Ireland success in 1989, having played also on the 1987 winning team. He is a hurling wing-half-back of outstanding quality and his exclusion from the All-Star hurling selection in 1994 caused a sensation. His thoughts on 1994: 'To win a club All-Ireland is the highest honour you can achieve. You're playing with lads you grew up and played with from U-10 level — lads like Brian Hennessy, Joe Erritty, Robert Shields, Mick and Noel Hogan, Gary Cahill... we are talking about the whole team basically. There may have been a year or two between some of us but we all played together. Brother Vincent played a huge part in all our careers by starting us off in the Brothers' National School here in Birr. He really drilled it home to us, the importance of practise, of continuing to learn the skills of the game. It took off from there.

'My father as well, was very influential. He never stopped talking about the game, bringing us to games and a lot of his interest rubbed off on me. We got the hurling from both sides — my mother is Susan Dooley from Coolderry, who won a Leinster Camogie medal with Offaly. 1994 was an unbelievable year. The club All-Ireland crowned a huge year for the County Offaly as a whole. We were on a great high after winning the All-Ireland against Limerick and then to have the honour of winning Offaly's first ever club All-Ireland finished a super year. No words can convey the sense of pride we had in our town, in our club and in our club colours of green and red. Returning for the second half, we all recognised how poorly we had sealed in 1948 by the late Fr John C. Ryan, a young and enterprising curate, who came to the parish in 1947. Hitherto Borris and Ileigh fielded two senior teams in the North Tipperary Championship. From then on it was to be Borrisoleigh which healed of a long standing rift in the parish. The first of six Tipperary Senior Hurling titles was won in 1949.'

Kenny era

'That was the era of the Kennys, Seán, Paddy and Phibbie, Jimmy Finn, Phil Crowley. Fr Ryan was highly respected in this area and was known as one of the Ryan giants, natives of Kilcommon. Jimmy Finn was starting his career then. The half-back line of that team was Phil Crowley, Billy "Stephens" Stapleton and Jimmy Finn. We won again in 1950 and 1953, three Tipperary titles in five years, with more or less the same crop of players. They were considered to be the best bunch of hurlers ever to leave the parish of Borris. Seán Kenny, who captained Tipperary to all-Ireland success in 1950 was a powerful man, a great leader and motivator supreme. Jimmy Finn was a great ground hurler; never lifted a ball he didn't have to. He was selected as right half-back in the Team of the Century and captained Tipperary to All-Ireland success in 1951. We had other great Tipperary men in Philly Ryan, Ned Ryan and Tim Ryan of that era of the 1950s.'

The 1980s

'Twenty-eight years elapsed before we won our fourth county title. We had good teams in between but the blend wasn't right. In 1981 I remember scenes of tremendous celebration when we won. I was on that team which beat Roscrea fairly well. We won it again in 1983. That year is best remembered for our tremendous tilts with Midleton in the Munster club final at Kilmallock. The speed of the ball in those two epic games (draw and replay) was unbelievable. Both clubs went on to win All-Irelands later. Then on to 1986 — a marvellous year for the club and parish. It's a tremendous distinction for a club to lay claim to an All-Ireland title and will always remain in our memory. An injury laid me low and though I fought to get fit, I didn't recover in time to make the panel. But I was so happy at our club's success. It has come to be a tradition now that when winning Borrisoleigh teams bring home the Cup I sing the local anthem *Lovely Fair Ileigh* written by a local man and capturing the spirit and geography of the locality. The writer of the song, Pat Mahon, was a gifted scholar, a cooper by trade and had great feeling for the parish and its people. The man of the house Mick Coen, married to Biddy's daughter Bridget, was on all winning teams in the 1980s. It is always well received and I've seen many a tear shed as I sang it. The kiln field is in old Ileigh and it is where the older players used to hurl before we had the more elaborate facilities we now enjoy (the Bishop Quinlan Park in Borrisoleigh, opened officially on 29 July 1984).

'Hurling is a way of life in this area. Nothing else brings as much joy into the lives and hearts of the people of Borris as to see a Borris team doing well. We had other great hurlers in Borrisoleigh between the two golden eras — Liam Devaney who won five All-Ireland medals and of course Noel O'Dwyer and the Stapletons Tommy and Gerry. Liam Devaney is the singularly most honoured player ever in the parish but he missed out mostly on the really great Borris teams, apart from being on the winning 1953 team. His input into hurling here didn't end with his playing.'

THE 1985 COUNTY FINAL

Borrisoleigh won the 1985 Tipperary Senior Hurling Final, defeating All-Ireland champions Kilruane MacDonaghs by 0-14 to 0-7 on 28 September before an attendance of 10,000. Michael Dundon (*Tipperary Star*) wrote: 'The key to Borrisoleigh's success was the gambit of playing Philip Kenny at full-forward and he won the man-of-the-match award.' Borrisoleigh led at half-time by 0-7 to 0-4 and aided by the wind it hardly seemed enough but Philip Kenny continued his tormentor role aided by the superlative Richard Stakelum and the Stapletons Gerry and Timmy, who were unbeatable. On 16 November in Limerick Borrisoleigh defeated Claughaun (Limerick) by 2-10 to 1-9 when Michael Dundon (*Tipperary Star*) wrote: 'Fortified by a goal in each half, and sustained by a determined defence, the Tipperary champions won the day with Philip Kenny once again the mainstay of the attack helped especially by Aidan Ryan, who had a fine first half, and the free-taking accuracy of veteran Noel O'Dwyer (0-5 in all).' Then on Sunday 29 November, at Limerick again, Borrisoleigh won for the club its first Munster crown, defeating Clarecastle by 1-13 to 1-9. Michael Dundon was there to record it: 'This looked like a cakewalk in the first half as Borrisoleigh led at half-time by 1-8 to 0-2 where Noel O'Dwyer had his best outing of the year. Others to shine were Richard Stakelum and Francis Collins, who

All-Ireland winning team and modelled myself mostly on Pat Hartigan, Martin O'Doherty and John Horgan, lads that always impressed me. 1986 was a great year for us. In 1981 we were beaten by Mount Sion because we were forced to play the game too soon after winning the County Final. We had to play the game on the Saturday after winning our first county title in 28 years. So we had done a lot of celebrating and suffered as a result. After that we lost to Midleton in Kilmallock in a replay. So in 1986 we said this was one we wouldn't let slip. My greatest thrill in the whole year was beating Kilruane in the County Final.'

Borrisoleigh, All-Ireland Champions 1987
Back row: *Rory Kinane (Selector), Conor Stakelum, Jerry Stapleton, Timmy*
  Stapleton, Richard Stakelum, John McGrath, Noel O'Dwyer,
  Timmie Ryan, Bobby Ryan, John McGrath (Selector).
Front row: *Noel Maher, Philip Kenny, Michael Ryan, Francis Collins, Mick*
  Coen, Francis Spillane, Aidan Ryan, mascot in front Aidan
  Coen.

Photo by Paddy Prior.

15
Roscrea: First In Hurling

Long life to the great Mick Minogue, too,
I pray that he'll never grow old,
His name will be linked here with hurling,
When tales of the great games are told

With Francis Loughnane by his side there,
The centre-field area held tight,
Their brilliance we'll always remember,
Those stars of the famed Red and White.

These lines from a poem by Roscrea native Pat–Joe Whelan reflect a county final victory over Carrick Davins. The red and white colours of Roscrea have always earned respect in Tipperary hurling but especially in the late 1960s and early 1970s. Mick and Maisie Minogue were my hosts in Roscrea for a very enjoyable visit to the North Tipperary hurling stronghold organised through the good offices of Tipperary PRO, Liz Howard.

MICK MINOGUE

Mick Minogue was a stalwart player on the great Roscrea team of the era mentioned. He took me on a ramble back. 'I remember losing the 1963 County Final to Thurles' Sarsfield's in Nenagh. We were a wee bit unfortunate then because we had to field without our left half-back Owen Killoran. We lost in 1967 too, fielding without the two Loughnanes, Francis and Harry. My first game with Roscrea was in 1955 so I was well seasoned by then. We were there or thereabouts in the great years of Toomevara in the 1960s. We won our first Tipperary title in 1968. We won it that day for all the great Roscrea teams which went before us, who contested so many finals and lost. In all I won five Tipperary medals 1968–1969, 1970, 1972 and 1973. For many years I was Treasurer of the club working closely with "Mr Roscrea GAA" John Joe Maher, who was Secretary to the club for 47 years and I followed John Joe in that position for a year. The man was popular in Roscrea and far outside, a tremendous servant to the GAA. It was his life. We were fortunate that Fr Bert Carey became Chairman of our club and he helped to bring unity to it. We had other great servants in Martin Loughnane, Joe Cuddy, Billy Brussells and Willie O'Reilly, a man who gave his life to promoting the juveniles in Roscrea, helped by Kieran McNicholas, and earlier still Christy Maher.

'I remember talking to Kieran Carey the day after we both won our first county medal and he said he'd give his five All-Ireland medals for the first Tipperary senior medal with Roscrea. We thought of the great Roscrea men who never had that honour. Men like the Ryans of Sheehills, Jack, Mick and Dinny all great stars in the 1940s and 1950s. Mick Ryan was an outstanding hurler but mostly lived outside Tipperary. Two other brothers Roddy and Donie also played. Fanny Rowland was very small but the greatest hurler I've seen. Martin Loughnane was another genius who was still playing and winning medals at 50. Billy Brussells, Mikie and Joe Fletcher, Tony Hannon, Timmy Bergin and Charlie Downes were others. The club All-Ireland is another great memory and more precious now when we think back and realise we were the first, even though we had lost out in Tipperary earlier that year. The greatest honour always for me was the first day I ever put on the red and white of Roscrea. It was always my dream. Roscrea hurling was always kept simple. Good ball control, deft touches. Very like the Cork style — quick and intelligent.'

ALL-IRELAND 1971

1971 was the middle of a great hurling time in Roscrea. As 1970 Tipperary champions (the end of a three-in-a-row) the Munster and first All-Ireland title beckoned. Munster had been running an official title prior to the inauguration of the club All-Irelands and their 1969–1970 title was being held simultaneously almost with the official 1970–1971 one. Roscrea won the first of two Munster titles (the 1969–1970) on Easter Sunday 1971, defeating Glen Rovers of Cork in a thriller by 3-6 to 1-9 in Tipperary. Meantime the 1970–1971 title race had begun with a runaway win over Kilmoyley (Kerry) on 7 February 1971 by 10-9 to 1-8. Then two weeks later at Roscrea's own St Cronan's Park, Ballyduff–Portlaw (Waterford) were overcome by 3-10 to 1-10. It was much stiffer opposition this time as Roscrea had to field without Francis Loughnane, Jackie Hannon and Mickey Nolan. The Waterford champions led at half-time by 0-8 to 0-3 after being wind-aided, but three goals, one by Harry Loughnane and Joe Tynan's two sealed the game for Roscrea. The *Nenagh Guardian* selected Mick Minogue as man-of-the-match. 'Bereft of his regular mid-field colleague Francis Loughnane, he 'lifted' his game in response to the extra demands made upon him and the crisp certainty of his striking was Roscrea's salvation while the wind was against them.' The winners were well served in defence by Tadhg O'Connor and Kieran Carey. Jody Spooner's second-half display was a revelation.

It was mid-August before Roscrea won their second Munster club title (1970–1971) in Limerick on a Wednesday evening by 4-11 to 1-6 against Clarecastle (Clare). Two goals inside a twenty second spell midway through the second half by Donie Moloney (capt.) and Joe Cunningham ended the game as a contest which was nip and tuck until then. Kieran Carey excelled at full-back, ably helped by Brendan Maher and Tadhg O'Connor. Mick Minogue and Donie Moloney dominated mid-field and in a rampant attack, Francis Loughnane, Joe and Liam Spooner were outstanding. Roscrea led at half-time by 1-6 to 1-3 (Loughnane scoring 1-5). So Roscrea had won two Munster club titles in the same year. One of their players, Tadhg O'Connor, was captaining Tipperary to win an All-Ireland title, the first Roscrea man to do so, while O'Connor and Loughnane were to be honoured in the first ever All-Star selection.

The All-Ireland was won and Roscrea once again qualified for the Tipperary County Final but this time they came a cropper to Moyne–Templetuohy, losing by 2-8 to 0-6. They were still in line for the first ever club title and after travelling the long journey north they defeated Loughgiel Shamrocks by 15 points on 14 November 1971. St Rynagh's (Banagher), who had also lost the Offaly crown, were Roscrea's opponents in the final which was played on 19 December in Birr, when Roscrea hurling received its greatest ever Christmas present, winning by 4-5 to 2-5 to crown a quite momentous hurling year for club and county. *The Guardian's* introduction did justice to the occasion. 'The pages of hurling history rolled back in Birr when at the same venue where the very first All-Ireland Senior Hurling Final was played back in 1888, the first All-Ireland Club Final was played and as in that historic first final of 1888, victory came to Tipperary.'

The losers St Rynagh's made Roscrea fight every inch of the way in a thrilling victory. Frank Murphy of Cork refereed the game excellently. A huge thunder storm around noon threatened play but conditions improved. Roscrea with wind advantage led at half-time by 2-4 to 0-1. Scores were slow a-coming for Rynagh's though now favoured by a strong breeze and Roscrea matched them score for score almost.

In that first half Mickey Nolan and Joe Tynan doubled on Tadhg O'Connor frees for Roscrea's goals. In the second half, when Rynagh's went on the offensive, half-backs Patsy Rowland and Tadhg O'Connor starred. *The Guardian* gave them their due: 'this pair more than anybody else deserve the credit for victory because of their assuredness and skill to repulse whatever came their way.' Kieran Carey's 'hard pulling and effective clearing knocked the sails out of many a Banagher hope'. Mick Hogan, Brendan Maher and goalkeeper Tadhg Murphy did all that was asked of them. Mick Minogue especially and Donie Moloney ruled mid-field. 'Minogue continues to amaze with his speed and sense of position and he gave one of his outstanding performances' (*The Guardian*). The man-of-the-match in attack was Francis Loughnane: 'his concentration on placing fellow forwards paid off,' (*The Guardian*). Jackie Hannon and Joe Cunningham completed a fine half line in attack, Joe Cunningham and Joe Tynan's goals after solo runs being the icing on the cake. Tynan's sense of position like Minogue's, was perfect. Mickey Nolan made a welcome return and Billy Stapleton teamed up well in this first ever club decider. This was the winning team:

Tadhg Murphy

Mick Hogan Kieran Carey Brendan Maher

Patsy Rowland Tadhg O'Connor Jimmy Crampton

Mick Minogue Donie Moloney (capt.)

Francis Loughnane Jackie Hannon Joe Cunningham

Joe Tynan Mickey Nolan Billy Stapleton

TADHG O'CONNOR REMINISCES

It was a momentous year for Tadhg, captain of Tipperary's winning All-Ireland team of 1971. 'It was a great time for Roscrea, for North Tipperary hurling. We felt we were special. For the previous ten years or more we had been winning minor and U-21 county titles for Roscrea pretty regularly. These young players were moving on to the senior team. Lads like Mickey Nolan, Mick Minogue, Kieran Carey, a man I looked up to so much, John Dillon, Mick Hogan were all seasoned. I came on to the 1967 team after being a minor in 1966. Up front we had Francis Loughnane, Jackie Hannon another great player. Then the young starlets like Joe Tynan, Joe Cunningham, magnificent scorer and a citeog, Barney Hogan, Donie Moloney. Practically everyone of us wore the Tipperary jersey at some level. We lost in 1967 and won our first ever title in 1968. The late Fr Bert Carey, our Chairman, a lovely man, was very influential then.

'1971 was a mixed up kind of year. We were very involved at county level in both National League and Championship. We lost to Moyne–Templetuohy in the County Final after we had won the All-Ireland inter-county title. We may have taken the whole thing too much for granted but we had had so many celebrations after bringing the Liam McCarthy home. John Joe Maher cried when we brought the Cup home. Still let's not take from Moyne–Templetuohy. They were a very good team, having travelled the juvenile route like ourselves. I often feel I didn't derive full satisfaction out of captaining the senior All-Ireland team that year because I was relatively young and inexperienced. As to the club All-Ireland we had to play Loughgiel Shamrocks up in Antrim and it was tough enough until our final flourish. Patsy Rowland was outstanding that day. A very fine hurler who minded himself and always prepared well. We stayed in Dundalk and the Loughgiel people gave us a marvellous time.

'Roscrea and Rynagh's had a great relationship in those years. Tony Reddan had been involved with them and they were a fine ball-playing team. We often played them and we knew each other's style. We generally won out in the end. Joe Cunningham, Jackie Hannon were two of our stars. I always loved Roscrea hurling. It was a great club to be associated with. We were always encouraged to play the game. Keep it open, never get physical. Let the ball travel. Hurling was a way of life for all of us.

'As to my greatest club memory it has to be beating Thurles Sarsfield's in Thurles in our first county title win in 1968. The Stadium erupted when we won. Everyone was carried shoulder high after the game. I was a Pioneer then and I showed up for work next day. One of the few that did.'

FRANCIS LOUGHNANE

Francis Loughnane's pub in Roscrea is festooned with GAA photographs old and new. Greyed somewhat, he still has the powerful arms which stroked over so many scores for Roscrea and Tipperary. '1968 was a great achievement for the town, winning a county title at last after being beaten in several finals over the years, some controversially. At one stage we won six minor county titles in a row and I played on four of them. Harry my brother was on two of them. My uncle Martin was a substitute on the Tipperary 1945 team and John Joe Maher rated Martin as a hurling genius. Thurles Sarsfield's were a smashing team in those days — Jimmy Doyle, the famous Tony Wall, Seán McLaughlin, Paddy Doyle and Mick McElgunn and we beat them in Thurles in 1968. That was my greatest honour ever. In all I won six county titles, all six titles which we won 1968 to 1970, 1972 and 1973 and our final title in 1980. I played in 13 finals. We were starved for success in the 1930s, 1940s and 1950s. Men like Joe Fletcher, Martin my uncle, Bill Brussels, Fanny Rowland, a beautifully skilful hurler and a naturally fit man, Timmy Bergin another outstanding man. I was only eleven or twelve years of age and used to look up to those men no end. The man who most inspired me was John Joe Maher. It was he who kept me at it. He often kept the club floating out of his own pocket.

'My greatest memory of playing for Roscrea is of the great team spirit of our club. The year we beat Kilruane in the County Final (1973) was one of my best games and in the 1968 Final I remember striking up a great understanding with Barney Hogan, a great character of our team, leading to two great points from Barney but Thurles copped on to our move fast and tended to cover Barney. We trained very hard then and in some of those sessions I had some great duels with Mick Hogan. Often as hard as a County Final

'As to my greatest score many of them were made for me. Against Moneygall once in a North Tipperary game which we won by a point, I remember scoring a lot of points when everything seemed to go right and I scored 0-14 in all, from frees and from play. The club championship has grown out of all proportions but it has snags. Sometimes a team wins a county title and has to play again inside a week in the first round of the Provincial title. There should be at least a two-week break. I was thrilled to be selected for the AIB Jubilee team, having thought all my hurling achievements were over years ago. I owe a lot to hurling for Roscrea and Tipperary. I was always proud to wear the jersey and I'm grateful to all the men who coached me along the way. You owe everything ultimately to your club and the red and white means so much to me. At the moment I'm training the senior team and there is nothing I'd like more than to see us getting back on top again.'

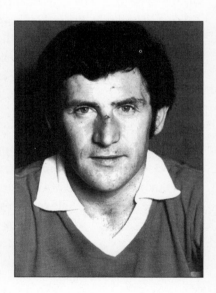

Francis Loughnane   *Tadhg O'Connor*

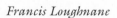

16
Christy's Glenmore

Glenmore is a little village nestling at the foot of a very steep hill about one mile off the main Waterford–New Ross speedway. A cluster of houses, just one public house, The Glen Bar, and a church half-way down the steep hill this is Glenmore. Christy Heffernan, the gentle giant of Kilkenny hurling from not so long ago, is its Matt the Thresher. When queried on the gentle giant image, he responded: 'There is only one answer to dirty play — put the scores on the board and win the game if you can.'

HISTORY OF THE CLUB

Tom Ryall, Kilkenny PRO, filled me in on the club's history. Glenmore, on the Wexford border, was a famous football club until recently, now sharing Kilkenny's Football Roll of Honour of 18 titles with Railyard. In all, the club won three junior hurling titles over the years, the last one in 1980, the forerunner of the great senior teams to follow. The Kilkenny Senior Hurling title was first won in 1987 and repeated three times since in 1990, 1992 and 1995. The All-Ireland crown was won in 1991 but it was the defeat of Glenmore in 1989, when losing the Kilkenny Senior Hurling Final to Ballyhale Shamrocks which helped them no end later. So the emergence of Glenmore as a real club hurling power is of relatively recent vintage and the Heffernans and O'Connors particularly have been closely associated with the club's success.

Glenmore also had Michael Phelan and Liam Walsh, who wore the black and amber. Christy Heffernan became the darling of Kilkenny when starring in Kilkenny's All-Ireland win of 1982.

THE BIG YEAR

Glenmore won the 1990 Kilkenny County Senior Hurling Final, easily defeating Clara by 3-15 to 2-6 with the winners' most famous son Christy Heffernan delivering two shattering blows in the 27th and 29th minutes of the first half, plucking goals out of virtually nothing to leave Glenmore in front at half-time by 3-6 to 0-5. The winners' half-back line of Liam Walsh, Des Ennett and Willie O'Connor particularly excelled. It was a memorable weekend for Christy Heffernan, whose wife Pat gave birth to a baby boy on the eve of the game. Georgie Leahy, the Glenmore trainer conceded that the match was much easier than expected: 'Glenmore were unlucky last year but they proved themselves today.'

On through Leinster to a final tilt with Camross (Laois) which Glenmore won by 0-15 to 1-9 at Athy on 25 November. John Knox (*Kilkenny People*) wrote: 'The ability to evaluate shrewdly the events as they unfolded and to make quick and positive changes stood to Glenmore who eventually cracked teak-tough Camross in an energy-sapping Leinster Club Hurling Final. The losers, a fiercely determined outfit with nothing but winning on their minds, took a lot of beating in a game that was always tense for the players and gripping for the large attendance. The losers led at the break 0-6 to 0-4. All the Glenmore half-time changes upped the performances of Michael Phelan, Pat Barron, John Flynn and Des Heffernan. Inspired by the already flying O'Connors, Eddie, Willie and P.J., Liam Walsh and Michael Alyward, a wonderful spell of six unanswered Glenmore points, leaving the score at 0-14 to 0-8, won the day. It was tough but when Glenmore needed to move ahead, they did so with style.'

Dunloy Cuchulainns were defeated in the All-Ireland Semi-final in Nowlan Park, on 24 February 1991, by 1-18 to 1-10 but the winners needed to produce some of their very best hurling to subdue the Antrim champions in a thrilling game. Dunloy brought over 2,000 followers to Nowlan Park and really tested the mettle of Glenmore. Inspired by a dazzling Michael Phelan and their captain Ray Heffernan, who shot 0-11, the winners eventually got on top to qualify for a final tilt with Patrickswell (Limerick).

THE FINAL

Glenmore joined the hurling élite on 17 March 1991, defeating Patrickswell at Croke Park by 1-13 to 0-12. John Knox (*Kilkenny People*): 'Tradition was turned on its head at Croke Park when the game battlers from Glenmore turned in a performance laced with passion and desire to topple mighty Patrickswell in a totally absorbing All-Ireland Club Hurling Final.' It was even-steven for much of the first half but as half-time approached Glenmore eased into a 0-8 to 0-6 lead at the break. John Knox's star was Christy Heffernan: 'It was his 33rd minute goal that proved crucial. The indomitable full-forward owned the skies whenever Glenmore rained the ball in around the square, and just to remind us once again of the tradition within the parish, he actually booted home the vital goal. It wasn't a one-man show. The O'Connors, Willie and Eddie dazzled. Ray Heffernan (capt.), Eddie Aylward, Liam Walsh and Denis Mullally had exceptional moments. John Heffernan had one of his finest hours. Michael Phelan helped sway mid-field in the second half.' Ray Heffernan, the captain, was a happy man as his score tally of 0-5 was the same as when he starred for Kilkenny minors in winning the 1981 All-Ireland Final over Galway by 1-20 to 3-9. 'It means so much more to win with your club. It's a wonderful feeling,' said a delighted Ray. The winning team was:

Michael Deady

| Eddie O'Connor | Ned Aylward | P.J. O'Connor |
| Liam Walsh | Willie O'Connor | Des Ennett |

Ray Heffernan (capt.)　　Michael Phelan

| Denis Mullally | Pat Barron | Des Heffernan |
| John Heffernan | Christy Hefferan | John Flynn |

Substitutes: Michael 'Foxy' Phelan for John Flynn, Michael Aylward for P.J. O'Connor. One of their former pals who used to play with them at U-10, U-12 and juvenile levels flew from New York. Michael Duggan and his wife Trudy enjoyed the occasion which was almost too emotive.

BIG CHRISTY'S THOUGHTS

Christy Heffernan is 39 years young and won his fourth Kilkenny Senior Hurling Championship medal in 1995. 'The first County Final win of 1987 was the sweetest of all. A great feeling really because Glenmore is such a small club. When I started off playing with them we couldn't win a first round junior game. That was 1974 and I was a teenager. Winning the All-Irelands with Kilkenny in 1982 and 1983 was great but I was much younger then and didn't fully appreciate it. Returning to that 1987 County Final win, we beat Ballyhale Shamrocks in it and we owed them one for a hammering we received from them in 1985. To make it better I captained our lads in that first county title triumph. We had great celebrations after that first triumph. I'm a fair old weight but that didn't deter our fans from chairing me off. Bonfires galore at home and great celebrations in our local the Glen Bar. It compared favourably with 1982 when I had the honour of bringing the Liam McCarthy Cup to our village. Brian Cody was captain that year but it was my honour to bring it to Glenmore.

'Winning the club All-Ireland was of course very sweet. When you see old men crying with joy you know it had to be special. Tom Ryan was one. I don't think he ever played but he never missed a game. Séamus Dunphy and Michael Lynch were others. Michael had done trojan work for our success at under age. Glenmore as you know was a well-known football area in the old days. My grandfather Jack Doherty was a well-known footballer and played for Kilkenny. At one stage up to 12 locals played for the county team.' At this stage Tom Ryall interjected that Jack Doherty, Christy's Grandad was on the last Kilkenny senior football team to contest a Leinster Final in 1922.

1989

'Actually I won a Kilkenny Senior Football title in 1989, our first football title in the area for 35 years. We were going for the double that year, an achievement we really craved but fortune didn't favour us. We were beaten in a thriller by the Shamrocks (Ballyhale) three weeks later by a lost time goal. We were holding on and Shamrocks were pressing us hard. Willie O'Connor had possession and it was taken off him. Then followed a lot of scrambling and the ball broke to Paul Phelan, who goaled. I wanted the ground to sink and swallow me up. Our double dream was over. They went on to win the All-Ireland. The next year we won the county title and we were really fired to win the All-Ireland as well. That defeat by the Shamrocks in 1989 was a huge help, though it didn't seem so at the time.

'Our hardest game that year was against St Rynagh's in the Leinster Semi-final. They had Roy Mannion, Aidan Fogarty, Martin Hanamy, Kieran Flannery in their lineout. I was sorry my father wasn't alive to cherish our All-Ireland victory but he was alive for the 1987 county title win. Georgie Leahy was our trainer and he kept us motivated all the way through. We knew what we were up against in Dunloy. After Christmas that year Georgie had a hernia operation and after just two or three days out of hospital he was at training. That's the spirit of the man. The weather conditions were atrocious. On snowy nights we could hardly get to the field but we stayed at it and it paid off against Dunloy. Signs on we didn't train at all this year (1996) and Dunloy beat us well. In 1991 it was different and we went on to win the final as well. The club All-Ireland is a great competition, more parochial than the inter-county All-Ireland and very community orientated. You're winning an All-Ireland with the lads you see every day, the lads you drink with. You've known them all the way through. As a team you were one and winning the Club All-Ireland cemented that bond of friendship. There were three brothers of mine on that team, Ray, John and Des and the O'Connors are cousins too so we were a close-knit bunch.'

Glenmore, All-Ireland Club Hurling Champions 1991
Back row: Des Heffernan, Christy Heffernan, Michael Phelan, Pat Barron,
Denis Mullally, P. J. O'Connor, Des Ennett
Front row: Eddie O'Connor, Willie O'Connor, John Flynn, Liam Walsh,
Michael Deady, Ray Heffernan (capt.), John Heffernan, Eddie
Aylward, Mark Flynn (Mascot).

17

Thomond Versus Stack's

The power of the third-level colleges, which surfaced in the early days of the All-Ireland Senior Football Club Championships is now a thing of the past. The lure of student work overseas is a major factor. Which is why Thomond College's winning of the Limerick Senior Football Championship title in 1977 was a singular achievement and their subsequent All-Ireland victory from a small pool of players even more extraordinary.

FOUR AND A HALF HOURS

There have been many marvellous club confrontations since the birth of the club All-Irelands in 1971 but none surpassed the four meetings of Austin Stack's and Thomond College (Limerick) in 1977–1978. The first game took place in Páirc na nGael, Limerick, on 11 December and resulted in a 2-6 all draw. Seán Kilfeather (*The Irish Times*) wrote: 'Mike Sheehy came off the substitutes' bench during the second half to put Austin Stack's back into a match they thought they had lost. With excitement at a high pitch and the supporters of both sides yelling encouragement, the final whistle brought an end to a splendidly contested game'.

Game number two took place the following Sunday at Páirc Uí Chaoimh. Thomond led again at half-time by 3-3 to 0-5. Once again Mike Sheehy was a star, contributing 1-6 in all, in an inspiring display. Thomond held sway at mid-field thanks to Brian Talty (Galway) and Tony Harkin. The real stars of the game were Thomond wing-half-backs, Mayomen Denis O'Boyle and Martin Connolly. Up front Thomond's kingpins were Richie Bell (Mayo) and Pat Spillane, where John O'Connell scored two splendid goals.

Thomond's only score in the second half was a brilliant individual Pat Spillane point. In the end Stack's owed much to substitute Pat Moriarty, who scored the equalising point. Referee John Moloney (Tipperary) didn't insist on extra time due to failing light. The final score was Thomond College 3-4 Austin Stack's 1-10.

Christmas intervened for game number three which was again at Páirc Uí Chaoimh, on 15 January and ended finally after extra time on the score Austin Stack's 3-15 Thomond College 2-18. Paddy Downey (*The Irish Times*): 'In Munster last night followers of Gaelic football were pondering the question—will it be this forever, will they go on in perpetual deadlock, in replay after replay, changing teams from year to year? Great scores, swaying fortunes, lost opportunities on both sides, all the stuff of sporting drama, before the sides finish deadlocked at the end of extra time.'

Once again Mike Sheehy was Stacks' saviour supreme. He pointed a long-range free some 15 seconds from the end of normal time to gain parity and then 75 seconds from the end of extra time goaled a penalty for the equaliser. Brian Talty was the Thomond star, though he tired in extra time. Up front Pat Spillane, the captain, led by example and Westmeath's Mick Kilcoyne also starred, while in defence Mick Houston, Seán O'Shea and Brian McSweeney excelled. The score at the end of normal time read Austin Stack's 2-9 Thomond College 1-12.

The end of it all came after game four at Páirc Uí Chaoimh the following Sunday with Thomond winning by 3-8 to 2-5. Seán Kilfeather (*The Irish Times*): 'After four and a half hours of football Thomond's easy win left us wondering how it was the Kerry champions made such a fight of it.' The winners built up an early lead of eight points, led by seven at half-time and stretched it to 11 in the second half, inspired by the Spillane brothers Pat and Mick, Brian Talty and Richie Bell, who held sway at mid-field and Longford's Seán O'Shea at full-back, who had a stormer. The half-time score read 2-4 to 0-3, the Thomond goals coming from Richie Bell and a cheeky Pat Spillane effort. John Moloney of Tipperary, who refereed all four games, contributed in no small way to the whole saga.

MUNSTER FINAL

Thomond won the Munster Final again in Páirc Uí Chaoimh on 5 February, defeating Nemo Rangers by 0-12 to 1-3. Paddy Downey (*The Irish Times*)

wrote: 'Match practice is the best training of all. The four semi-final games had sharpened and polished the skills and the teamwork of the Limerick champions for the contest. The winners were also fitter and faster than their opponents.' The standard of football never equalled that of the four-game-marathon and a waterlogged pitch didn't help. The pace quickened in the second half and the quality improved. In what Paddy described as 'an outstanding side', Mick Spillane starred, helped in defence by Seán O'Shea, Mick Houston and Brian McSweeney, while up front Michael Kilcoyne, Jimmy Dunne and Johnny O'Connell impressed.

In the All-Ireland Semi-final on 5 March at Limerick's Páirc na nGael, Thomond's shooting boots almost let them down. The final took place in Croke Park on 26 March and proved to be an anti-climax as Thomond cruised to an ever so easy win over St John's (Belfast) by 2-14 to 1-3. The disparity between the sides was quite amazing, considering that both teams had travelled long and arduous roads *en route* to the final. St Johns proved no match for the well-drilled Thomond College outfit. Playing against the wind, Andy McCallin, the St Johns' sharpshooter, astonishingly missed an easy early free. Thomond surged ahead to lead by 2-4 to nil before McCallin goaled from a penalty. In the second half Andy had a chance to goal a second penalty for a foul on Mickey Darragh but this time the Thomond goalkeeper, Liam Murphy, saved. Brian Talty and Tony Harkin held sway at mid-field despite being opposed by St Johns' star player, Peter McGinnitty of Fermanagh. Declan Smyth (Galway), Richie Bell and Jimmy Dunne posed all sorts of problems for the St Johns' defence, where Pat Spillane was also a constant threat, scoring 1-4 of the winning total. At half-time Thomond led by 2-6 to 1-0, Pat Spillane getting the first goal with Mick Kilcoyne getting the second after a great Richie Bell shot was blocked. The winners were worthy if easy champions of Ireland. This was the team:

Liam Murphy (Cork)

Michael Houston	Seán O'Shea		Eddie Mahon
Mick Spillane	Brian McSweeney		Martin Connolly
	Anthony Harkin	Brian Talty	
Jimmy Dunne	Richie Bell		Declan Smyth
Mick Kilcoyne	Pat Spillane (capt.)		John O'Connell

Substitute: Denis O'Boyle (Mayo) for Martin Connolly.

115

DENIS O'BOYLE LOOKS BACK

Denis O'Boyle, the substitute, who came on in that final, and was a star half-back in the four-game saga against Austin Stack's earlier, remembers those days with fondness. He is now a Physical Education teacher in St Colman's College, Claremorris and, like many of his counterparts scattered across Ireland, is involved in GAA coaching at many levels.

'We had a very successful team in Thomond the year prior to our All-Ireland win, full of stars like Brian Mullins, John Tobin, Pat Spillane, Liam Farrelly (Wexford) and Fran Ryder but they didn't participate in the club scene. Side by side with that we had a second Intermediate College team which was very successful — a second team of which I was captain. So it was largely a mixture of both of these teams which formed the All-Ireland winning one.

'We decided at a club meeting to enter the Limerick County Senior Football Championship, having been inspired by UCD's All-Ireland successes earlier. The year before we had won practically everything at College level so the time was ripe. The people in charge of us were David Weldrick (Coach), John O'Halloran from Cork, himself a former star and our great motivator, and Joe McGrath was involved also in the video analysis area. We were a very small bunch but the key point was we lived, worked, ate and played together. We came as close as you can get to the professional approach. Before we knew it we were in the now famous saga with Austin Stack's, a team full of household names whereas our team would average at about 21 years of age or less. The rivalry between us, while keen, was healthy. At the end of one of those games Mikey Sheehy had to goal a penalty to equalise. It was tense. Yet our goalkeeper, Liam Murphy, asked Mikey, "Which side are you putting it today?" Mikey nonchalantly, replied, "I'll send it to your right!" which he did. That incident showed the friendly spirit between the sides as well as the super confidence of the great Sheehy.

'We had a pool of about 25 players available to us out of 50 men in the College. Some of those available to us opted to play for their own home clubs. For a time we had difficulties over the eligibility of Brian Talty and Declan Smyth who had been in the USA. Gerry Dillon needs a special mention because he was very much part of the team early on.

'The excitement of winning was different as many of us went our separate ways from Croke Park. Afterwards we celebrated at a presentation night in

Limerick which was memorable. The late Richie Bell was a great member of that team and a great friend. The number of those former team-mates who attended his funeral was testimony of the great camaraderie and team-spirit he helped to foster. How often the two of us hitched to Limerick for training sessions after our day's work!

'Pat Spillane was great. Pat always had difficulty seeing the play at the other end of the field. Maybe that's why he chased everything! He had tremendous skill, didn't like losing. Winning that All-Ireland has created a great bond between us. David Weldrick was way ahead of his time in coaching methods. Every session was different. It gave us all a tremendous concept of how to prepare Gaelic teams. We prepared systems of play for all situations and everyone on the team covered for somebody else.'

Pat Spillane (capt.)   *Brian Talty in action in Croke Park*

18

Portlaoise

PORTLAOISE AND TOM PRENDERGAST

The silken football skills of dark-haired stylist Tom Prendergast will be forever linked with Portlaoise's All-Ireland Senior Football club success of 1983. Portlaoise had an impressive club football record, both at home and in Leinster, before the Andy Merrigan Cup was won. In the 1982 County Final at Portarlington, Annanough were beaten well by 1-13 to 0-4 on 3 October. In doing so Portlaoise brought off the senior double (Hurling and Football) for the second successive year. The winners were in devastating form, led by 0-8 to 0-2 at half time before one of their dual stars, Pat Critchley, scored the only goal of a one-sided game.

Then followed wins over Two-Mile-House (Wexford) by 0-12 to 1-5, over Granard Saint Mary's (Longford) by 2-18 to 1-12, over Sarsfield's (Kildare) by 1-11 to 1-6. In the latter game an opportunist goal from Tom Prendergast after 19 minutes had a big bearing on the outcome.

Described as 'one of the finest games ever played in the competition' Portlaoise defeated the Dublin champions, Ballymun Kickhams, at Dr Cullen Park, Carlow by 1-8 to 0-7 on 28 November. A magnificent second-half performance gave Portlaoise their third Leinster crown, though success at half-time looked very remote for them as they led by 0-3 to 0-2 although aided by the wind. It was the brilliant play of Tom Prendergast and Éamonn Whelan, both Laois stars, which was significant in fashioning the victory.

St Finbarr's

Beating the Barrs of Cork in the semi-final at Portarlington on Sunday 6 March was a marvellous feat. The score 0-7 to 0-6 tells the story of an agonisingly close game on a day of high winds, which certainly didn't help the forwards. The Barrs have an unrivalled record in club All-Ireland fare. Five times champions of the land they are the only club with dual titles— three Football (1980, 1981 and 1987) and two Hurling (1975 and 1978) and the only football club besides UCD to win All-Ireland titles back-to-back. The game was played at the Mill Field, Portarlington, before an attendance of 4,000.

The Leinster Express's sub-heading read 'Gerry Browne's late point the match-winner in thriller'. The scenes that followed Tony Jordan's final whistle demonstrated that the heartbreaks of 1972 and 1977 were well and truly forgotten as both players and supporters could not conceal their boundless joy at the prospect of a long overdue title for "The Town".' Victory was secured in the 25th minute of the second half when Gerry Browne gained possession from Bernie Conroy's probing free kick and pointed to give Portlaoise the lead.

St Finbarr's won the toss and played with the very strong breeze at their backs but it was Portlaoise who dictated the scene, as the Munster men tended to over-elaborate, and led at half-time by 0-5 to 0-2 with Jimmy Bergin at full-back proving a master and both Bernie Conroy and Mick Lillis giving exhibitions of half-back play at its best. The Barrs came back against the wind and drew level (0-6 each) with a point from their best forward, Jamesie Callaghan, with six minutes to play. Then followed Gerry Browne's match winner and the celebrations. *The Leinster Express* singled out Jimmy Bergin as the day's star ably helped by Mark Kavanagh, Mick Lillis, Colm Browne, Éamonn Whelan and Mick Dooley, while up front Pat Critchley and Liam Scully (capt.) were best. Tony Jordan was praised for an 'exemplary display of refereeing'.

The Final

The final against Clann na nGael (Roscommon) took place in McDonagh Park, Cloughjordan, on Sunday 20 March and resulted in a pretty decisive win for Portlaoise on the score 0-12 to 2-0. Martin Breheny (*Irish Press*) wrote: 'Portlaoise overcame both their own inaccurate shooting and the

support for their style of play from way outside Portlaoise. That was the year of the brilliant game we lost to Austin Stack's of Tralee. One of the best games ever played in O'Moore Park and still talked about both here in Laois and in Kerry. There were so many brilliant scores and the atmosphere was electric with the issue in the balance to the end. Tom Prendergast set the place on fire with two great goals. I often regret we don't have them on video to recapture their magic.

'The club was growing in confidence all the time: getting experience and maturing into a strong cohesive unit, winning successive Laois titles in 1981 and 1982, and the third Leinster club crown in 1982. This time, come hell or high water, we were after the All-Ireland and had the confidence to do so. Bill Phelan had been trainer of the team from 1976 to 1981 but Colm Browne took over then. The selectors were Jas O'Reilly (Chairman), Bill Phelan, Paschal Delaney, Mick MacDonald and myself. Our club had been in an All-Ireland Final as a club representing the county Laois and been beaten by Bohercrowe (Tipperary) in 1889. So we were in a sense re-enacting history. We would have loved to have played the final in Croke Park but the club All-Irelands hadn't established themselves then and weren't in the glamorous position they now enjoy. There was a marvellous sense of satisfaction at achieving the All-Ireland goal.

'In the late 1970s while I was still Chairman, I spearheaded a special Committee to look into ways of promoting hurling in the club in tandem with football. We found it very difficult and there was a lot of negative reaction. We got Jimmy Doyle of Tipperary to help us out. Tom Lalor and others had kept the hurling flag flying over the years. We got to the County Final in Jimmy Doyle's first year in 1980 before losing to Camross. We went on to win the hurling title from 1981–1984, our first since 1943. At this stage we have won 20 football and nine hurling titles and have produced some great hurlers like John Taylor, the Bohanes and Pat Critchley who became an All-Star. We are very proud of maintaining such a high standard in the club in both codes in the 1980s. One of my great regrets is that we never won a Leinster club hurling title, though we narrowly lost to a late goal in the dying seconds by Rathnure once in a final.

'We've got our own club grounds in the late 1970s which we called after Bill Phelan and we built our own Club Centre in the early 1980s called after Paschal Delaney. Club development has continued apace and we now have a number of pitches. In both hurling and football we have continued to promote the games at juvenile level and this continues to reap rewards. The club championships have developed themselves without too much help from the GAA. The club is the heart and soul of the organisation and while the county is very important, the club championships have opened up a new avenue for successful club teams and their supporters. As to the future they will only develop further and the sponsorship of AIB is a great boost to the competition.'

Portlaoise, All-Ireland Club Football Champions 1982/1983

Back row: Mick McDonald, Éamon Conroy, Seán Dunne, Éamon Whelan, Mick Lillis, Ger Rowney, Mick Mulhall, Mick Dooley, Jimmy Bergin, Mark Kavanagh, Joe Keenan, Seán Bergin, John Bohane, Bernie Conroy, Teddy Fennelly.

Front row: Bill Phelan, Noel Scully, Billy Bohane, Gerry Browne, Tom Prendergast, Liam Scully (capt.), Noel Prendergast, Brian Rankin, Pat Critchley, Colm Brown (team trainer), Jas O'Reilly, Tony Maher.

19

The Fennellys & Ballyhale

Ballyhale Shamrocks, formed in 1972, is an amalgamation of two junior teams at the time, the adjoining villages of Ballyhale and Knocktopher. Success came to the club almost immediately with the winning of the Kilkenny junior hurling title in 1973, the Intermediate in 1974 (gaining the club senior status), as well as three U-21 titles in a row 1972–1974. The club battled bravely for success at senior level before their first title win of 1978. Altogether the club now has nine Kilkenny titles, and three All-Irelands, sitting alongside The Rockies of Cork at the top of Ireland's club roll of honour. Tom Ryall, Kilkenny PRO, in tribute to the Fennelly clan: 'It is fair to say that the rise of Ballyhale Shamrocks coincided with the coming of the Fennellys on stream. They became the backbone of the team, although at the start of the club in 1972 most of them were in their teens. In time all seven boys were on the winning All-Ireland teams of 1981, 1984 and 1990, Michael, Kevin, Liam, Brendan, Ger, Seán and the youngest of the boys, Dermot. The latter wasn't old enough to make the 1978 first county title winning side. It is doubtful if any other family feat surpasses the Fennellys' achievements. Not alone did they win hurling honours but all seven brothers won Kilkenny Senior Football Championship medals three times. Their own father, Kevin, was a fine hurler in his own right, playing with the Kilkenny minors as captain in 1940 and the juniors in 1949. In 1943 he helped Stoneyford to Kilkenny junior hurling success, along with six other brothers. So it was a case of, "Briseann an dúchas…" when his own sons did likewise later.'

THE THREE ALL-IRELANDS

Shamrocks drew the 1980 Kilkenny Senior Hurling Final with Muckalee/Ballyfoyle Rangers on the score 3-10 to 2-13. It was a battle supreme on a heavy surface between the style of Ballyhale and the passion of Muckalee. A tremendous cheer greeted Tom Moran's drawing goal from a penalty. In the replay, also at Nowlan Park two weeks later, the Shamrocks roared back in style to win by 3-13 to 1-10.

In the Leinster Final, Coolderry (Offaly), fell by 3-10 to 1-8 at Athy, when Shamrocks won their second Leinster crown. The winners had defensive heroes in captain Richard Reid, Watty Phelan and Seán Fennelly, with goalkeeper Kevin Fennelly a commanding last line of defence. In the All-Ireland Semi-final at Ballycastle, the local McQuillans were beaten by 2-11 to 0-12. Ballycastle pounded them non-stop against the wind in the second half when Maurice Mason was a tower of strength. In the end, long range points from Brendan and Ger Fennelly and the industrious Michael Kelly saved the day. Six Donnelly brothers starred for the losers in this Donnelly-versus-Fennelly battle.

Shamrocks won their first club title defeating St Finbarr's of Cork by 1-15 to 1-11 in Thurles on 17 May 1981. John Knox (*Kilkenny People*): 'By playing hurling of a rare sort, the players from the small Southern parish of about 260 houses, have now gained national recognition for the stylish hurling they have been producing regularly in Kilkenny. All seven Fennellys including substitute Dermot were great, but Brendan was the star supreme, scoring 0-11 (four frees and one penalty). Liam wasn't far behind with Kevin brilliant in goal. The entire total of 1-15 fell to three Fennellys, Liam scoring 1-1 and Ger 0-3 (one free and one "65"). But it wasn't just the Fennellys. Richard Reid played a captain's part when the pressure was greatest and Frank Holohan was also top class, while Liam Dalton starred in his task of keeping tabs on Jimmy Barry-Murphy.' The winning team was:

Kevin Fennelly

| Watty Phelan | Liam Dalton | Richard Reid (capt.) |
| Frank Holohan | Maurice Mason | Declan Connolly |

Johnny Walsh   Seán Fennelly

| Michael Fennelly | Patrick Holden | Ger Fennelly |
| Brendan Fennelly | Liam Fennelly | Michael Kelly |

TITLE NUMBER TWO

Shamrocks' fifth Kilkenny county title success in 1983 was 'a show of real class' (*Kilkenny People*). The defending champions tore 'The Village' (James Stephen's) apart in a mad scoring burst approaching the break and went on to win well by 2-14 to 1-8, displaying 'a vigour and zeal exclusive to them' (John Knox, *Kilkenny People*). The winners led at half-time by 2-11 to 0-4. Though forced to field without Brendan and Ger Fennelly, John Knox singled out the family for special plaudits 'The Fennelly family from Castlebanny can wallow in the glory of it all. Five of these talented hurling sons performed and one was better than the next.' He went on to praise stand-in goalkeeper forty-two-year-old Ollie Harrington, Maurice Mason who was great under the dropping ball and Seán Fennelly who was outstanding at mid-field. Regular goalkeeper Kevin Fennelly played a captain's part in attack, scoring 0-4 from frees.

In the Leinster Final, played in December 1983 in Athy, Shamrocks won a thriller against Kinnity (Offaly) by 3-6 to 0-9. The teams were level four times and Shamrocks took control in the final ten minutes after Liam Fennelly scored two opportunist and timely goals. Once again the Fennellys accounted for all Ballyhale's total Frank Holohan was a pillar in defence and Ollie Harrington manned the 'bearna baol' efficiently.

EXPERIMENT

The GAA experimented in 1984, playing semi-final and final on the same weekend, similar to Intervarsity competitions but this didn't suit club teams and was quickly forgotten. On Saturday, 14 April at Navan, Shamrocks defeated Ballycastle McQuillans by 3-14 to 2-10 in a match of contrasting halves. The first was tough, bruising and, at times, wild. The second threw up some stirring hurling as Ballycastle took the game to Shamrocks and were only beaten by a determined late burst which saw the winners score seven points to one in the final 11 minutes. It was very much a battle of the Donnelly clan (seven brothers) against the Fennellys (six) with the latter coming out on top.

Imagine the Ballyhale team waking up next morning to take on Gort in the final at Birr who won their semi-final also on the Saturday. Men with tired sore limbs. The game ended in a draw 1-10 each. In the second half Liam Fennelly was sprung from the sideline after recovering from a broken ankle and this had the double effect of unsteadying Gort and giving life to the Shamrocks. At the finish it was a 59th minute spectacular point from Dermot Fennelly which earned Shamrocks a draw. Kevin Fennelly scored a remarkable 2-12 over both days. Both sides turned down the playing of extra time. Two very tired teams trooped off the field to settle the issue on another day.

In the replay on 3 June at Thurles, Ballyhale won club title number two by 1-10 to 0-7. Heavy showers made conditions difficult but the Kilkenny lads took their chances better. Gort hurled with the breeze in the first half but in the 27th minute with the scores at 0-4 each Ger Fennelly got the decisive goal and Shamrocks went on to lead 1-5 to 0-4 at the break. The Fennellys once again accounted for Ballyhale's entire tally. This was the team:

Ollie Harrington

Frank Holohan	Liam Dalton	Watty Phelan
Michael Fennelly	Maurice Mason	Seán Fennelly

Johnny Walsh   Tommy Phelan

Brendan Fennelly	Ger Fennelly	Michael Kelly
Dermot Fennelly	Kevin Fennelly	Liam Fennelly

Substitute: Liam Long for Liam Fennelly.

TITLE NUMBER THREE

On Sunday, 1 October 1989 on the same day as Glen Rovers defeated Sarsfield's to win the Cork County title, Shamrocks had an incredible win over Glenmore by 2-11 to 1-13. After trailing for most of the way, Ballyhale drew level at 1-11 each with four minutes to play. Approaching full-time they found themselves two points in arrears. Thirty seconds into lost time their big-hearted central defender Paul Phelan burst up-field, started and finished an attack which yielded Shamrocks' winning goal. It was a famous eighth Kilkenny title for Shamrocks and a shattering blow to Glenmore which inspired them later. Glenmore were well on top in the first half but a timely goal by Brendan Fennelly just before half time took a very bare look off Shamrocks' total to leave it 1-8 to 1-3 in Glenmore's favour at half time. The eventual winners kept nibbling away at Glenmore's lead until they clinched it with Paul Phelan's goal at the end through a crowded goalmouth.

In their fourth Leinster title win over Cuala (Dublin) by 2-11 to 0-7 at Athy, Frank Holohan and Tommy Shefflin were outstanding.

In the All-Ireland Semi-final on 11 February at Ballinasloe, the day Joe Cooney was held up by floods, Ballyhale Shamrocks defeated Sarsfield's (Galway) by 2-8 to 0-12. Despite very wintry conditions in Duggan Park, Ballinasloe, there were passages of excellent hurling in this game. In the end it took a brace of points from Ger Fennelly to clinch victory.

Joe Cooney's late arrival certainly affected Sarsfields' play in the first half when favoured by the strong breeze, they led by 0-7 to 1-0 at half time with Michael 'Hopper' McGrath in scintillating form. After seven minutes of the second half Ballyhale forged ahead with a Dermot Fennelly goal. Still with four minutes to go as in the County Final the sides were level 2-6 to 0-12. Then came Ger Fennelly's brace of points, the last one a magnificent 75 yards free and Shamrocks were into another final. On the same day Ballybrown (Limerick) just edged out Loughgiel by 0-9 to 0-8 in the other semi-final.

St Patrick's Day had now become All-Ireland Club Final day. In the final, Shamrocks defeated Ballybrown by 1-16 to 0-16 in yet another thriller. Tom O'Riordan (*Sunday Independent*) gave pride of place to Ger Fennelly who 'masterminded his side's third victory in the All-Ireland club series before 16,000 people in a thrilling game. It was Fennelly's old head which calmed things when Ballybrown held sway and led by six points six minutes from half time. Then Fennelly stepped up to a 50 yard free and his well hit shot went all the way to the net but Ballybrown still led 0-12 to 1-5 at the interval.'

Ballybrown lost their way in the third quarter and fine points by Brendan Mason, Brendan and Ger Fennelly and Tom Shefflin had them level before Jimmy Lawlor put them ahead. That surge won the day and the Shamrocks held on for a deserved third success. This was the team:

Kevin Fennelly

Michael Fennelly	Frank Holohan	Watty Phelan (capt.)
Dick Walsh	Paul Phelan	Seán Fennelly

Ger Fennelly   Tom Shefflin

Tommy Phelan	Jimmy Lawlor	Dermot Fennelly
Brendan Fennelly	Liam Fennelly	Brendan Mason

GER FENNELLY

I had long desired to meet one of the great Fennelly clan and when Tom Ryall took me to Knocktopher to the home of Ger Fennelly, I was thrilled to meet a very humble sportsman and spend a lovely evening in the company of his family: wife Carmel and children, Caitríona, Maresa, Paul, Gerard, Keeva and Geraldine. A hole the size of a sliothar was in one of the front windows and when I enquired, yes it was the result of a sliothar on that very evening and lucky for the youngsters the parents understood. 'It often happened to myself at home when we were young. And we'd try to blame the younger lads,' Ger said.

Ger captained Kilkenny to win the U-21 All-Ireland in 1974, having won a minor All-Ireland medal in 1972, and went on to captain Kilkenny to senior All-Ireland success in 1979. He went on to win All-Irelands with Kilkenny again in 1982 and 1983 and was the first of the famous Fennellys to hit national headlines. Younger brother Liam became a very successful captain later. Where did they get all the hurling interest? 'It was always hurling in my parents' families and we grew up with it. We started off in Piltown National School at a very young age before moving to the family home at Clonbanny, Ballyhale. Our most precious presents from Dad were hurleys. I remember often cleaning them after use. We were lucky enough to have plenty of other young boys of our own age all around us and we hurled together every night till it got dark. My mother used to blow a whistle to bring us in for bed. Those games were great. We often played for sweets with lads like Maurice Mason and the Reids.

'As to the All-Irelands we were brought on to a wider stage meeting the Barrs from Cork, some very strong Antrim teams, Blackrock, Sarsfield's, other strong teams in Leinster, Ballybrown and Sylvie Linnane's Gort. It was a great comfort to have so many brothers playing because we knew each others play inside out. In the early days we all lived at home and had hurling for breakfast, dinner and supper literally. Dad was involved with the club then and he was master of it all. As for Mam, all she'd be worried about was that we wouldn't get injured. She'd insist on us wearing helmets and she used to pray a lot during games.

'My greatest club memories are of the first County Final win of 1978 and our first All-Ireland club win in 1981. It is a very proud feeling to be part of a small parish and see five or six buses lined up in the village on the morning of an All-Ireland Final, transporting almost the entire community behind the local team. We ourselves travelled in a bus too. As to particular feats, I remember Brendan scoring freely against the Barrs in 1981 and the most thrilling win of all has to be the County Final win over Glenmore in 1989 with the last puck of the game. The club All-Irelands give chances to players to play in Croke Park in exciting games before big crowds that they'd never otherwise get. People like my own brother Brendan for instance. As a family we are scattered a bit now but we are still very close and meet often. Playing the game gave us a great outlook on life and we have made friends with people across the land. Finally, I'd like to pay tribute to local teacher Joe Dunphy who did so much to create young hurlers and to our trainers Tom Ryan from Dunamaggin, Martin Óg Morrissey and Tommy Hearne of Waterford. We now have our own club field in Ballyhale but we never had one during our All-Ireland winning years, using the Friary field as our training grounds. By the way it wasn't all boys in the Fennellys. Our greatest fans were the two girls Teresa and Monica.'

Ballyhale Shamrocks, Triple Senior All-Ireland Club Champions
*Back row: Ger Fennelly, Frank Holohan, Liam Fennelly, Michael Fennelly,
         Dick Walsh, Sean Fennelly, Jim Lawlor*
*Front row: Dermot Fennelly, Kevin Fennelly, Brendan Fennelly, Tommy
         Phelan (capt.), Watty Phelan, Tommy Shefflin, Paul Phelan,
         Brendan Mason.*

20
Castleisland Desmonds

The death-knell sounds, alas, for whom,
As Downey floats it in
And Donie Buckley in great style
Has scored and done his thing
Marino souls cut to the core
Dreamt of things that might have been
But Desmonds are All-Ireland champs
In every hill and glen.

The Castleisland Desmonds had a tortuous route to win the Kerry Club Championship of 1984, qualification for which was achieved by Castleisland by finishing joint second in the 1984 County League. First Castleisland defeated Austin Stack's in a playoff; then there were other playoff wins over Beale, Rathmore, in the quarter-final, Valentia, the Division I League winners in the semi-final and finally the South Kerry champions, St Mary's of Caherciveen in the final after a replay in which Arthur O'Connor starred. This was Castleisland's third Kerry Club championship in four years.

MUNSTER CHAMPIONSHIP

A goal by substitute Willie O'Connor, who had just replaced Christy Kearney, won the day at Fethard on 9 December against the home club on the score 3-7 to 1-8. Fethard led for most of the game, were in front 1-6 to 0-5 at half-time but a strong Castleisland comeback in the second half, influenced chiefly by Kerry minor Martin Downey, who scored 1-4 in all, saw the Desmonds through to the Munster Final.

In the Munster Final at Bruff on the Sunday before Christmas Castleisland won the title, defeating St Finbarr's of Cork by 2-6 to 0-9 atoning for a Munster Final replay defeat against the same opposition two years previously. The winners were hampered with injuries to Donie Buckley, Willie 'Dom' O'Connor and John Lyons but the spirit in training in the December mud was keen and hopes were high. Once again Castleisland came from behind with goals by Phil Horan and substitute Willie 'Dom' O'Connor to inspire a great victory. After being out of football for over a year Pa O'Callaghan made a fine comeback. Peadar O'Brien (*Irish Press*) described it as 'a splendidly contested final'. At half-time it looked as if Castleisland would win handily enough as they held St Finbarr's to level scoring despite having played against an extremely strong breeze. The Barrs rallied into the wind and led by three points in the final ten minutes. A Martin Downey point followed by Willie 'Dom's' goal, flicked to the net from a Michael O'Connor lob, did the trick. Peadar's heroes were: Michael O'Connor at mid-field, the terrier-like 'Dom', whose goal won the day, and the *Irish Press* man-of-the-match was M. J. Kearney.

Clann Na nGael

The Desmonds players trained under former Kerry star Dave Geaney on Banna Strand in early January. Dr Geaney was selected as Talbot Team-manager-of-the-month for December and the All-Ireland Semi-final game on home soil against Clann na nGael (Roscommon) was eagerly awaited. Then two weeks before the game Arthur O'Connor broke his leg and the atmosphere was shrouded in gloom. The performance by both teams was disappointing and they failed to snatch winning late points. The disappointment was even greater for the home side, who never got to grips with the game. Clann led by 0-5 to 0-3 at half-time. Towards the end a Mikie O'Connor penalty conversion put Desmonds in front but Éamonn McManus Jnr got the equalising point for Clann. The final score was Clann na nGael 0-7, Castleisland Desmonds 1-4. They trained extra hard for the replay on 18 March in Clann's own grounds at Johnstown.

I remember travelling by train from Dublin to Athlone *en route* to Galway, meeting up with Seán Kilfeather (*The Irish Times*) and sharing a taxi to the game with the well-known pressman from Sligo. Many Castleisland supporters had travelled on the long journey north on a bitterly cold March day. Seán Kilfeather opened his piece for *The Irish Times*: 'Briseann an dúchas…' Surely enough the old Irish proverb carried much wisdom. In Johnstown a son of the great Tadhgie Lyne, named as Diarmuid in the programme but 'Domo' to his supporters, showed all the class and guile of his breeding by scoring 2-2 as Castleisland won the replay by 2-6 to 0-8.' Nibs of sleet blown by a vicious March wind numbed the senses and made playing conditions very difficult, Billy Lyons played a captain's part for the winners, helped by Diarmuid Ó Ciardhubháin, Mike O'Connor and Dermot Hannafin but 'Domo' Lyne was the star supreme, getting his goals at vital times. This was undoubtedly Desmonds' greatest display in the whole campaign and hopes were high that the mighty St Vincent's of Dublin, who boasted many of the Dubs stars of that era, would be beaten in the final in Tipperary Town on Sunday 24 March, just six days after the victory over Clann.

Gerry McCarthy (*Irish Press*) under a banner headline 'Desmonds Rob St Vincents' wrote: 'Daylight robbery is alive and thriving. St Vincent's and all connected with the Dublin champions will forever be convinced of this after they had victory snatched from their grasp at Tipperary. The game was in its concluding minutes and Desmonds trailed by two points. A despairing last attack by the Kerry representatives appeared to have foundered, when a St Vincents' defender cleared the ball over the sideline literally inches from his own left wing corner flag. Willie O'Connor took the kick and floated the ball into the Vincents' square. Hands reached for it and Vincent Conroy failed to bring off a clean fetch. The ball bobbed about in the air and suddenly it was in the net, despatched there by Donie Buckley. The Dublin champions were shattered and all of Castleisland descended onto the playing area to celebrate the fact that the country cousins had defeated the fancied city men.' The final score read: Castleisland Desmonds 2-2 St Vincent's 0-7. (Half-time 0-3 to 0-1 in favour of St Vincent's). No Kerry team ever gives up hope no matter how forlorn the chances. Charlie Nelligan was superb between the posts. It was as Éamon O'Sullivan, Kerry and Castleisland Desmond's PRO, described 'a moment of imperishable triumph'. Certain defeat had been turned into glorious victory. This was the team:

Charlie Nelligan

D. Ó Ciardhubháin Billy Lyons (capt.)   Willsie King

Pa O'Callaghan   Michael John Kearney   Denis Lyons

Mikie O'Connor   Dermot Hannafin

'Dom' O'Connor   Christy Kearney   'Domo' Lyne

Johnny O'Connor   Donie Buckley   Philip Horan

Substitutes: Martin Downey for Johnny O'Connor, John Lyons for 'Domo' Lyne. Team-manager and Sole Selector, Dr Dave Geaney, Trainer Donal 'Duke' O'Connor.

REFLECTIONS OF THE MANAGER

Dave Geaney, the Castleisland Manager/Sole Selector is a former Kerry star, whose father Con also wore the Kerry jersey with pride. A medical doctor with a thriving practice in his native town, his interests are Gaelic football and racing outside the routine of family life and work. 'I had a trainer with me and a good one in Donal O'Connor. We had a tremendous set up in that. Even though I was the Manager and Sole Selector, I always sought Donal's advice and we had an outstanding player in Mikie O'Connor, who was a born leader both on and off the field.

'People say we were lucky to beat Vincent's in the final, in the sense that we didn't get the winning score until the last two minutes of the match but on balance we put up a great performance on the day. It was a lovely way to win it because the goal came at a period when there was no coming back from it.

'A tremendous amount of work goes into the winning of an All-Ireland on the part of the players, trainer, club and management. We had learnt over the previous few years that we were capable of doing it. We had lost two previous Munster finals, to Nemo Rangers on our first foray and in a replay to St Finbarr's of Cork in the second. The Nemo loss was a learning experience and our close call with the Barrs showed remarkable improvement.

'The year of our triumph we beat the Barrs in the final. You have to be able to beat a Cork team if you want to win an All-Ireland, because their standard is so high. We were quite fortunate to draw with Clann na nGael in our own pitch. We didn't know what to expect really as it was our first introduction to the All-Ireland series and they were used to it. They had a fine team and were very unlucky not to win a title. I think everybody who opposed them over the years would have loved to have seen them go all the way.

'Coming back to the final we were lucky again with the timing. We beat Clann na nGael on their pitch on a St Patrick's weekend Bank Holiday Monday and were in the final again six days later. We were in an All-Ireland Final and nobody had a chance to think about it and get excited. So we went there with no great pressure on us. The whole thing gave a great lift to the town. A great morale booster for the area and we had a huge support in Tipperary for the final, from the town, the hinterland and the county itself.'

The Team

'There was a great bond between us all. We had a huge inspiration from the goal in the person of Charlie Nelligan. His performance in the final was his greatest ever display. The late Bill Lyons was our captain and full-back. He was a real inspiration and knew when to mix it and when to play football. Mikie O'Connor and Dermot Hannafin formed a fine mid-field partnership. O'Connor led by example at all times. Since then I've come to realise what it means to have a good leader on a team. In the forwards, we had Donie Buckley, who scored the winning goal and will always be remembered for that. A man who kept his feet firmly on the ground and still gives his all to the game. "Domo" Lyne's two goals against Clann were vital too. Pa O'Callaghan, Michael John Kearney were in the backline. Nobody passed them. Christy Kearney was up in the forward line with Philip Horan. We had forwards who'd match anybody for scoring power.

'Winning the Munster Final, beating the Barrs at Bruff was probably my greatest thrill. We developed a great friendship with Clann na nGael. Club to club can develop great bonds. Each respects the other and this competition has created many such bonds. I'd like to see it finished before the year is out. It would mean running it off on a regular basis in the months of October and November. The final could even be played in December.

'Our trainer Donal O'Connor had a lovely quality about him. We had great back-up from the club itself, its officers Jack Nolan, John Pender and Seán McCarthy. We played a lot of challenge games before the All-Ireland series with UCG and there was never a problem. Winning the All-Ireland gave a lift to the many great players from the past like Mikie Joe O'Sullivan,

Timmie O'Sullivan, Tadhg McGillacuddy, my own Dad (Con Geaney), Tom Óg Burke, Dermot Hannafin, (father of Dermot), Tadhgie Lyne, (father of "Domo"), some of whom are now dead and gone, and to the men who trained juvenile teams up along the way like Tommy Broder and Larry Dowd. The lads who sowed the seed. I'm still team-manager and still have ambitions. It has to be a tonic. Sure I wouldn't be at it unless I enjoyed it!'

CHARLIE NELLIGAN

He was busy in his Killarney bakery when I called but as always found time to talk and still has the big endearing smile and the twinkle in the eye. How does he compare the club All-Ireland with his inter-county achievements with Kerry? 'Winning the All-Ireland club title was fantastic. I would certainly put it equal to winning my first All-Ireland medal with Kerry. Had I won only one All-Ireland medal with Kerry, the thrill would be the same. I'm not being smart Jack, but it's great to have both. In my eyes they are both the same. The only difference as I see it, with the club, every day you walk down the street you meet fellows you win the club title with. With the county it's different John Egan is in Cork, Pat Spillane is in Kenmare. Since our team broke up in 1986 I think we have only met as a group once.'

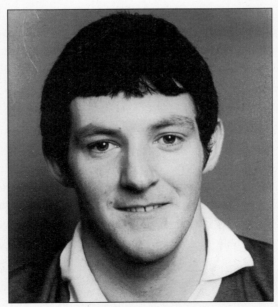

Charlie Nelligan

21
East Kerry's First

Divisional teams have long been part of Kerry club football, as Kerry County Secretary Tony O'Keeffe explains in the chapter on Austin Stack's. Although a Divisional team may still win out the Kerry County Senior Football title, a club, as such, may only represent the county in the All-Ireland club scene and they have a special club title as distinct from the county title to decide for Kerry in such circumstances. So it has not been possible for a divisional team to win a club All-Ireland for some years now.

East Kerry, roughly the Killarney area of Kerry, has its own East Kerry Board which runs its own East Kerry Senior Football Championship for the O'Donoghue Cup annually, honouring the late Dr Patrick O'Donoghue of Glenflesk. Seán Kelly, the present Kerry County Board Chairman, is a former East Kerry Board Chairman. The Board published its own history entitled *The Clear Air Boys* edited jointly by Donal Hickey and Tony Leen in 1986, honouring on its cover its four All-Ireland winning captains Dick Fitzgerald (1913–1914), Johnny Culloty (1969), Donie Sullivan (1970) and Ambrose O'Donovan (1984).

The glorious era of county championship football success for East Kerry began in 1964 when it was decided that a team from the Division would contest all grades of the Kerry County Championships that year and to the delight of all involved, the East Kerry senior team reached the County Senior Final before yielding to Shannon Rangers. 1965 was to be even better. The first ever Kerry Senior Football Championship title was won in a replay against Mid-Kerry and the minor title was added also. The Munster Senior Football title of 1966 was achieved against Clonmel Commercials. A short

This was the winning team:

Éamon Fitzgerald

| Donie O'Sullivan | Derry Crowley | | Jim Gleeson |
| Ger Cullinane | Noel Power | | Ger O'Donoghue |

Pat Casey   Pat Moynihan

Paddy O'Donoghue Dan O'Keeffe   Denis Healy

Denis Coffey   Michael Gleeson (capt.)   Dan Kavanagh

Substitutes: Tom Looney (Dr Crokes), Mikey Lyne (Legion), Weeshie Fogarty (Legion), Jimmy Hegarty (Glenflesk), Johnny O'Mahoney (Gneeveguilla) Trainer: Donie Sheahan (Dr Crokes)

DONIE O'SULLIVAN REFLECTS

Donie O'Sullivan was one of the great all-time Kerry corner-backs, an All-Star corner-back in the initial years 1971 and 1972 and one of the longest dead ball kickers the game has seen. 'I won four County titles with East Kerry 1965, 1968–1970. Mick Gleeson, Derry Crowley, Ger Cullinane and Pat Moynihan were on all those teams. Up to 1969 we had eight clubs represented. After winning in 1969, three of the eight clubs opted out of the East Kerry team and we were represented in 1970–1971 by five clubs, the three Killarney teams Spa, Legion and Dr Crokes, plus Glenflesk and Gneeveguilla. In the three county finals 1968–1970 we beat Waterville, who had a great club team with Mick O'Connell of Valentia also playing for them. Mick O'Dwyer, the great O'Connell, who was half a team and Cork's Mick O'Neill, a Garda Sergeant stationed there, were their strong men. Overall we were that bit stronger but we had some royal battles, most notably the 1969 decider when we were fortunate to win.

'Looking back on the All-Ireland success it meant an awful lot to us as most of us had been around for a good span of time having played in four Munster championships, winning three in all. Our toughest game was against Muskerry who had beaten Nemo Rangers, a club on the way up then. In the final against Bryansford we got the goals at the right time but they had a lovely team. Our full-forward line of Mick Gleeson, Dan Kavanagh and Denis Coffey was as good as any inter-county grouping. They were on top of their form just then, all great men to score.

'Winning the first ever All-Ireland club title is the great memory. We knew we were making history in one way. Also it was a case of *carpe diem* (grab the day) our last hurrah. I don't remember any great euphoria after winning in the now accepted sense. Many of us worked elsewhere. So there was no homecoming as such. When we won our first county title now that was different and there was a huge reception for us then in Killarney, but they had got used to us winning.

'Now 25 years after it was a great honour to be selected for the AIB Jubilee Team. Difficult to select such a team. I enjoyed the occasion very much and met many old friends. That gave us the idea of holding a Silver Jubilee Dinner for our team in Killarney on 17 May 1996. John Kelly, Chairman of the East Kerry Board got the idea first and former County Treasurer Murt Galvin did much of the organisation. We had a wonderful night of nostalgia. One of the players I hadn't met since that day in Croke Park, Denis Healy, was there. We probably celebrated more than we did the night we won it in 1971! I don't remember when we received our medals but we got them OK. Donie Sheahan, our trainer, is still a chemist in Killarney and an enthusiast to this day. That enthusiasm was very infectious, and there never was any tension. Our back-up from officials, trainer and selectors was superb. I remember one night in the Imperial Hotel in Tralee our group were lamenting the fact we never won the Railway Cup and one of the East Kerry lads, Johnny Culloty, remarked: "Whatever about the Railway Cup, we'll never win a county championship!" That was about 1964 but how wrong he was!'

MURT GALVIN'S THOUGHTS

Murt Galvin, Kerry County Treasurer from 1967 to 1984 remembers coming back to Killarney with the Shield in 1971. 'It was an exceptionally cold day in November. We had a fair good support at the game from Kerry people in Dublin and its environs but very few travelled up with us on the train. When we arrived back that night in Killarney at about 11.30 p.m. there were two people at the railway station, the father of one of the players and the player's brother. The competition hadn't taken off at all with little coverage of the event. Coming home that night we might as well have been out playing a club game in Duhallow or Rathmore.

'I was delighted to be part of the organisation of the Silver Jubilee Dinner for the team recently as I had much experience of it in my days with Kerry in the 1970s and 1980s. All bar two of the panel were in attendance. Fourteen of the panel had worn the Kerry jersey in some grade. Wonderful to note that most of that team are still in East Kerry, all of them holding down good jobs, many of them very involved in the GAA still. The men in charge then, Brendan Walshe and Denis Fenton, did a wonderful job in uniting players from five clubs into a winning formation. At times it is difficult enough to manage one club but to achieve unity and success with five is much more difficult.'

From left: Donie O'Sullivan, Denis Coughlan and Francis Loughnane taken at the All-Ireland AIB GAA Silver Jubilee Awards in 1996.

22

Austin Stack's: Tralee

'The Austin Stack's are Champions, once more they hold the Cup,
Through years of disappointments, they never once gave up;
Behind that famed tradition, so proudly handed down,
Those sons of famous fathers, brought glory to their town.'

The first verse of a poem by Jimmy Cullinane commemorates the winning by Austin Stack's of the Kerry Senior Football Championship in 1973 after a long wait of 37 years. In 1926 the Kerry County Board insisted that Tralee on its own was too strong and divided the town into three clubs namely Rock Street (Austin Stack's), Boherbee (John Mitchel's) and Strand Road (Kerins-O'Rahilly's). All three clubs had their golden and bleak eras afterwards but the rivalry provided some of the greatest club games ever seen in Kerry.

Who was Austin Stack? He was active during the years 1879–1929, when he reorganised the Tralee John Mitchel's club to win eight consecutive Kerry Senior Football titles 1902–1909. A regular member of the Kerry team from 1902, he captained Kerry to win the 1904 All-Ireland. Subsequently he became Kerry's most honoured and respected official and as well as the Rock Street club, Tralee's magnificent GAA Park also bears his name. The Austin Stack's teams down the years bristled with Kerry stars. Men like the Landers brothers 'Roundy' and Purty, the great Joe Barrett, full-back of renown, Bill Gorman, 'Pedlar' Sweeney, Miko Doyle — all illustrious names. The Stacks were kings of Kerry football in the late 1920s and early 1930s, Joe Barrett captaining Rock Street to win four county titles in football and two in Senior hurling. Miko Doyle captained the 1936 Senior Football title winning team. Then came the lull until the young babes of 1973 won for Rock Street its sixth of eleven Kerry crowns. This is where our story begins.

With the coming of Austin Stack's as a football power in the 1970s it was inevitable that an All-Ireland club crown would come to Tralee. It came in 1977 but in the history of the club All-Irelands, Austin Stacks' involvement in the replay saga with Nemo Rangers in 1975–1976 (three games in all) and the epic four–game saga with Thomond College, Limerick, helped give the competition a new status and brought much needed prestige to the scene.

1977

Austin Stack's won the 1976 Kerry Senior Football Championship for the third time in four years on Sunday 3 October, defeating Kenmare in a bad tempered and ragged game by 1-14 to 0-7 at Fitzgerald Stadium, Killarney. An easy-looking goal from Jackie Power set Stack's on their way. Then an incident involving Stacks' mid-fielder Dinny Long, the Cork star, incensed the Kenmare supporters who barracked him incessantly subsequently. But the Rock Street mid-fielder revelled in it all and dominated the game thereafter helped by a staunch half-back line of Fintan Lawlor, Anthony O'Keeffe and Ger Power. Stack's led by 1-6 to 0-4 at half-time. In the second half after an early Kenmare point, the winners won comfortably.

Team trainer Jo Jo Barrett (the current *Evening Herald* GAA correspondent), now set his sights on the All-Ireland crown and planned a rigorous training programme which quite often involved training at Banna Beach or Ballybeggan Racing Park. The first step was the defeat of Croom (Limerick) in Tralee on 30 November by 1-13 to 0-4 with Ger Power the star of the day and Paddy Moriarty very impressive in attack.

St Finbarr's of Cork were next to fall, again at Tralee, on 12 December on the score 1-7 to 0-8 but as always against Cork opponents there were many anxious moments before victory was achieved. *The Kerryman* described the win as 'nothing short of grand larceny'. Éamon Horan described the drama thus 'time had just run out when Stack's were awarded a free close to their own goal; this was quickly taken and it eventually spun off an opponent and into Ger Power's grasp. The All-Star wing-back booted a long ball upfield. Ever elusive, Mikey Sheehy moved onto it despite some close policing and duly found full-forward Billy Curtin in front of the Barrs citadel.

144

As the red-haired full-forward gained possession he was submerged in a sea of light blue jerseys and went crashing to the ground. Confusion reigned for some ominous seconds before referee George Ryan of Tipperary signalled a penalty. Suddenly from being a closed case, this game, which had been dominated for long periods by the Corkmen, assumed an entirely new and totally unexpected dimension. There was only a point between the teams despite the dominance of the Barrs (0-8 to 0-7). Would Mikey Sheehy opt for a draw or go for it? The Kerry stalwart decided on all or nothing and amidst nerve-tingling tension ran up to the ball and banged the ball into the roof of the net leaving goalkeeper Donal Kelliher bewildered and beaten. It was one of the most extraordinary turnabouts imaginable in sport!'

Fate had smiled on Austin Stack's. 'I had my mind made up that I was going for the goal,' said a delighted Mikey Sheehy afterwards as he congratulated Billy Curtin for taking his pass so well. Jo-Jo Barrett had indicated he should go for it but team captain John O'Keeffe would have settled for a draw

Austin Stacks' next game, also in Tralee, saw them defeat Kingdom (London) by 2-16 to 0-7 on 30 January. The sticky underfoot conditions failed to limit the silken skills of Mikey Sheehy who scored the only goals of the game in a personal tally of 2-6. Ten thousand people packed themselves into O'Moore Park, Portlaoise, for the semi-final with the local team in a game which ebbed and flowed at an alarming rate. In the end Austin Stack's won a classic game by 1-14 to 2-6. A Tralee rally in the final minutes saw them get back on level terms with a Mikey Sheehy pointed free four minutes from time before the final surge to glory.

Portlaoise led at half-time by 1-3 to 0-5 after a fine first half in which both sides did remarkably well in controlling the ball despite the hazardous underfoot conditions. In the second half, Tom Prendergast scored a smashing goal which is still the talk of Portlaoise and Tralee, which sent 'the whole of O'Moore Park into a frenzy of tribal excitement' (Éamon Horan, *The Kerryman*). Stack's played great football after Mikey Sheehy's equaliser. They engulfed their opponents in wave after wave of blistering football, the speed and fury of 'which had to be seen to be believed' (Éamon Horan). Paudie McCarthy (substitute) shot the winner in the 58th minute after a Ger Power centre. With half a minute of actual playing time left John O'Keeffe set up the move which Timmy Sheehan finished to the net for the final crunch blow. Over 500 Austin Stack's fans travelled by special train for the game and it was a happy trainload set off for the journey home.

to go just two points separated the teams. Then Pat O'Shea struck for a very valuable point in the 57th minute but Paul Curran answered with a beauty, one of his best points ever. In the 59th minute Vincent Carney pointed a free to leave a point in it. Crokes survived a last gasp attack and held on to win.

Con Houlihan (*Evening Press*) described it as 'a hard sporting game and a credit to two fine clubs'. Jim O'Sullivan (*Cork Examiner*) paid high praise to 'John Galvin at centre-back, full-back Liam Hartnett and goalkeeper Peter O'Brien all of whom inspired confidence'. Michael Ellard (*Evening Echo*) quoted Eddie 'Tatler' O'Sullivan, the Crokes' trainer as being 'over the moon'. 'In all my years I have never seen a greater reception accorded a winning Kerry team than the homecoming of Crokes to Killarney last night.' The winning team was:

Peter O'Brien

Brendan Keogh	Liam Hartnett	John Clifford
Seán Clarke	John Galvin	Colm O'Shea

Connie Murphy   Noel O'Leary

Connie Doherty	Danny Cooper	Seánie O'Shea (capt.)
Pat O'Shea	Vince Casey	Ger O'Shea

'TATLER JACK'

Eddie O'Sullivan trained the Crokes to All-Ireland success. A very colourful character, his heart has always been stuck in the GAA. His hostelry 'Tatler Jack's' in Killarney is known far and wide. A native of Castleisland he spent many years working in New York before returning to Killarney to set up business in Ireland's beauty spot. Whence the 'Tatler Jack' name? '"Tatler Jack" Walsh was a rambling house in Lyracompane, where they told stories and sang songs and what have you and I chose that name. I'm known as "Tatler" for some time now. In 1975 when I returned from America I got involved with the Crokes through people I had met in America, like Denis Coffey, Tom Looney and Paudie O'Connor.'

Reflections

'We lost the County Final to Kenmare in 1987 in a replay, our first County final since 1914. In 1988 we reached the final again and lost again to St

Kieran's. We were young and up-and-coming but the two final losses in a row put us back a bit. And we won the County title at last in 1991 against my own club Castleisland Desmonds. From there on we took it one step at a time. First it was the Barrs in Ballincollig, as good a team as we met in the two years we won out in Munster.'

Did you ever feel like throwing it there? 'After the County Final loss to Kenmare in 1987, I was involved as a selector with Kerry in 1982 when Séamus Darby got the goal but the goal scored by Kenmare at the end of our game was worse. It had been such a long wait. We had a great backroom staff of men like Jackie Looney, Tadhgy Fleming, Donie Leary — all great workers and they felt we could do it. My two selectors then were Tadhgy and Donie. The Chairman of the club was Mike Neeson and John Keogh was Secretary.

'We stayed in the Grand Hotel, Malahide for the final. We said that we would do ourselves justice on the day. Nobody talked of winning. We played well on the day and won. If we held our nerve, I felt we'd win. It gives me pride now that we played our best football ever on the most important stage. Connie Murphy had the game of his life. When we lost Danny Cooper we found we couldn't use our trump-card Mike Buckley, a man who had given us great service and for whom Croke Park held no fears. I regret we weren't able to use Mike because of the circumstances but the man is still playing with us. We had three trains for the game and filled them all, two regulars and one special. Bringing home the Cup to Killarney is something I'll never forget. There were bonfires in Rathmore first. The crowd was as big as when Kerry brought home Sam because it was a St Patrick's Night and a great night for a celebration.

'I trained a combined Killarney team to win the County Senior Football Championship title in 1983 but training Crokes on their own to County Final and All-Ireland success was so much better. When I came to Killarney first I was well accepted in town and the Crokes club were very good to me. I'm back in charge again after a lapse of a year and we're building a young team again. We have had a storied history, men like Tadhgie Lyne and Tom Long, Donie Sullivan, the Kavanaghs, both generations, Teddy O'Connor, John Moynihan, who was a wonderful clubman in the 1950s, and Dick Fitzgerald, who lived down the lane near me here. The rivalry with Legion and Spa is great. Tom Long is a great friend and was one of the reasons why I joined the Crokes. The Legion have always been a great club in their own

> *"Through life and death he had hardly aged.*
> *There always was an athlete's cleanliness*
> *shining off him and except for the ravaged*
> *forehead and the blood, he was still that same*
> *rangy mid-fielder in a blue jersey*
> *and starched pants, the one stylist on the team*
> *the perfect clean unthinkable victim."*   (Séamus Heaney)

'There were other lads like Kevin and Éamonn Mulholland and they all came through to win championship after championship and become the kingpins of Derry football, winning 17 Senior titles to date. Our longest sequence was a four-in-a-row and we had many great battles with Newbridge of the Gribbens, Ballymacguigan of the McKeevers and Dungiven for whom Joe Brolly's father Patsy was a star. The founder of the club was Edward Scullion (no relation) and others who worked closely with him would have been Brian Toner, Jim Brown and an unsung hero in the person of Mick McErlean, who lined the pitch, put out the flags and the nets and was literally Bellaghy's greatest supporter. The Griffin brothers, Seán, Jim and Paddy were other great men in the early days along with another neighbour of mine Charlie Molloy. John Joe Diamond, father of Laurence and Tommy and grandfather of Karl, was big into team-management then, which was known in those days as a trainer.'

ALL-IRELAND YEAR

'When our 1972 All-Ireland year came along it was nearing the end of my club days. Tommy Diamond was at right-half-back in front of yours truly at right-corner. The 1971 County Final win was against near neighbours Lavey. Then there followed wins over Ballybofey at Magherafelt by 1-10 to 0-7 on 3 October 1971, Ardboe at Dungannon by 3-6 to 1-8 on 24 October, Teemore by 0-9 to 0-3 at Dungannon on 7 November and on 12 December victory in the Ulster Senior Football Club Final by 1-11 to 0-5 over Clan na nGael (Lurgan) at Dungannon. Captain Laurence Diamond won the toss and with wind and sun advantage Bellaghy took over and led 1-9 to 0-2 at half time. Chris Browne, Frankie O'Loane, Tommy Diamond and Tom Quinn were the stars, moving on to a facile win before 2,000 shivering fans.

The semi-final in Magherafelt against Portlaoise on 23 April 1972, was a very close affair with Bellaghy winning by 1-11 to 1-10 in a pulsating game played in perfect conditions. Throughout the hour, the teams were level on five occasions. It took Bellaghy some time to settle but they took control at half-back through Tommy Diamond, Hugh McGoldrick and Chris Browne and led at half time by 1-6 to 0-5. Portlaoise rallied early in the second half to take the lead with five unanswered points. Bellaghy struck back to regain the lead. Five minutes to go and Portlaoise in front by a point. With four minutes to go Frankie O'Loane got the equaliser. He too engineered the winning point placing Hugh Donnelly for the winner. Phew!

THE FINAL

Bellaghy's final opponents UCC were beaten in Croke Park in another thriller played on Friday night 12 May by 0-15 to 1-11. Con Kenealy (*Irish Independent*) described the game 'as a thriller, especially in the second half during which the sides were level on no fewer than five occasions.'

UCC were powered by men like Moss Keane, Séamus Looney, Paudie and Brendan Lynch, Dan Kavanagh also of Kerry and were expected to keep the title in Munster. Gerry McGuigan (*Belfast Telegraph*) describes the closing scene: 'Bellaghy's best football of the hour was reserved for the last three minutes. Picture the scene as Kerry ace, Brendan Lynch found strength enough in an injured left leg to send UCC into the lead for only the second time with a point after fifty-seven minutes.

'With a series of swift passes the ball travelled to the other end of the field where Tom Quinn was pushed down near the goalmouth. Up stepped Frankie O'Loane with his trusty left boot to steer over his seventh point of the match for the equaliser.

'Hugh McGoldrick broke up a UCC attack and sent Brendan Cassidy away. The pint-sized Cassidy had time to steady himself from forty yards and shot over the all important point for victory.'

Glensman (*Sunday Independent*) thought Larry Diamond had a tremendous game at mid-field. Con Kenealy gave the honours to Tom Scullion, Hugh McGoldrick, Frank Cassidy, Larry Diamond, Frankie O'Loane, Tom Quinn and Brendan Cassidy. Perhaps the finest tribute of all was paid by Dan McAreavy, the well-known Armagh journalist/teacher to: 'Harry Cassidy's astute management; Brendan Cassidy's golden point; Larry

157

captained the side and was my star of the day as seven medals in all came to the McGurk household was used. The occasion was used to honour Anthony who came on as a substitute near the end for his brother Colm and rounded off a brilliant career by winning an All-Ireland medal at last.

Martin Breheny (*Irish Press*) under a heading 'Lavey Simply Exceptional' praised Lavey 'for doing the simple things exceptionally well and anchored their effort around two goals scored at critical stages of either half'. Salthill's poor shooting didn't help them. For the winners 'John and Colm McGurk, Henry Downey, Damien O'Boyle, Brian McCormick and Don Mulholland all excelled and it was also a very special day for forty-three-year-old former Derry star Anthony McGurk, who finally clinched an All-Ireland medal'. This was the team:

Brendan Regan

Damian Doherty   Anthony Scullion   Brian Scullion

John McGurk(capt.)Henry Downey   Kieran McGurk

Damian O'Boyle   James Chivers

Fergal Rafferty   Brian McCormick   Hugh M. McGurk

Don Mulholland   Séamus Downey   Colm McGurk

Substitute: Anthony McGurk for brother Colm.

Team-Manager: Brendan Convery.

A writer in the *Mid-Ulster Observer* under a heading 'Small is Beautiful' put it all in a nutshell: 'Two truths emerge from the unforgettable Lavey experience. One is that there are very few people in a parish like Lavey who are not involved in some way in the team which represents their community. Another is that Lavey were not just representing themselves on 17 March 1991 — they were representing what is at once the greatest strength of the GAA and the greatest single contribution it makes to our national life — the pride of the small parish. Lavey's triumph is not just a joy for Lavey — it's an encouragement to us all'. Exactly my sentiments too!

JOHN MCGURK REMINISCES

John McGurk is an accountant. Just thirty now he was plagued by injuries in 1996 but hopes to return to fitness and new battles. He had a box of cuttings of all the 1991–1992 Lavey games and a clear memory of every game in the series. Most people will remember his winning point against Dublin in the All-Ireland Semi-final of 1993. He isn't a big man but is built close to the ground. 'Our club was founded after Bellaghy around 1940. We won our first Derry Senior Football Championship in 1944 and there were only a few Derry clubs in existence at the beginning — Bellaghy, Lavey, Newbridge, Ballymacguigan... mostly South Derry clubs, a post war rural development really. In all Lavey has won eight Derry Senior Football Championship titles, four of which I have been part of. My memories of that year were the close games in Derry with Castledawson and Dungiven. Here in Derry it is nearly all local derbies. We developed the habit of getting on top at the end of games, with fortune favouring us at times. Dungiven have possibly been our greatest rivals in Derry. I was proud to lift the McLaughlin Cup. A Derry title means a lot to all of us.

'In the Ulster series St Columba's (Glencolmcille) ran us close but we just moved ahead at the end. At this stage we were getting to know each other pretty well and we never panicked at the end of games. We had developed the knack of thinking we could win games even when we were up against it. Because we had won so many games at the late stage of a game we felt we could do it in a tight finish. Sarsfield's (Armagh) were a very good outfit also, favouring a short passing game, and a scrambled goal at the end won it for us. That was some scramble — there must have been ten players in the square when the ball hit the net. A game right to the death that one. Brian McCormick got the goal using his right foot, which he usually used for standing on and it just crawled over the line. We played Kingscourt in the Ulster Final, a team coming to the end of its tether, a team on top in Cavan for many years previously and led by a wonderful player and character Jim Reilly. We beat them well but to their credit they played it sporting to the end. Afterwards their attitude was one of fellowship and this extended to their supporters also. Our clubs are friends since.

'Tírconaill Gaels provided us with the most epic game of them all. We did a Lazarus act in normal time with brother Anthony's late goal. We got strong again in extra time where our fitness was a telling factor. Brendan Convery was our Manager and Paddy Chivers our Trainer. Paddy was involved with us all, training us from U-14 right up. That duo were excellent that year in that they didn't take an absolute lot out of us through the training. We were kept fresh and eager. We did a lot of ball work and we didn't leave our best on the training ground. The Gaels team had stars in James McCartan (Down), Ollie Reid (brother of Donal), Timmy Connolly (Antrim), Mattie McGleenan (Tyrone), John Duffy (Donegal) and Tommy Maguire (Fermanagh).

'Our semi-final with Thomas Davis (Dublin) in Celtic Park, Derry was a big occasion. Paul Curran and David Foran were the big men on a fine team in a David and Goliath situation, the immensity of a Dublin suburb against a small rural parish in Derry. Again a close one and we really appreciated the guard of honour provided for us as we left the field. They took their defeat like Kingscourt very well and there is a wonderful relationship between our clubs, so much so that many Lavey people went to Dublin to support them in the final a year later. Dublin teams generally have great character about them.

'We travelled to Dublin on the eve of the final, leaving Lavey with about 300 people out to cheer us off. We were clapped out of our village and a convoy of cars followed the team bus as far as Magherafelt. That is one of my greatest memories. We have a video of that day which I love watching, our orange and black colours everywhere. We watched a video of the Salthill against Ballinamore Seán O'Heslin's game that night just to acquaint us with the Salthill lads. Next morning our PP, Father O'Donnell said Mass for us in our hotel, the Dublin Airport Hotel. Father O'Donnell had supported us all along the way in his weekly Church bulletins! Our fans were starting to arrive. And we were so relaxed. Croke Park would suit our style of play. It's a big pitch. We like to run. We were fit. Our Manager Brendan Convery was not one for psyching players up. His motto all along was: "Go out and play without fear. Take chances. Keep attacking. Keep trying." We played as well that day as we could have. My greatest memory is of lifting the Cup and looking down and seeing the whole parish of Lavey down below me. A parish of about 1,300 people (300 houses). We went home that night and the whole scene was unbelievable from Cookstown home. Cars were waiting all along the road. Home eventually to our own Clubhouse at 11.30 p. m. with the Cup. I was glad Anthony came on and was part of our success. No one was happier than he that day. That win in 1991 helped Derry to change its style of play, of favouring the Lavey possession game in preference to the long ball, with wonderful results for Derry subsequently'.

After the interview John took me to the Lavey field and Clubhouse. Some players were out pucking a sliothar while an aerobics class for ladies was in full swing in the spacious Hall bedecked with team photos and trophies. Later on John escorted me some eight miles of my journey in case I got lost. Just a measure of the courtesy I was afforded in Derry.

Lavey, All-Ireland Club Champions 1991

Back row: *Damien Doherty, Brian McCormick, Don Mulholland, Damien O'Boyle, Brendan Regan, Fergal Rafferty, James Chivers, Anthony Scullion.*

Front row: *Ciarán McGurk, Brian Scullion, Hugh Martin McGurk, John McGurk, Henry Downey, Colm McGurk, Séamus Downey.*

26

UCD's Back-to-Back Titles

1974 AND 1975

It was a glorious time for UCD; winning two Dublin Senior Football Championships in a row in 1973 and 1974 and going on to take the Leinster and All-Ireland crowns; also winning the Sigerson Cup three years running 1973–1975 as well as reaching the Dublin Senior Football Championship final of 1975 against St Vincent's, which was never played. All of this was achieved under the management of Eugene McGee of Longford, who was later to halt Kerry's five-in-a-row ambitions with the Offaly team of 1982. In these early years of the club All-Irelands, UCD, UCC and Thomond College, Limerick, participated with great success despite difficulties in fielding teams during holiday periods. All this has changed now with the mass exodus of third-level student footballers and hurlers to the USA during summer holidays and the growth in third-level inter college competitions. In winning the successive club football All-Irelands of 1974 and 1975, UCD became the first club to do so, a feat also achieved by St Finbarr's of Cork in 1980 and 1981.

DUBLIN COUNTY FINAL 1973

On Sunday, 27 August 1973, UCD defeated old rivals St Vincent's in Parnell Park by 1-11 to 0-10 to reverse the result of the previous year's County Final and halt a St Vincent's four-in-a-row bid. In what Gerry McCarthy (*Irish Press*) described as a 'best forgotten final', UCD won their fourth ever Dublin title in a game more remembered for some disgraceful scenes in the final ten minutes than for the quality of the fare served up.

'On the run of play UCD should have won by a cricket score but they had to work hard to hold on in the finish. John O'Keeffe ably helped by Benny Gaughran lorded the issue at mid-field in the first half against the wind and led at half-time by 0-6 to 0-5. Jimmy Keaveney and Paddy Hallinan manned mid-field for the start of the second half before Des Foley came from full-forward in a swap with Hallinan but all to no avail. UCD's light forwards made little impression and it was 0-7 each after 37 minutes and UCD edged two points ahead ten minutes later before Paddy Kerr punched a breaking ball from a Benny Gaughran free for the decisive goal. Then followed the two free-for-alls which 'left a bad taste in the mouths of spectators'.

At Croke Park on 4 November, UCD were almost caught napping by the Wicklow champions Carnew Emmets but after being led by 1-5 to 0-5 with 13 minutes remaining they raised their game and with successive points from Jackie Walsh, Ray O'Donoghue and Benny Gaughran came back to level pegging. The replay at Aughrim on Saturday 1 December 1973 was described by Mick Judge (who played mid-field with Benny Gaughran that day) as: 'The Battle of Aughrim. It was "Dinny" O'Connor who lobbed the goalkeeper to earn us a narrow win. We were literally on the ropes with no support and a very partisan home support. We were lucky to survive that one in more ways than one!'

Then followed an easy win over Raheens (Kildare) by 4-13 to 0-5 at O'Toole Park and a Leinster Club Final win over Cooley Kickhams (Louth) in a hard-fought game by 1-6 to 0-7 on 3 March 1974. Earlier UCD had retained the Sigerson Cup, their 27th Sigerson success, defeating UCG at Newbridge on 24 February by 0-16 to 1-5 with Kerryman Jackie Walsh the outstanding player afield. Another easy win followed in Ballina against Knockmore by 4-13 to 0-4. J. P. Kean started the rot with an early goal while substitute Dinny O'Connor scored a hat-trick. In the other semi-final Clan na nGael (Lurgan) defeated UCC by 3-7 to 1-10.

DRAWN FINAL

But on 18 March 1974 at Croke Park the well fancied star-studded UCD team of county stars were lucky to survive the challenge of Clan na nGael on the score 1-6 each. The game was televised live and the Northern team brought a huge support to Croke Park. The early departure of All-Star mid-fielder John O'Keeffe through injury made a huge difference. Still it was a drab performance by the students who had to rely on the accuracy of Jackie

Walsh from frees to survive and a late point from opportunistic Ollie Leddy to avoid defeat. What Clan na nGael lacked in all round skill they made up for in dedication and a firm belief in their ability to bring the title North.

The replay took place on Sunday, 28 April at Croke Park on the same bill as the Sligo versus Roscommon National Football League Semi-final and this time UCD won convincingly enough by 0-14 to 1-4. The game didn't rise to the exciting heights of the first one and despite playing into the breeze UCD, with few wides, led at half-time by 0-6 to 1-1. Kevin Kilmurray of Offaly was having one of his most industrious hours at mid-field after switching with Ollie Leddy, ably helped by veteran UCD man Benny Gaughran of Louth, who had an outstanding second half. After eleven minutes of the second half the score stood 0-9 to 1-2 after points by Leddy, Denis O'Connor and a magnificent Jackie Walsh free from way out. Now Clan na nGael rallied but missed some crucial scores. UCD went on to win convincingly. After the game Clan na nGael crossed the field to applaud their huge support and then formed a guard of honour for the winning UCD team as they left the field. Peadar O'Brien (*Irish Press*) gave man-of-the-match billing to UCD corner-back Mick Judge who 'played the game of his life in a rock-like defence. Judge was head and shoulders over everybody as he calmly repelled repeated Lurgan attacks.' Special tributes were also paid to Éamonn O'Donoghue (Kildare) for his sterling performance at centre-half-back. The Andy Merrigan Cup was presented by Father Seán Kitt representing Andy's club Castletown (Wexford) and then handed by a smiling Donal Keenan (a former UCD star himself) to a very happy Paddy Kerr of Monaghan. This was the winning team:

Ivan Heffernan (Mayo)

Mick Judge (Galway)	Garrett O'Reilly (Cavan)	Frank Donoghoe (Galway)
Pearse Gilroy (Cavan)	Éamonn O'Donoghoe (Kildare)	Paddy Kerr (capt.) (Monaghan)

Ollie Leddy (Cavan)   Benny Gaughran (Louth)

Enda Condron (Laois)	Kevin Kilmurray (Offaly)	Jackie Walsh (Kerry)
J. P. Kean (Mayo)	Denis O'Connor (Cork)	Pat Duggan (Dublin)

THE 1975 WIN

The Dublin County Final of 1974 wasn't played until 1 December 1974 and St Vincent's were again UCD's opposition for the third successive year. This time there were no unsavoury scenes and UCD won convincingly by 0-12 to 1-3. It was a disappointing final watched by an attendance of 4,000. St Vincent's started well and were three points up but then lost Bobby Doyle through injury. John O'Keeffe and Paddy Kerr got on top at mid-field and UCD led at the break 0-5 to 0-3. In the second half, with the help of the wind, the winners tacked on three points before being pegged back by a Jimmy Keaveney penalty goal. UCD then took over and Jackie Walsh punished every infringement within scoring distance with his uncanny free-taking which saw him score nine times from ten attempts. Pádhraic Puirséal (*Irish Press*) praised Walsh 'who stole the show' and Paddy Kerr as 'the most industrious player afield'. A week later in Newbridge UCD were lucky to defeat Carbury (Kildare) by 1-3 to 0-5.

On 12 January 1975 UCD had an easy win over Éire Óg (Carlow) in Carlow on the score 2-13 to 0-6, Ollie Leddy and J.P. Kean getting the goals. On 26 January at Croke Park the students were very lucky to beat Ferbane in the Leinster Final by 2-7 to 1-9. It was 0-4 apiece at half-time but with three minutes to go the score stood 1-9 to 1-5 in favour of the Offaly men. Sixty seconds later Jackie Walsh got his boot to a Pat Duggan centre and lashed the ball to the net. Just on time his brother Barry pointed a 40 yards free and time was up when the bould Barry did likewise for the winner from another 40 yards free. In defence Garrett O'Reilly, Connie Moynihan and Gerry McCaul starred.

In the All-Ireland Semi-final on 23 February at Roscommon, UCD had a comfortable win over Roscommon Gaels by 0-12 to 1-2. Pádhraic Puirséal, a UCD graduate himself, wrote in the *Irish Press* that 'the Connacht champions over the hour won just as much of the ball as UCD but could not match the victors for teamwork accuracy and expertise'.

The weekend before the final UCD retained the Sigerson Cup in Belfast winning their three games on successive days to bring their total of knockout victories in a row to 39. Now without three top stars in Kevin Kilmurray, Paddy Kerr and Ollie Leddy they faced the 1973 All-Ireland champions Nemo Rangers on 16 March in Croke Park and put two All-Irelands back to back on the score 1-11 to 0-12.

J.P. Kean Goal

Once again UCD showed all their great fighting qualities to win. Séamus Leydon the veteran Galway star was Nemo's most polished player first half. It took a remarkable J.P. Kean goal after a great run to keep UCD in touch and see them behind 1-4 to 0-8 at the interval. By the end of the third quarter Nemo led by 0-12 to 1-5. A Pat Duggan point started the now almost inevitable UCD revival. Jackie Walsh ranging the entire field had two points from frees. Barry, his brother, levelled scores with nine minutes to go. Three minutes later Jackie gained UCD the lead from a free from an acute angle. Pat O'Neill then got the insurance point from a J.P. Kean pass after Nemo had failed to equalise from a scorable free. The winning team was:

Ivan Heffernan

Michael Judge   Garrett O'Reilly   Con Moynihan

P.J. O'Halloran   Éamonn O'Donoghue   Frank Donoghue

Mick Carty (capt.)   Pat O'Neill

Brendan Dunleavy   J.P. Kean   Jackie Walsh

Barry Walsh   Pat Duggan   Brendan Heneghan

Substitute: Enda Condron for B. Heneghan

Michael Judge Looks Back

Michael Judge, corner-back on both successful teams is a native of Caherlistrane, County Galway and a popular financial business executive in Tuam. Like all of his counterparts on that very successful UCD team, Michael is still an avid GAA supporter of both his club Caherlistrane and his county to whom he gave many years of distinguished service.

'We had a marvellous team of household names in those years and I was very lucky to be on the team, being the only non-inter county player selected (my selection for Galway came later). Indeed some of our substitutes were inter-county players. Our trainer then, you'd call him team-manager now, was Eugene McGee of Longford. He built up this team into a great combination. He had a most unusual style of management in that he was close to nobody. If he was close to anybody it would be to the lesser known names like myself. That was one of his great strengths. He was an excellent manager, a great motivator and a mighty man to give the team pep-talk. He always picked the right words and before the off he went to each individual on the team saying the appropriate words to each player. He struck a chord with everyone of us. He was the finest team-manager I encountered. Basically he had no favourites. Best of all he was greatly admired by everybody.

Thinking back on those years we had great duels with Clan na nGael of Lurgan in 1974. We were lucky to draw the first day. Clan had a huge support both days and we had little if any support. It was a great achievement to win out in Dublin both years as we often hadn't full teams for some of the earlier rounds and it took some organisation on Eugene McGee's part to get us through it all. We had some mighty battles with St Vincent's. And possibly the hardest of all with Ferbane which was powered by Tony McTague and the Lowry brothers. Barry Walsh saved us that day with two great points. I cherish those two All-Ireland club medals but I'd have to include my Galway Junior Championship medal of 1976 won with my native Caherlistrane. In a different sort of way Caherlistrane tended to mean so much more. I was born there, grew up and became a man there. I was only passing through UCD, but what a lovely journey.

I was lucky to get on the UCD team because I transferred from UCG to continue my Agricultural Science studies in 1973. Éamonn O'Donoghue asked me to play for UCD's U-21 team almost immediately. Éamonn and myself became firm friends. If Eugene McGee was the big man behind us, the big man on the field in those days was Éamonn. The great success of UCD must be attributed to Eugene McGee and Éamonn O'Donoghue.'

Éamonn O'Donoghoe (Kildare), the great inspiration of the UCD team receiving an award from former Olympic 1500 gold medalist, Ronnie Delany

UCD, All-Ireland Club Champions 1974 (replay)

Back row: Ollie Leddy, Dinny O'Connor, Garrett O'Reilly, Ivan Heffernan, Frank Donoghue, Pearse Gilroy, Kevin Kilmurray.

Front row: Enda Condron, Michael Judge, Bennie Gaughran, J.P. Kean, Paddy Kerr (capt.), Pat Duggan, Jackie Walsh, Éamonn O'Donoghoe.

Missing from photo are: Joe Waldron, P.J. O'Halloran and John O'Keeffe who played in the drawn final.

172

27

The Boys Of Blackrock

I met an old hurler now sixty and six,
Who played centre-forward and under the sticks
He played with the Islands, the Redmonds, and Barrs
He had medals to prove it with old battle scars
He could play don't forget, although an old crock,
But the best men he met were the boys from Blackrock.

'Down by the fishing village; at the pier-head; round the Convent Road; at the quarry in Ballintemple, and Boreenmanna we practised hip to hip. To see the Blackrock hurl was a revelation. They never caught a ball after a lift, they never dallied with a ball. Their swing was long, but crisp and graceful. They drew on "lightning balls" off left and right showing a command of ash that was astonishing. Hurling was in their blood.' So wrote Paddy Mehigan (alias Carbery), himself a Blackrock hurler in the period 1904–1909, of his beloved Rockies, champions of Cork Senior Hurling on 29 occasions, All-Ireland Senior Hurling club champions three times 1972, 1974 and 1979. This is an historic club which shares with Ballyhale Shamrocks the honour of winning three Senior Hurling club titles. The club is unique in that it won two All-Ireland Senior Hurling titles in the early days, representing Cork in victory in 1893 and 1894.

CHURCH ROAD

The club has a permanent home and valuable property in Church Road and an impressive GAA social centre to befit its status, which was officially opened in 1982. Down the years the Rockies provided great hurlers for Cork. You don't need to be a Corkman to have heard of Eudie Coughlan, the Ahernes, 'Gah' and 'Balty', Jim Hurley, 'Marie' Connell, 'Hawker' Grady and that most respected player and official Seán Óg Murphy. There were lean times too with few Cork titles coming but there were always great hurlers like John Quirke and Mick Cashman, father of Tom and Jim, who led the Rockies to county success in 1956 after a break of 25 years. Another in 1961 and then came the glorious '70s with three All-Ireland, five County and Munster titles right up to Blackrock's 29th title in 1985.

THE FIRST ALL-IRELAND

The Rockies beat the Barrs in the 1971 County Final by 2-19 to 5-4 in a tough struggle where Ray and Frank Cummins were outstanding. Then followed victories over Claughaun (Limerick) in Church Road by 2-18 to 2-11 on 24 January 1972, Newmarket-on-Fergus on 9 April at Kilmallock by 5-14 to 2-5 and Blackrock's first ever Munster Club Final victory over Moyne–Templetuohy (Tipperary) also at Kilmallock on Tuesday 25 April. The best of these games was against Claughaun which Michael Ellard (*Cork Examiner*) described as 'an enthralling second-half drama in which a heroic Blackrock defence stole the honours.'

In the Newmarket-on-Fergus game, the Clare lads led at half-time by 2-4 to 0-5 but Blackrock, with the wind behind them in the second half, won comfortably in the final quarter, Pat Moylan scoring 1-9 again as he had done against Claughan earlier.

The Rockies were lucky to come out of Duggan Park, Ballinasloe on the score Blackrock 3-7 Tommy Larkin's 2-8. It was a do-or-die effort by the Rockies in the closing ten minutes that produced the decisive score when Donal Collins lashed the ball to the net from thirty yards. An interesting substitute for the losers was Cyril Farrell, who scored a crucial point. The winners could thank Pat Casey, Pat Geary and Frank Norberg who was the best back on view.

THE FIRST TITLE

On 14 May in Walsh Park, Waterford, Blackrock won their first club All-Ireland defeating Rathnure (Wexford) of the Quigley's by 5-13 to 6-9.

Michael Ellard (*Cork Examiner*) wrote: 'Salute Blackrock, the hurling club champions of Ireland. Many glorious triumphs have made their way to the little fishing village of Cork but none so historic as this. Blackrock can proudly fly the banner of victory. They emerged from the throes of intimidation in this gruelling encounter to record a spectacular victory.' Leading at half-time by 4-5 to 3-4 the winners survived a barn-storming rally by the Wexford men who nearly pulled the game out of the fire and it took a point from a '70' by Pat Moylan four minutes from time to win.

John Rothwell was the winners' star, scoring two great goals in the first half to answer big Dan Quigley's two, while Dave Prendergast notched the two other goals and Donal Collins also shone in attack. Pat Moylan was in vital control and at mid-field Michael Murphy's great hurling brain was seen to advantage. John Horgan did well when switched to full-back to mark Dan Quigley getting most help from Frank Norberg and in particular Simon Murphy. This was the team:

Bernard Hurley

Pat Casey	Pat Geary	John Horgan (capt.)
Simon Murphy	Frank Cummins	Frank Norberg

Michael Murphy   Pat Kavanagh

Donal Collins	Ray Cummins	Pat Moylan
Brendan Cummins	John Rothwell	Dave Prendergast

THE SECOND TITLE

On 20 January 1974 Blackrock pipped Roscrea (the first ever All-Ireland club champions of 1970–1971) in a brilliant game at Roscrea by 5-6 to 4-8 after a rip-roaring second half when the score changed with bewildering rapidity and ended in a crescendo of excitement with the winners coming from four points behind to gain a one-point victory. The switching of Frank Cummins to centre-half-back in a swop with John Horgan worked wonders and the Kilkenny star played some tremendous hurling.

It was close again on 17 February at Bruff when Newmarket-on-Fergus fell by 1-13 to 0-14 and again it was a pity there had to be a loser in this memorable Munster Final which produced another thrill-a-minute second half of admirable skill, sportsmanship and excitement in which Frank

Cummins, John Horgan and Jack Russell were outstanding in the vital last twenty minutes. Jim O'Sullivan (*Cork Examiner*) praised the excellent refereeing of John Moloney and the fine state of the Bruff pitch. In the semi-final, subsequently, Blackrock were never extended in their own grounds at Church Road by St Johns (Belfast) and won easily by 5-12 to 1-5. It was to be much different in the final against old rivals, Rathnure.

Jim O'Sullivan (*Cork Examiner*) under a heading 'Rockies Force Draw in Thriller' wrote about Blackrock's draw with Rathnure on the score 2-14 to Rathnure's 3-11 on St Patrick's Day in Croke Park. 'The combined display of Blackrock and Rathnure hurlers in the All-Ireland Club Hurling Final gave the ailing St Patrick's Day programme its biggest lift in years and highlighted once again the attractiveness of the club championships. It produced a game more than worthy of its new stature and was so competitive as to make a draw an acceptable result.' Blackrock missed chances galore but it was they who had to fight back to level with a pointed free from Pat Moylan in the 58th minute after Dan Quigley had scored his third goal for Rathnure with three minutes remaining. Big Dan scored a remarkable 3-6 (1-6 from frees) with brother Martin also outstanding. Scores were level six times in the first half which ended all square at 1-7 apiece.

THE REPLAY

On 28 April in Dan Fraher's Field in Dungarvan the Rockies won title number two in another storming finish by 3-8 to 1-9. Michael Ellard (*Cork Examiner*) was enthralled by Blackrock's: 'Last ditch rescue operation in which they turned imminent defeat into a sensational victory and brilliantly robbed Rathnure of the honours in a barn-storming finish to a hotly contested final replay.' Six points down with nine minutes remaining Blackrock seemed to have shot their bolt. Summoning up all the resources of courage at their disposal, they shrugged off the effect of tired limbs and aching muscles to whittle away the intimidating deficit and then bravery was rewarded when Donal Collins and Éamonn O'Donoghue struck two golden last minute goals to win the title for the second time in three seasons. Right-corner-back John Rothwell was the man-of-the-match with a talented display of defensive hurling at its best. Goalkeeper Timmy Murphy made a series of brilliant saves under pressure. Pat Geary never put a foot wrong at full-back.

This was the Blackrock team:

Timmy Murphy

John Rothwell   Pat Geary   John Horgan (capt.)

Frank Cummins   Conor O'Brien   Frank Norberg

Pat Moylan   Jack Russell

Pat Kavanagh   John O'Halloran   Donal Collins

Dave Prendergast   Ray Cummins   Éamon O'Donoghue

Substitutes: S. Kearney for Pat Kavanagh, Danny Buckley for S. Kearney

TITLE NUMBER THREE 1979

In the County Final at Páirc Uí Chaoimh, Blackrock had a big win over Glen Rovers by 4-12 to 1-7 with superb performances from Ray and Frank Cummins, captain of the day John Horgan, Tom Cashman and Pat Moylan. The Cork club's first scalps in Munster were Kilruane McDonaghs whom they beat by 3-11 to 1-8 while in the Munster Final at Páirc Uí Chaoimh, Newmarket-on-Fergus were beaten by 3-8 to 1-8 after a harder game than indicated by the score.

Now followed one of the most historic trips ever embarked on by the Green and Gold Blackrock team and supporters on a 600 mile round trip to Ballycastle in North Antrim. From the time of the arrival of the 50 strong Blackrock party in Central Station, Belfast through the tour of bunting bedecked Ballycastle, where the streets were lined with people welcoming the men of Cork, to the game itself won by Blackrock by 5-12 to 2-9 for Ballycastle McQuillans with late scores by Cummins and Moylan to the final official function and the farewells, this was a never to be forgotten experience where great friendships were forged which last to this day.

CLASH OF THE GIANTS

The final, three weeks later in Semple Stadium, Thurles, between the giants of club hurling, saw Blackrock win their third All-Ireland defeating Ballyhale Shamrocks of the Fennellys by 5-7 to 5-5. After an even first quarter Blackrock got on top with two fast Ray Cummins goals in the second quarter. When Tom Lyons got Rockies' fifth goal in the third quarter

Blackrock held on for title number three. It was a great moment for Ray Cummins, Frank Norberg, Frank Cummins, Ray Kavanagh, Donie Collins, John Horgan and Pat Moylan who were part of all three All-Ireland triumphs in the 1970s and for youngsters like Tom Cashman, Tom Lyons and Danny Buckley it was the climax of a wonderful achievement as all three had won All-Ireland Féile na nGael medals at the same stadium seven years earlier. This was the team:

Tim Murphy

Frank Norberg   Conor O'Brien   John Horgan

Dermot McCurtain   Tom Cashman   John O'Grady

Frank Cummins   Andy Creagh

Donie Collins   Éamon O'Donoghue   Pat Moylan

Éamon O'Sullivan   Ray Cummins   Tom Lyons

Substitute: Danny Buckley for Andy Creagh

Sean Kilfeather (*The Irish Times*) praised Ballyhale Shamrock's 'plucky fightback which turned what had been a one-sided contest into a nailbiting one' but in the end, before a crowd of 3,000 most of whom favoured the Shamrocks it was the 'faster, fitter and more adaptable (at overcoming the poor ground conditions) Blackrock side' which won the day.

FRANK CUMMINS REFLECTS

One of the most modest men, it is difficult to get Frank Cummins to talk of his exploits down the years. A giant of a mid-fielder and always a sportsman supreme, he won seven All-Ireland senior medals with Kilkenny in the period 1969–1983. 'I'm not a good man to reflect on games but I'll never forget the mighty battles we had with Rathnure and all the Quigley lads. They were a hard team to beat. I found it hard to psyche myself up to play against my own home area of Ballyhale in the third final.

'In my younger days I won a Kilkenny junior medal with my local village of Knocktopher in 1965 (I won a minor title that year too). Ballyhale and Knocktopher later amalgamated to form the Shamrocks. I joined the Gardaí in 1967 and after being posted to Cork was persuaded to join Blackrock by Terry Kelly, another Gárda and a former Cork star. Thus began my association with the Rockies in 1970. I had heard a lot about this famous club and never thought I'd be privileged to play for them. They made me welcome from the start and I became part of the whole set up. Men like the Chairman of the time Ned Cotter who is still hale and hearty, Florrie O'Mahony, Ger O'Leary, Father Mick O'Brien, Michael Flaherty, Joe McGrath, Jimmy Brohan, Tommy O'Sullivan and many others paved the way for me.

'As to the players it was marvellous to play alongside Ray Cummins, Hoggy (John Horgan), Éamon O'Donoghue, Pat Moylan, another Kilkennyman Conor O'Brien, Dermot McCurtain and Tom Cashman. Ray Cummins, the best full-forward in Ireland in both codes. As I said I found it hard to motivate myself for the Ballyhale final as I had an old grá for the home place and I deeply appreciate a presentation of a watch they made to me during my playing career. I'm still an avid follower and was so sad when my old team-mates Ted Carroll and Ollie Walsh died last year. My son Alan now hurls at U-21 level with Cork and plays for the Rockies. The club hasn't been the force of late it once was but there are signs of a revival.'

Frank's wife Madeleine is a staunch supporter too. They live in Clogheen with their four children. 'It was a great time in our lives when Frank played. I missed the whole thing a lot when he gave it up. But now Alan has started and already has won a Fitzgibbon Cup medal.' At this stage Frank took over again: 'Our greatest opponents here in Cork were the Barrs and the Glen, especially the former. Anytime you beat the Barrs in a final you've earned it.'

Frank Cummins, the great Kilkenny mid-fielder, was on all three winning teams with the Rockies.

Blackrock, Senior All-Ireland Club Champions 1971

Back row: Pat Casey, Brian Tobin, Brendan Cummins, Pat Kavanagh,
Paddy Geary, John O'Halloran, Pat Moylan, Andy Creagh, Mick
O'Loughlin, Donal Collins, Dave Prendergast, Maurice Duggan
(trainer).

Front row: Bernard Hurley, Frank Norberg, Ray Cummins, Frank
Cummins, John Rothwell, Simon Murphy, John Horgan (capt.),
Michael Murphy, Neil O'Keeffe, Willy Cronin.

Blackrock, Senior All-Ireland Club Champions 1979

Back row: Joe McGrath (trainer), Conor O'Brien, Ray Cummins, Andy
Creagh, Donal Collins, Frank Cummins, John O'Grady, Éamonn
O'Donoghue.

Front row: Tim Murphy, Dermot McCurtain, Tom Cashman, John Horgan,
Pat Moylan, Tom Lyons, Frank Norberg and Éamonn O'Sullivan.

28

Midleton Magic

Midleton is a thriving Cork County town about twenty miles east of Cork City. The return to hurling greatness of Midleton in the 1980s has been one of the features of modern Cork hurling. In the vanguard of that return was John Fenton, a superb and stylish striker of a ball, who captained Cork to Centenary All-Ireland glory in 1984. He traced Midleton's hurling history with me.

'We won the Cork Intermediate Championship in 1978 and at our AGM we decided by one vote to go senior. That was a major decision for it gave us experience of the big-time and we had a group of young fellows, interested and dedicated, all willing to learn. The start of it came on 8 October 1983 when we beat the Barrs in a County Senior Final to win our third ever Senior Hurling Championship (the previous ones were 1914 and 1916) after a long wait of 67 years. For the record, Midleton won for Cork its first ever All-Ireland football title in 1890, something we are very proud of. That October day of 1983 will never be forgotten by Midleton people. We had played the Barrs four years in a row in the County Semi-final prior to this, never getting closer than a draw in 1982. These were all great games of hurling and when success came against the Barrs eventually, it was the icing on the cake. St Finbarr's at the time were the masters of Cork hurling but we were very willing apprentices. The Barrs versus Midleton rivalry of the entire 1980s kept Cork hurling alive and vibrant. It was country against city and the other great club rivalries of the past had tended to go down.

'We inherited a hurling tradition in Midleton in our youth. People we are indebted to are Seán Hennessy, father of Kevin, who gave much time to us as juveniles, Michael O'Neill, Bawnie O'Sullivan, the Mulcahys; later on we had Nealie Horgan, Paddy Fitzgerald, Joe Desmond, Patrick Horgan, Patrick Crotty, and lots of others who helped to keep the game going. We were very lucky too to have two wonderful Christian Brothers in Midleton CBS, namely Brother Moran in the 1960s and 1970s and Brother Cunningham who retired last year. The influence of these two men on hurling in Midleton for the past 30 years is immense. We all went through their hands and we owe it all to them. In 1983 we won our first Munster Club title defeating Borrisoleigh after two great games but fell to Gort in the semi-final. We won the Cork Senior Hurling Championship title again in 1986 and retained it in 1987.'

MARCHING TO GLORY

To win out in Cork in 1987 Midleton had to beat St Finbarr's yet again. It was in an epic semi-final which they won by 2-9 to 2-8. Michael Ellard (*Cork Examiner*) described the game as 'Fabulous, a victory born out of raw courage, and for pure passion, drama and excitement surpassed anything of the previous games between them. The glory went to Midleton because of the freetaking expertise of John Fenton and the greatness of Pat Hartnett as Midleton held on to win.' In the County Final on 25 October, Midleton defeated Na Piarsaigh at Páirc Uí Chaoimh by 2-12 to 0-15 in another epic before 21,194 spectators. After a one-sided first half Midleton led by 2-6 to 0-5 at the interval. This all changed in the second half as Midleton strove to contain Na Piarsaigh. Once again John Fenton delivered the goods. Michael Ellard (*Cork Examiner*) praised Fenton 'who scored several points of vintage quality — a real artist who scored all of Midleton's second-half total of 0-6 and a quite outstanding save of Midleton's goalkeeper Ger "King" Power from a ferocious drive from John O'Sullivan. The greatest save I've ever seen in a County Final'.

There was no rest for the Cork champions, who a week later at Cusack Park, Ennis, defeated Clarecastle by 3-12 to 2-11. They were forced to field without star goalkeeper Ger Power (injured) but substitute goalkeeper Colman Quirke did well. Next to fall were Ballyduff (Waterford) at Midleton on 14 November with the score 2-13 to 2-5. In this game Midleton struggled but a Colm O'Neill goal just on half-time was a major boost and saw Midleton lead by 2-6 to 1-3 at half-time. In the final quarter the Cork champions pulled away to win well in the end. In the Munster Final at Kilmallock on Saturday, 5 December, Midleton triumphed by 1-12 to 1-11 over Cappawhite of Tipperary. Jim O'Sullivan (*Cork Examiner*) wrote: 'It was a pity there had to be a loser in this excellent Munster Final with scores level for the eighth time and a minute remaining. If Midleton were a little lucky, in that a goal-keeping mistake led to the "65" which John Fenton pointed to decide the game, they worked harder to earn their second title after they had Kevin Hennessy sent off twelve minutes from time.' Ger Power was back in goal and was outstanding. Brothers John and Pat Hartnett, together with John Fenton also shone for the winners.

CUSHENDALL

The semi-final clash with Antrim champions Cushendall meant a round trip of over 700 miles from Midleton on 14 February 1988. Midleton won in the end by 3-11 to 2-5. The *Irish Press* man-of-the-match was John Fenton, ably helped by full-back Mick Boylan, centre-back Seán O'Brien, mid-fielders Tadhg McCarthy and Fenton and forwards John Hartnett, Ger Fitzgerald and Kevin Hennessy. The game was played on a very heavy pitch and a big contingent of Midleton supporters enjoyed their Northern visit no end. All was now set for the final with Athenry St Mary's in Croke Park on St Patrick's Day. The Galway lads had accounted for Rathnure easily in the other semi-final by 2-14 to 0-5 with veteran P.J. Molloy scoring 0-11 of their total.

THE FINAL

Under a headline 'Glory For Midleton' Jim O'Sullivan's (*Cork Examiner*) account of Midleton's win by 3-8 to 0-9 led off: 'The combination of two early Kevin Hennessy goals, superb defensive play in the second half and inspired goal-keeping from team captain Ger Power proved too much for Athenry. It was a struggle for much of the second half, in the face of constant pressure, and not until Colm O'Neill kicked a goal two minutes from time, could they be absolutely certain of victory'.

John Horgan (*Evening Echo*) paid tribute to 'captain Ger Power and sterling defender Denis Mulcahy who were magnificent'. The story that began with an Intermediate title win ten years earlier could not have had a happier ending. John Fenton had announced his retirement from inter-county hurling before the Club Final. So it was a fitting farewell to a hurling artist's great career. This was the winning team:

Ger Power (capt.)

| Denis Mulcahy | Mick Boylan | Sylvie O'Mahony |
| Edser Cleary | Seán O'Brien | Pat Hartnett |

Tadhg McCarthy   Mick Crotty

| John Fenton | John Hartnett | John Boylan |
| Ger Fitzgerald | Colm O'Neill | Kevin Hennessy |

Substitutes: Gerry Glavin for M. Crotty Vincent O'Neill for J. Boylan, Gerry Smyth for S. O'Mahony.

There was a marvellous homecoming for the team on the Friday night after the final led by the Holy Rosary Brass and Reed Band, from the Old Distillery Road through the Main Street to the Courthouse, scene of many celebrations and political gatherings in the past. It was Midleton's greatest day of sporting celebration.

JOHN FENTON'S MEMORIES

'If there was one game in which I think we came of age in senior club hurling, it had to be our 1986 Cork Senior Hurling Semi-final win over the Barrs. We won at the end by nine or ten points, whereas all the previous ones were close. There was one incident in that 1986 game which highlighted our coming of age. Ger Cunningham came up from the Blackrock end goal to the City end goal to take a penalty which went over the bar and before he reached his Blackrock end goal we had scored a goal. Ger Power took a quick puck-out; Kevin Hennessy got it and passed it to me and I scored from about 30 yards out just as Ger got back on the line. We had at last got the savvy to play senior club hurling. What other teams like the Glen or the Barrs or Blackrock could do to us before we were doing it ourselves now. I mean that in the very best sense not in any kind of gloating fashion.

'The game against the Barrs in 1987 was another typical game in our saga of the 1980s. Pat Hartnett always enjoyed those battles and he was fabulous that day. To think that this man never won an All-Star Award is an indictment of that selection system. In the County Final against Na

Piarsaigh — another terrific game — I saw the greatest save effected by our goalkeeper Ger Power. We were struggling to stay in the game in the middle of the second half when John O'Sullivan let go for the bottom left hand corner from about twenty yards out. People often talk of Gordon Banks' save from Pele in 1970 but Ger Power dived the full length of the goal and not alone saved but caught the ball. I've seen the video a few times and everybody including Na Piarsaigh officials and John O'Sullivan himself were jumping in expectation of the seemingly inevitable goal. That save inspired us to win.

'We were lucky enough to defeat Cappawhite in the Munster Final. We trained hard for the game against Cushendall. I remember one Wednesday evening in a group of 25 players training on a snow covered pitch in Midleton when we could hardly see the ball. Our weekend in Cushendall (we brought a special train and a number of buses North) will go down with the 1983 County Final as one of the special memories. We have kept up our great friendship developed then with annual under-age visits. We stayed two nights in the area and they appreciated the fact that we spent time with them unlike other teams who travelled North and couldn't return home fast enough.

'For the final we stayed in the Kilternan Sports Hotel. P.J. Molloy was Athenry's top man at the time. We were thrilled to win out in the end. We were very lucky with that team. We had won three All-Ireland seven-a-side titles in 1982, 1983 and 1985 and that helped. In the All-Ireland Final of 1986, which Cork won, there were five Midleton players on the team — Pat Hartnett, Denis Mulcahy, Kevin Hennessy, Ger Fitzgerald and myself. Ger Power was Ger Cunningham's equal and that is high praise. We had the three Boylan brothers, Dave Mick and John, Tadhg McCarthy a fine midfielder, Mick Crotty, Sylvie O'Mahony, a great corner-back, Seán O'Brien at centre-half-back, John Hartnett, a substitute for Cork in 1984, Colm O'Neill, who played hurling and football for Cork. You had to be good to get on that Midleton team. The men in charge were Father Denis Kelleher, Paddy O'Brien, Séamus O'Farrell, Oliver O'Keeffe and myself (the selection committee in 1983); and in 1987–1988 we had Pat Fitzgerald, Joe Desmond and Father Kelleher in control. Pat Fitzgerald (Ger's Dad) was a Cork star himself in 1966. Ger captained Midleton to win the county title again in 1991 and went on to lead Cork in 1992. When we were growing up Pat Fitzgerald was our idol and I remember the time he brought the Liam McCarthy Cup to our school. That inspired us all and sitting with me in the school that day were Pat Hartnett, Denis Mulcahy, Kevin Hennessy and Seán O'Brien. Pat was so happy when we won the Cork title in 1983. He put in a lot of time and effort into our training.

'Personally, Willie John Daly, who played hurling with my father Dan for Carrigtwohill, and who came to live in Midleton was a big influence on me. We often talked about hurling and I learnt a lot from him. You asked me for the greatest memories and I'm not demeaning the club All-Ireland win but that coming of age against The Barrs in 1986 and the 1983 County Final win stand out. It all started in 1983 really. I'd have to thank our wives and/or girlfriends who put up with an awful lot from us all during the 1980s and supported us all the way. Our field here in Midleton is called Clonmult Memorial Park after an infamous ambush in the time of the Black and Tans. That field was developed in 1963 and the Pavilion and ancillary amenities were opened in 1975. We are very proud of our facilities which include a practice pitch as well as a full length field and the Pavilion includes a bar, squash courts and Hall.'

Midleton, Senior All-Ireland Club Champions 1988
(with County, Munster and All-Ireland Cups)

*Back row: Joe Desmond, Michael O'Mahony, Gerry Smith, Denis Mulcahy,
Gerry Glavin, Colman Quirke, Pat Hartnett, Seán O'Brien,
Mick Boylan, Fr Denis Kelleher.*
*Middle: Pat Horgan, John Boylan, Colm O'Neill, John Hartnett,
Kevin Hennessy, Edser Cleary, Kevin Coakley, Ger Fitzgerald,
Paddy Fitzgerald.*
*Front row: Tadhg McCarthy, Mick Crotty, Sylvie O'Mahony, Ger Power
(capt.), John Fenton, Vincent O'Neill, David Quirke.*

29

The Spirit Of The Glen

How oft I've watched him from the hill move here and there in grace,
In Cork, Killarney, Thurles Town or by the Shannon's Race;
"Now Cork is bet; the hay is saved!" — the thousands wildly sing —
They speak too soon, my sweet garsún, for here comes Christy Ring.

Bryan McMahon's lines of tribute to Christy Ring, Glen Rovers' and Cork's greatest hurler have always appealed to me. Glen Rovers or The Glen, this wonderful club set in Blackpool, bids fair to be the greatest of all hurling clubs. Founded in 1916, the club won its first of 25 Cork Senior Hurling Club titles in 1934, winning eight in-a-row, Christy Ring winning his first of 14 Cork Senior Hurling Championship medals in 1941. Tremendous crowds (25,028 in 1962) saw them win their titles but then the club bristled with names famed in song and story — 'Fox' Collins, Paddy O'Connell, who through his coaching of juveniles helped to build the club, Jack Lynch, later to become Taoiseach, Jim Young, Din Joe Buckley, Dave Creedon, John Lyons, Paddy O'Donovan, Josie Hartnett, Vince and Joe Twomey, Joe Salmon, Éamonn Goulding, Patsy Harte, Jerry O'Sullivan, Seán Kenefick, Denis Coughlan... the list is endless.

ALL-IRELAND NO 1

Though the power of The Glen has dimmed somewhat in recent times, the club won its first club All-Ireland in 1973. The 12th November 1972 saw a most unlikely pairing for the Cork Senior Hurling Championship County Final after a year of upsets in Cork. Captained by Patsy Harte, Glen Rovers defeated Youghal in their first ever final by 3-15 to 1-10. A 1-6 total scored in the last five minutes flattered Glen Rovers. A miserable day of incessant rain and howling winds kept the attendance down to 7,873. Teddy O'Brien, at left-half-back was the outstanding player afield while Pat O'Doherty shone in attack.

On 11 March The Glen easily defeated Ballyduff (Kerry) in Tralee by 5-6 to 0-1 (with Frank Cunningham scoring four goals) and on Sunday 22 April, 1973 they won the Munster title defeating Roscrea in a thriller by 2-9 to 1-10. The sides were level five times during a game in which Teddy O'Brien and Pat O'Doherty starred once again with Denis Coughlan, having an outstanding game, playing a captain's part. Subsequently Glen Rovers had an easy win over Castlegar on 6 May by 6-9 to 1-7 in the Cork Athletic Grounds with Tom Buckley the star.

Controversy surrounded the final against St Rynagh's when the Activities Committee of the GAA turned down a request for a postponement by St Rynagh's. Glen Rovers were not interested in winning a title by default and pressed for a re-fixing of the final. This was granted but the final didn't take place until 9 December at Croke Park when The Glen won its first All-Ireland title by 2-18 to 2-8. *The Cork Examiner* was none too happy with the tactics of St Rynagh's and under a heading 'Glen Triumph Over Tough Tactics' paid tribute to 'the deadly marksmanship of Tom Buckley aided by Red Crowley, a man of a thousand battles, and Pat O'Doherty, who ruled the roost at mid-field'. The Cork City team led at half-time by 1-10 to 1-3 and had heroes in Finbarr O'Neill, Martin O'Doherty, Pat Barry, Michael O'Halloran as well as the trio mentioned.

The winning team was:

Finbarr O'Neill

Denis O'Riordan   Martin O'Doherty   Pat Barry

Jerry O'Sullivan   Denis Coughlan (capt.)   Michael O'Halloran

J. J. O'Neill   Pat O'Doherty

Patsy Harte   Red Crowley   Tom Buckley

Mick Ryan   Tom Collins   John Young

Substitutes: Michael Corbett for Denis O'Riordan. George O'Riordan, Teddy O'Brien, Liam McAuliffe, Frank O'Sullivan, Frank Cunningham, Tony Treacy, D. McCarthy.

TITLE NO. 2

On 3 October 1976, Glen Rovers defeated Blackrock by 2-7 to 0-10 before an attendance of 25,080. I travelled from Galway to see my first ever Cork Senior Hurling Championship Final and I wasn't disappointed. Paddy Downey (*The Irish Times*): 'At the Mardyke twelve months ago the famed spirit of the Glen barely flashed as the hurlers from Blackpool suffered a heavy defeat at the hands of Blackrock. But a year is a long time in hurling as in the 1976 final at Páirc Uí Chaoimh that spirit was still aflame. Glen Rovers surged through in the second half to score a splendid 24th title win'.

It wasn't the greatest of Cork finals. The first half was tense yet interesting as Blackrock, playing with the wind, led at half-time by 0-8 to 0-2. The second half provided a fierce battle as Glen Rovers rallied and fought back with great fire to win. A penalty goal scored by thirty-six-year-old Patsy Harte after 90 seconds of the second half brought the deficit down to three points. With ten minutes to go the game was finely balanced 1-6 to 0-9. Then in the 51st minute Glen Rovers took the lead for the first time when after Tim Murphy had parried a shot in the Blackrock goal from point blank range, Patsy Harte pounced for another goal.

Denis Coughlan suffered a severe facial injury (a complete accident) before retiring, but captain Pat Barry transferred to centre-half-back 'when his cool resolute hurling steadied affairs'. Glen's heroes were Finbarr O'Neill, 'whose agility has not been impaired by the passage of time', Martin O'Doherty, who held Ray Cummins scoreless from play, Teddy O'Brien, Patsy Harte, Pat O'Doherty, Red Crowley and Frank O'Sullivan. Overall it was the great spirit and teamwork of The Glen which was the difference. I have been to county finals in at least ten counties. Nothing ever touched the Cork Final for passion, atmosphere and sense of occasion.

On 21 November Glen Rovers defeated Newmarket-on-Fergus in a thriller at Newmarket-on-Fergus by 1-13 to 2-9. The Glen led by 1-9 to 0–5 at half-time but just managed to hold on in a spine-tingling second half powered by Finbarr O'Neill who was brilliant in goal, Martin O'Doherty, Teddy O'Brien and Denis Coughlan who was excellent in defence, Pat Horgan lording it at mid-field and Pat O'Doherty, Mick Ryan, and Tom Collins shining in attack.

RUGGED EXCHANGES

On 19 December in Limerick, Glen Rovers defeated South Liberties (Limerick) in a rugged encounter by 2-8 to 2-4. Paddy Downey (*The Irish Times*): 'There was a period in the first half when it seemed that the game might not finish — for lack of players. Referee Noel Dalton sent three players (two from South Liberties one from Glen Rovers) to the line for misdemeanours. The firm handling of Mr Dalton's authority brought the desired result and though the game continued in rugged style, cool heads prevailed.' Paddy blamed the conditions and the time of year for the unsporting behaviour. The ground conditions were dreadful for hurling and heavy rain at the start of the game created a sea of mud from end to end. Failing light didn't help either. 'Spectators were fortunate to have hurling of pleasing quality at all.'

South Liberties led at half-time by 1-3 to 1-1, Glen Rovers being 'the more accomplished team in ball control and positional play, South Liberties the stronger and more direct strikers'.

Credit was lavished on 'the elegant Denis Coughlan, who was the star of the game when moved to centre-half-back before the interval, the highlight of whose play was a mighty point from 85 yards'. Others to play well were Martin O'Doherty, the O'Sullivans Jerry and Frank, Donal Clifford, Pat Horgan, J.J. O'Neill and Pat O'Doherty. Glen Rovers almost got a fright from St Gabriel's, the London champions, on 6 February at rain-soaked Páirc Uí Chaoimh but a late goal from substitute Tom O'Neill helped avert a surprise result. The Glen won by 1-13 to 1-6 and in the semi-final in The Mardyke they had an easy win over Roscommon champions Tremane by 7–10 to 0-3.

In the final at Thurles on 27 March, Glen Rovers defeated the Laois champions Camross of the famous Cuddy family by 2-12 to 0-8. Seán Kilfeather (*The Irish Times*): 'The good name of gallantry was in safe hands at Thurles where Camross came to do battle with Glen Rovers. All the gallantry wasn't enough to earn the little Laois village the spoils of as fervent a fight as could be imagined and the Corkmen returned to the banks with the All-Ireland title that their superior skill and technique earned for them.

'March was at its worst in Thurles. Still all through both sides displayed ground hurling of such accuracy and sweetness that greybeards in the stand were throwing their caps in the air to greet the return of the style of play they thought was long since dead. All through, Glen Rovers half-forward line of Patsy Harte, Red Crowley and Pat O'Doherty, were quick and direct in their approach and seemed to relish the hip-to-hip clashes as much as the Laoismen. Vince Marshall, too, was in his element in the corner. Pat Horgan and J.J. O'Neill won the mid-field battle, Teddy O'Brien was outstanding at corner-back.' The winning team was:

Finbarr O'Neill

Jerry O'Sullivan   Martin O'Doherty (capt.) Teddy O'Brien

Frank O'Sullivan   Donal Clifford   Denis Coughlan

Pat Horgan   J.J. O'Neill

Patsy Harte   Red Crowley   Pat O'Doherty

Mick Ryan   Tom Collins   Vince Marshall

Substitute: Liam McAuliffe for T. Collins, Tom O'Neill, Frank Cunningham.

DENIS COUGHLAN LOOKS BACK

'The Glen lies in the heart of Blackrock. The eight-in-a-row of county titles 1934–1941 is a record never likely to be equalled. Our colours are green, black and amber and we got the name Glen Rovers, through our association with Goulding's Fertilisers Company, which is situated right in the heart of a glen and gave so much employment to local people and many Glen Rovers players. The Glen always had great men. The two Buckleys, Connie and Sonny, would have played in all the eight-in-a-row titles. Paddy "Fox" Collins was one of the gentlest of men and a terrific hurler by all accounts. He was a great hurley maker too. Jim Young, Joe Hartnett, Jack Lynch, John Lyons, Dave Creedon, a host of stars in The Glen then. Joe and Vincie Twomey and Christy Ring of course. Christy came to the Glen in the early 1940s and became even more Glen than The Glen men themselves. It was absolutely wonderful to observe his total dedication to Glen Rovers at general meetings long after he retired.

'I played with Christy in 1964 (as a substitute, getting a few early round games) and won my first county title with the club in 1967. As youngsters we used to go up to the Glen field to watch the seniors training. It was a great honour to play alongside the man. I got to know him well from 1969 on. The best speech I've ever heard in a dressing-room came from Ring at half-time in our semi-final win over Blackrock in 1969. We were in trouble and he lifted us all.

'Looking back at our two All-Ireland wins, the organisation was somewhat haphazard then. We were aware it could be good. Our Munster Final win over Roscrea in 1973 was a great game. It was Easter Sunday and I had the great honour of receiving the Cup from Mick Mackey, whom Christy Ring had prevailed on to do the honours. I'm sorry I haven't a photograph of that unique presentation. The final as your know was delayed and that took from it. The 1977 team had nine of the winning 1973 team and organisation had improved a lot.

'Playing for the Glen was a great honour. We all aimed at that and then to be on a team alongside Christy Ring, Joe Salmon, Jerry O'Sullivan, Denis Riordan, John Young... all household names. Hurling was in my blood. It is a way of life in Blackpool. You made The Glen team if you could and it was expected of you to win County titles.

'Christy Ring's death in 1979 coincided with the demise of The Glen as a top hurling power, which may of course have been coincidental. We didn't win a county title from 1979 to 1989. His influence was greatly missed. He had an uncanny idea of the game and its players and was gifted on the sideline at training or during games. I'll never forget his funeral. Christy's final journey on a Sunday from Ballinlough to Cloyne (20 miles) took three to four hours to reach Cloyne. A funeral to compare with those of Michael Collins, Terence McSweeney or Tomás McCurtain.

'People talk of the spirit of the Glen. It's hard to define and is probably something handed down through generations. You never give up or accept defeat. All Glen teams have a great will to win. I was born and reared on that. In my time no player epitomised it more than the late Jerry O'Sullivan. He came on in 1959 and was still going strong in 1979. During that time he showed what playing for the Glen should mean to everybody. Typical of him he was a junior selector when he was over 40 and the team were short and of course Jerry lined out. He got a heart attack and died with a Glen Rovers jersey on him.

'The present Glen field was handed over to us by Goulding's in 1970 and we've developed three pitches to include football and camogie. Our Clubhouse is a wonderful structure and a great social centre for the area.'

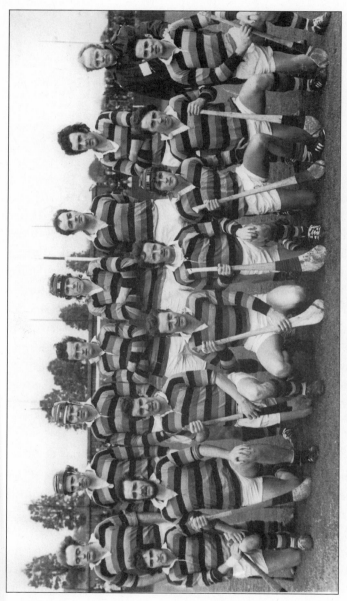

Glen Rovers, All-Ireland Club Champions 1973

Back row: Denis O'Riordan, Pat O'Doherty, Fr Paddy Barry, George O'Riordan, Martin O'Doherty, Denis Coughlan,
Liam McAuliffe, Jackie Daly (trainer).
Front row: J0-Jo O'Neill, Michael Corbett, John Young, Patsy Harte, Finbarr O'Neill, Tom Buckley, Teddy O'Brien, Jerry O'Sullivan.

30

St Vincent's of Dublin

They won their first Dublin Senior Football Championship in 1949 with a team which included Dublin greats like Olly Freaney, Kevin Heffernan, Nicky Maher, Denis Mahony, Norman Allen, Dessie Ferguson, better known as 'Snitchy', and Jimmy Lavin. Then followed the Golden Age of the 1950s which produced nine Dublin Senior Football and four Senior Hurling Championship titles with many of the same personnel, the senior double being achieved four times in 1953, 1954, 1955 and 1957 and a record seven-in-a-row of Dublin Senior Football Championship titles 1949–1955 inclusive. In that decade, too, we saw the three Tuam Stars versus St Vincent's challenge games, and a famous December club hurling game against Glen Rovers in 1953 won by the Dublin club by 3-11 to 2-11. In all St Vincent's have amassed 24 Dublin Senior Football and 13 Senior Hurling titles, a truly remarkable record for one of the greatest club teams of all time.

JIM CROWLEY'S THOUGHTS

Jim Crowley, one of the St Vincent's and Dublin stalwart footballers of the 1950s traces the club's early history. Jim won ten Dublin Senior Football Championship medals in the Golden 1950s era. He married Mary O'Leary, sister of Cathal, another Vincent's and Dublin footballer of that era. 'The start of St Vincent's can be laid at the door of two men and their presence in the Marino Parish, namely Rev. Dr Fitzpatrick (a Laoisman) and Brother Ernest Fitzgerald, at more or less the same time. The club was founded in 1931. There was a big housing estate in Marino at the time and Dr Fitz, as he became popularly known, and Brother Fitz saw the need to have some

194

activity for the young people growing up in the parish. For the first few years the club had a very ordinary beginning but eventually it began to make its way in minor hurling and football, winning a few championships but the goal was to have senior hurling and football teams representing the club. Many of the minors in St Vincent's at that time would have gone to school in O'Connell's School and St Joseph's Marino or "Joeys" as it was known. I went to school at Coláiste Mhuire in Parnell Square. I got on the Dublin minor team of 1947 alongside Kevin Heffernan and Cyril Freaney and it was Kevin invited me to play for St Vincent's after the minor grade with Coláiste Mhuire. I lived in Whitehall just a mile or so up the road from Marino. So it was a great adventure for me starting off with the junior team and eventually making the senior team in 1950, the year after St Vincent's won its first Senior title defeating Garda, powered by men like Brendan Lynch, Tom Langan and Paddy Kennedy in the final. We won everything for eight years from 1948–1956, League and Championship including the record seven-in-a-row Senior Football Championship titles before UCD and the young Erin's Hopes team from St Patrick's College, Drumcondra put a halt to our gallop.

'Around this time of the rise of St Vincent's, Dublin didn't have a great inter-county team. They won the 1942 All-Ireland and after that came a lean period. Native-born Dubliners saw St Vincent's like the Phoenix rising from the ashes. They saw it first in the great rivalry between St Vincent's and other fine club teams in Dublin at the time like Seán McDermotts, Westerns, UCD, Garda, Banba and Air Corps, mostly made up of country lads working in the city. You didn't have the same exodus out of Dublin every weekend as today. The cream of the country's footballers were based in Dublin. Men like Peter Donoghoe, J.J. Cassidy, Tom Sullivan, Tom Dillon, Tom Dunleavy, Seán Flanagan, Pádhraic Carney.... It was a great time in Dublin football — city against country really. Great bite in it and the crowds came back to club football. I remember people coming straight from work to see championship games played on summer evenings. Men with the signs of toil still on them.

'During that fabulous unbeaten run Westerns came closest to beating us but a draw was as close as they got. On a famous November day in 1956 we were beaten at last by UCD in a Dublin League game. An old friend Séamus Conaty (Cavan) played that day in Parnell Park and he often reminds me of it still. In those days the Dublin team was often comprised of country lads who, once they had played for Dublin, often declared for their native counties later. When St Vincent's won the Dublin 1949 title it was decided that the county champions would select the Dublin team. St Vincent's had a club policy to try as far as they could to play native-born Dubliners on the county team, so that there would be continuity and better empathy with supporters. That took off then and a new following for Gaelic football was generated in the city. When Cork beat Dublin in the 1952 National Football League Final (Home) by 1-3 to 0-5, there were 14 St Vincent's men on the team but it was even more memorable a year later when we beat Cavan, the All-Ireland champions at the time, again with 14 Vincent's men on board and better still, clad in the St Vincent's jerseys to avoid a clash of colours with Cavan. That was the first National Football League Final ever won by Dublin. The lone outsider that day was Tony O'Grady (Air Corps) in goal.

'We had a great *esprit-de-corps* then. Very few, if any, took alcoholic drinks. You trained hard to hold your place. Mossy Whelan was my mid-field partner. Pound for pound the best man you could play beside. Mick Moylan known for the long kickout. Jimmy Lavin was a sound full-back. The Mahonys, Denis and Tim were there too. The great Nicky Maher who played with his glasses on with goggles over them. All these lads were wonderful kickers of the ball. They used to vie with each other in the taking of '50s'. Liam Donnelly was one of the best dual players ever. Some of the forwards were household names. Olly Freaney, Kevin Heffernan, Dessie Ferguson, Jock Haughey, Johnny Joyce — what players! Later came the Foleys, Des and Lar. Later still was the era of Tony Hanahoe, Jimmy Keaveney, Brian Mullins, Bobby Doyle, Gay O'Driscoll, Pat O'Neill and Fran Ryder. There would be a family row if I didn't include Cathal O'Leary another great player from that era, a wonderful athlete and a brilliant fielder of a ball.

We still keep up our contacts. We meet sometimes at club and county games. Some of us play golf together. Strangely enough Whitehall Colmcille's now have a strong club for whom all my sons have played. The Christian Brothers set up a school here too and my four sons were educated by them. Three of them went on to win minor All-Ireland medals. I'd love to see club football return to the glory of the 1950s. I still recall the marvellous football of Mayo's Tom Langan against St Vincent's. I marvel at the wonderful goals he scored against us. He once left three of us standing with a hop and a side-step just under the old Cusack Stand. The games we had with Tuam Stars in Croke Park and Tuam in 1957 helped sow the seed.'

This then was the early history of St Vincent's. When the era of the Dubs arrived in 1974 and Heffo launched a new managerial style, his great Dublin team was bolstered by a very strong St Vincent's. It was inevitable that when the club All-Irelands came into being that St Vincent's would make a big effort to win a title. In 1975 the Dublin Senior Football Championship was awarded to St Vincent's, as UCD (All-Ireland champions for the two previous years) failed to field a team on the appointed day. A big doubt existed as to St Vincents' further participation in the All-Ireland series that year as the club has never recognised the county title award of 1975. But the participation of St Vincent's was finally resolved when the Chairman Jack Gilroy and his Directors decided to play not as county champions but as nominees of the County Board.

1976

In the early rounds St Vincent's had a somewhat lucky win over the Kildare champions (Carbury) before easily beating Newtownmountkennedy (Wicklow) on 16 November 1975 at Croke Park by 5-14 to 2-4, Jimmy Keaveney scoring 3-2 and Bobby Doyle 2-3. The Leinster Final was played in Athy on 18 January 1976 and the Dublin champions laboured unimpressively to overcome St Joseph's, a resolute Laois club team, by 3-9 to 1-8. The Laois champions took the game to Vincent's in the first half and at half-time it was level pegging. St Joseph's took the lead again at the end of the third quarter but in the final quarter it was one way traffic with goals from Mickey Whelan and Jimmy Keaveney.

On Sunday, 22 February at the Mardyke, St Vincent's had their greatest win that year, defeating Nemo Rangers by 0-10 to 0-3. The losers, from whom much was expected, 'were helpless as lambs in a slaughterhouse after their three epic games with Austin Stack's', (Paddy Downey, *The Irish Times*). It was no contest and the attendance of 5,090 appreciated the superb display of the Dublin team, whom Kevin Heffernan had trained to perfection. Six of the ten points came from Jimmy Keaveney frees. After playing with the wind, St Vincent's led at half-time by 0-5 to 0-2 and despite some profligate shooting, won well in the end. Brian Mullins and Bobby Doyle starred. 'The fetching of Mullins and his forward thrusts were the biggest factors in the rout of the Cork men while Doyle's contribution was enormous,' (Paddy Downey, *The Irish Times*). As always the latter roved all over the place and his flashing runs frequently dismantled the Nemo defence. Peadar O'Brien (*Irish Press*) also gave man-of-the-match billing to Brian Mullins who had expert assistance from Gay O'Driscoll, Mick Behan, Vinny Lambe, Fran Ryder, Tony Hanahoe, Mickey Whelan, Jimmy Keaveney, Bobby Doyle and Barney Reddy.

At wintry Portlaoise the final touches were put to the Vincents' success story when an absolutely rampant fifteen sent Roscommon Gaels reeling to the tune of 4-10 to 0-5 on 14 March 1976. Damien McElroy (*Irish Independent*) gave credit to the 'team performance of the winners powered by Gay O'Driscoll, Vinny Lambe (first half), Barney Reddy, Jimmy Keaveney and Bobby Doyle'. The winners ran riot in the final minutes with two goals from Tony Hanahoe and a point from Jimmy Keaveney. The losers had plenty of play but 'their forwards were well beaten by a superb St Vincent's defence', (Peadar O'Brien, *Irish Press*). This was the winning team:

Norman Bernard

Dave Billings	Gay O'Driscoll	Mick Hannick
Mick Behan	Vinny Lambe	Brendan Pocock

Brian Mullins   Fran Ryder

Barney Reddy	Tony Hanahoe (capt.)	Mickey Whelan
Leslie Deegan	Jimmy Keaveney	Bobby Doyle

Substitute: P.J. Reid for M. Hannick.

TONY HANAHOE RECALLS

Tony Hanahoe well-known solicitor and former Dublin and St Vincent's captain, is one of the most respected and articulate of Gaelic football men. Despite a very busy work schedule, he has still an abiding interest in Gaelic football, his native Dublin and the fortunes of St Vincent's.

'As a youngster regularly going to Croke Park no one impressed me more than Ned Wheeler of Wexford. He was an outstanding giant of a man in a great team. Wheeler to me was the blonde crew-cut indestructible giant, who was fair but never dirty.

'I joined St Vincent's because I was at school with the Christian Brothers in Griffith Avenue. There was a natural progression from one to the other. I began with Vincent's early. I lived in Clontarf and there was great pride in the school at that time. When I was about ten I used to go to Croke Park early for games and often met another little guy with a gaberdine coat, whom I grew to know later as Jimmy Keaveney. The two of us were often there hours before the officials opened the gates. Jimmy hates me telling that one.

'My first year in St Joseph's Marino there was Des Foley's last year and our school won the Hogan Cup. We were the first day-school to do so. Lar and Des Foley were well-known in Joey's as huge sporting figures. They became big names in St Vincent's shortly afterwards. At that time Kevin Heffernan was still playing. Ollie Freaney had just retired. Cathal O'Leary, the Foleys, Jimmy Lavin and all that famous 1950s team were involved still and in the hurling Paddy Donnelly and Joe Drumgoole, both equally zealous people, were in charge. When I left school I played for the Dublin minors for a few years in each code and gradually got on to the senior squads. We were beaten by UCD in the Senior Football Championship in my first year, a pretty unusual occurrence then. The year was 1964.

'I won my first title in 1965 with a team which included Kevin Heffernan, Cyril Meehan, Jimmy Lavin, the Foleys, Blackie Coen, Mick Kissane, Des McKane — that's the era I entered. I was really taken by the great St Vincent's of the 1950s. I remember Denis Mahony crying in the back of my father's car up in Dundrum over the loss to Kerry in 1955 — my interest goes back that far. I went to all the games in Croke Park and saw all those games against Garda. I remember vividly up in Croke Park the crowd shouting at the Garda players "Where's your baton?" or "Take out your notebook".

'Lads who came on to the Vincent's team with me were Jimmy Keaveney and Brian Mullins' brother Seán. Then on to the 1970s when the era of the Dubs came along and those hectic games with Kerry.'

So how did the club St Vincent's fit into that whole unique and busy and hectic era? 'The club fitted in in a very significant way because there was always this contention in Vincent's — a demand for loyalty. A kind of omerta, a loyalty to club which was sacrosanct. Some people outside St Vincent's found this objectionable, feeling that St Vincent's people always gave loyalty first to the club and next to the county. At that time the people involved, Bobby Doyle, Brian Mullins, Gay O'Driscoll, Jimmy Keaveney and myself, tried very hard to apportion ourselves to both club and county. We always gave 100% to our club and none of that bunch ever felt special.

We had a great rivalry with UCD in the early 1970s in the years they won their two club All-Irelands and we won our lone one. In fact the County Final of 1975 was never played. The timing of the final coincided with UCD's examinations. In fairness there was credibility in their argument but we didn't accept a walkover and never count that year as a title won. We were reluctant even to take any further part in the All-Ireland club competition. Later on that year some team had to be nominated and after a fairly forceful meeting we decided that we'd represent Dublin and went on to win the title.

Winning that All-Ireland title was a great experience because it brought you out of an urban environment into fresh pastures. One game in which we beat Nemo Rangers in the Mardyke stands out. That was like a top inter-county game. Nemo had beaten us in one before and we developed a great friendship with them. We still have challenge games with them annually at different levels. As a result of that connection the Cork county team use our facilities for workouts prior to important Croke Park games.

The Competition

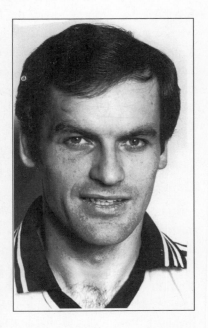

'I'm disappointed that the competition has to be played during the worst months of the year. The competition succeeds in spite of all the problems. It should be played, at a different time of the year. Central Council has the power to regulate. As to Vincent's today I would hope they could strive to maintain the same high standards of the past. We have a superb ground and facilities. It is important that leadership should be given to young people and sport should be used for the purpose for which it is ordained. There is very little point in having a successful social club unless you are able to put your teams out to compete. That is the kernel of what the Association is about.'

Tony Hanahoe — 'winning the club All-Ireland, a great experience'.

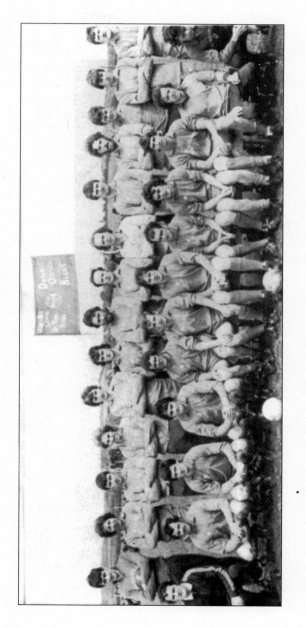

St Vincent's All-Ireland Club Champions 1976

Back row: Bobby Doyle, Mick Behan, David Billings, Norman Bernard, Barney Reddy, Vinnie Lambe, Tony Hanahoe, Brian Mullins.
Front row: Mickey Whelan, Mick Hannick, Fran Ryder, Brendan Pocock, Jimmy Keaveney, Leslie Deegan, Gay O'Driscoll.

31

The Barrs In Blue

What an amazing GAA club is the St Finbarr's National Hurling and Football Club, in existence even before the GAA was founded in 1884. It even possesses records of hurling games played as far back as 1875. In terms of the amount of Cork Senior Hurling Championship titles that they've won, they are second in line to the Rockies on 29, and share the honour with the Glen at 25. They are the only club to bring off the double (Hurling and Football) senior title achievement in the same year which they did twice, in 1980 and 1982. They also are the sole club to win club All-Irelands in both codes. Hailing from the Lough area of Cork City they were the standard bearers in showing the way to all other GAA clubs when their magnificent GAA Pavilion was officially opened in November 1970 by Connie Neenan, one of the club's greatest benefactors and friends. The Club Grounds at Togher, officially called Neenan Park, were opened in 1962. When I first visited the premises in the early 1970s I was privileged to be given the grand tour by Connie Neenan himself.

'I spend most days here in Togher watching the youngsters play in the evenings and meeting my friends in the Pavilion at night. After so many years spent abroad it is lovely to be back with your own in the place you were reared.'

Hurling came before football for the Barrs. The first Senior Hurling title came in 1899 while the first one in Gaelic football wasn't until 1956 and the total number of Senior titles won in football is now eight. The club has won five club All-Irelands in all, hurling in 1975 and 1978, football in 1980, 1981 and 1987. From the early days the club bristled with names like Moloney, Young, Sexton, O'Connell, Harrington, Sheehan, O'Leary, Ring, Neenan,

Canton, Dorney and O'Donovan. Titles came regularly enough to the Lough Parish. Later on names like Coughlan, Cronin, O'Connell, Buttimer, Kenneally, Horgan and Atkins were in the vanguard. The first great Barrs men I came to know through Michael O'Hehir's voice were Mick Kennefick, Tom Mulcahy, Seán Condon and Tony O'Shaughnessy. Then came the 1960s and hurling stars like Gerald and Charlie McCarthy, Peter Doolan, Denis Murphy, Tony Maher, Tony Connolly and Con Roche, and footballers of quality like Séamus Looney, Jimmy Barry-Murphy (one of the greatest dual men ever), big Christy Ryan (whose service to the club at both levels is paramount), Donal O'Grady, John Meyler, John Allen, Dave Barry, John Kerins, Michael Slocum... the list goes on.

THE FIRST HURLING TITLE

The Hurling title was first won in 1975. In the 1974 Cork Senior Hurling Final played in the Mardyke the Barrs ended a six-year drought by defeating the champions Blackrock by 2-17 to 2-14 in a barn-storming finish which saw the victors come from four points down with 11 minutes remaining. It was a case of the walking wounded with Barrs surprising the star studded Rockies. No one lit the torch which kindled the victory fire more than Con Roche despite a heavily bandaged injured knee. Later followed victories over Mount Sion in Waterford by 5-12 to 3-3, Kilmallock at the Mardyke in December by 4-12 to 0-9 and in the Munster Final over Newmarket-on-Fergus on 19 January 1975 by 0-7 to 0-3 which was a test of stamina and endurance rather than of hurling skill. Young Donal O'Grady was a dominant figure at centre-half-back and unfortunately the game ended the great service given to the club of Bernie Scully, who received a broken shin-bone.

In the semi-final the Barrs made the long trip to Ballycran (Down) by train and stayed the night in Down, a gesture appreciated by their opponents. The Barrs rattled in three early goals and won in the end by 8-8 to 3-10. Jimmy Barry-Murphy was their top scorer and star supreme. In the final at Croke Park on 16 March the Barrs defeated The Fenians (Kilkenny) by 3-8 to 1-6. In a fine second-half performance, man-of-the-match Jimmy Barry-Murphy, inspired the winners with the first of their three goals in the last quarter, the other two coming from Jerry O'Shea and Charlie Cullinane.

This was the team:

Jim Power (capt.)

Tony Maher	Seán Canty	Charlie Barrett
Bertie O'Brien	Donal O'Grady	Tony Butler
Gerald McCarthy		Con Roche
Éamonn Fitzpatrick	Jimmy Barry-Murphy	Séamus Gillen
Charlie McCarthy	Séamus Looney	Jerry O'Shea

Substitutes: Charlie Cullinane, Barnie Scully, Denis Burns, Barry Wiley.

THE SECOND TITLE

Three years later came another hurling crown. In the Cork Senior Hurling semi-final, played on a dull rainy August night (14 Saturday) before 7,900 spectators, the Barrs defeated the Rockies in what Michael Ellard (*Cork Examiner*) described as 'fabulously exciting' and 'on a par with the best seen in Cork for many a long day'. The Barrs' three greatest stars in this classic were Charlie McCarthy and Jimmy Barry-Murphy. The final against The Glen attracted an attendance of 34,000 on a day when the gates were broken down by the huge crowd seeking to gain admittance — the greatest attendance ever at an Irish club game in any code. The Barrs gambled on youth and tradition — eight of the panel were sons of men who had won county medals with The Barrs. Their gamble came off and they won convincingly by 1-17 to 1-5. Denis Burns, the winners' captain, was outstanding. Christy Ryan was a big success when switched to full-forward and in the second half, when favoured by the strong wind, the half-forward line of Barry Wiley, Jimmy Barry-Murphy and John Allen devastated The Glen who led at half-time by 1-5 to 0-6.

Victories over Portlaw (Waterford) by 5-7 to 3-9 in Portlaw, an easy semi-final win over Ballyduff (Kerry) in Páirc Uí Chaoimh by 3-11 to 1-4 and a drawn dramatic Munster Final in Tulla against Sixmilebridge at 3-5 apiece followed. A blanket of fog covered the field on 18 December, 1977, yet both teams kept 4,000 spectators on a knife-edge of suspense for the hour. Charlie McCarthy was the star this time and on 22 January in the replay at Tipperary the stars of Barrs' victory (by 2-8 to 0-6) were Tony Maher and Denis Burns.

The semi-final and final were played on the weekend of the 26th March. In the semi-final, at home in Togher, St Finbarr's defeated O'Donovan Rossa (Belfast) by 6-12 to 1-16. On the following day, St Finbarr's travelled to Semple Stadium, Thurles, and defeated Rathnure of Wexford by 2-7 to 0-9. It was a day of gale-force winds and Rathure led by 0-8 to 0-1 at the interval. It took 20 minutes of the second half for Barry Wiley to put the Barrs on level terms. A Jimmy Barry-Murphy goal from an upright rebound sealed the game in which goalkeeper Jim Power was the hero of the hour. The winning team was:

Jim Power

Charlie Barrett   Tony Maher   Denis Burns (capt.)

Donal O'Grady   Niall Kennefick   Jerry Murphy

Gerald McCarthy   John Cremin

John Allen   Jimmy Barry-Murphy   Barry Wiley

Éamonn Fitzpatrick Christy Ryan   Charlie McCarthy

Substitute: Bernie Meade

THE FIRST FOOTBALL TITLE

The Barrs became the first and only club to achieve national success in both games in 1980. The Lough men won the Cork County Final on 21 October 1979, defeating Castlehaven (in their first final) by 3-14 to 2-7. Castlehaven fought hard and brought the deficit to two points in the middle of the second half. A Mick Lynch goal put a damper on Castlehaven and inspired by man-of-the-match Christy Ryan and Jimmy Barry–Murphy, the men in blue were on their way. Later came wins over Loughmore–Castleiney (Tipperary) by 1-9 to 0-5 and a Munster title victory over Kilrush by 0-10 to 0-4 at Páirc Uí Chaoimh in which Christy Ryan, goalkeeper Bertie O'Brien and team captain Noel Aherne excelled.

Then followed an easy win over The Kingdom (London) by 3-17 to 1-3 and a hard-earned All-Ireland Semi-final win over Scotstown (Monaghan) in Clones on 11 May 1980, by 0-7 to 0-4. This was a bruising encounter. Mick Carey and Donal O'Grady were heroes in defence and Jimmy Barry–Murphy's genius in attack was never more appreciated by The Barrs' followers. In the final at Tipperary on 25 May St Finbarr's had an easy win over St Grellan's, Ballinasloe, by 3-9 to 0-8. Ballinasloe started well against the wind and but for the brilliance of Donal O'Grady had the Barrs in trouble. Then the genius of Jimmy Barry-Murphy shone like a beacon as he set up all three goals scored by Jamesie O'Callaghan and Finny O'Mahony. Jamesie O'Callaghan's goal of absolute splendour (with one minute to go) started with a Dave Barry dribble, then a pass to Barry-Murphy who placed Jamesie for the vital score. Christy Ryan had another splendid game at centre-half-back. The team was:

Bertie O'Brien

Donal O'Grady Gene Desmond Noel Aherne (capt.)

Dan Brosnan Mick Lynch Mick Carey

Christy Ryan Damien Philpott

Finny Twomey Richie Kenny Finny O'Mahony

Jimmy Barry-Murphy John Allen Jamesie O'Callaghan

Substitute: Dave Barry for D. Philpott.

TITLE No. 2

In the 1980 County Final, the Barrs retained their title, defeating UCC by 3–8 to 1-9 before a mere 4,500 spectators. Afterwards, loyal servant Christy Ryan (capt.) received the Andy Scannell Cup from the Board Chairman Paddy O'Driscoll. Dave Barry, Finny O'Mahony and Mark Healy were the stars. The Barrs' hurlers made it a double in Cork with eight of the footballers on duty. They did the same in Munster also, the Barrs' hurlers beating Roscrea 2-12 to 1-14 and the footballers overcoming Stradbally (Waterford) by 3-12 to 1-8. Earlier they had beaten Thomond College (Limerick) by 4–4 to 1-5. Three great goals in the second half against Stradbally by Jimmy Barry-Murphy, Finny O'Mahony and Dave Barry showed the Barrs were intent on keeping their crown. Meantime, the club's hurlers fell to Ballyhale Shamrocks in the final by 1-15 to 1-11 and a week later the footballers defeated Scotstown in Páirc Uí Chaoimh in a close semi-final encounter by 0-8 to 0-4.

FINAL AGAINST WALTERSTOWN

The final against Walterstown (Meath) took place on 31 May at Croke Park and the Barrs held on to their crown by 1-8 to 0-6. It was by no means an easy win. The winners owed a lot to the brilliance of goalkeeper Bertie O'Brien. The new ruling on the handpass in vogue tended to curtail movement. Inhibition set in and the game became a series of misses. With five minutes to go the Meathmen were just two points behind. A minute from full-time substitute Jim Barry ran into an open space, picked up an O'Mahony pass and shot the vital goal to finish it. Mark Healy played a trojan game at full-back and the left flank of Eugene Desmond and Mick Carey also held the fort. The winning team was:

Bertie O'Brien

John Cremin	Mark Healy	Eugene Desmond
Mick Carey	Christy Ryan (capt.)	Dessie O'Grady

Teddy Holland   Mick Lynch

Dave Barry	Richie Kenny	Finny O'Mahony
Jimmy Barry-Murphy	John Allen	Jamesie O'Callaghan

Substitute: Jim Barry

TITLE NO. 3

The Barrs actually lost the Cork County Final of 1986 on 28 September at Páirc Uí Chaoimh, falling to the Divisional side Imokilly by 2-4 to 0-9. They were disconsolate afterwards because of the palmed goal by Brian Lotty just two minutes from full-time which saw Imokilly take the lead for the first time. Even before a ball was kicked in the final, the Barrs knew they were to be Cork's representatives later in the club All-Ireland but they wanted to be in that position as champions. A good U-21 championship campaign subsequently helped them ride the storm and it was a determined Barrs' team which defeated Austin Stack's of Tralee on 9 November in Tralee by 0-11 to 0-5. In Fraher Park, Dungarvan, the Barrs showed marvellous spirit on 23 November when with a team of only 13 men they romped to a very impressive 2-15 to 1-5 win over Kilrossanty.

CASTLEBLANEY FAUGHS

On 15 February, St Finbarr's travelled to Castleblaney to take on the local Faughs on a beautiful spring day. The visitors playing football of great character led by two goals at the break, but the home team rallied in great style and it took a late drop kick point by Michael Slocum to save the day 1–12 to 2–9. It was back to Páirc Uí Chaoimh on 1 March for the replay. This time the pitch was mist shrouded but the game ran on similar lines in a contest to be savoured. The Barrs led by nine points early in the second half but back came The Faughs and The Barrs held on grimly to win a thriller by 3-5 to 2-7. A tremendous half-back line of Michael Carey, Kevin Scanlan and Bill O'Connell saved the day.

St Finbarr's defeated Clann na nGael (Roscommon) by 0-10 to 0-7 in the final. Seán Kilfeather (*The Irish Times*) described the game as: 'having plenty of honest effort in a bleak Croke Park. Clann na nGael made a brave effort to save the game in the final quarter against a staunch St Finbarrs' defence.' The experience of men like Christy Ryan, John Allen and Declan O'Mahony was invaluable. Michael Ellard (*The Examiner*) under a heading 'Super Blues Back-line Paves Way for Victory' described it as: 'a performance with character. It took great courage to win because of the atrocious weather conditions. In a truly magnificent Barrs defence, John Cremin and Bill O'Connell were heroic.' The team was:

John Kerins

John Cremin	John Meyler (capt.)	Gene Desmond
Mick Carey	Kevin Scanlan	Bill O'Connell

Paddy Hayes   Tony Leahy

Kieran McCarthy	Christy Ryan	Michael Slocum
John Allen	Declan O'Mahony	Tony Power

Substitute: Michael Barry.

It was a tremendous achievement for any club to win five All-Ireland titles (two hurling and three football). No man can lay claim to all five medals but three men almost did; Christy Ryan (three football, one hurling); Jimmy Barry-Murphy (two hurling, two football); and John Allen (three football, one hurling).

DONAL O'GRADY LOOKS BACK

Donal O'Grady, former Cork All-Ireland hurling full-back of 1984 is a Barrs' man through and through. The former popular Sunday Game hurling analyst is Principal of Youghal Vocational School. He won three All-Ireland Club titles with the Barrs — two hurling (1975 and 1978) and one football (1980) playing up to the end of the Munster campaign with the 1981 champion team, of which his brother Dessie was a member. He remembers his times with the Barrs: 'Believe it or not Dessie, my brother, and I first played in the North Cork Leagues with The Glen. We then played in the Lough Leagues with a team called Clarke's Road, when Gerald McCarthy was largely instrumental in persuading my late father Jim to start his two young sons playing for St Finbarr's. My father was a Barrs' man and that's how it started.

The first team from the club to influence me was our famous minor team of 1963 which lost to Blackrock in the final and included Gerald and Charlie McCarthy, Tony Maher and Con Roche. It was a mystery how that team lost. Then of course the Barrs' men on Cork's 1966 All-Ireland winning team were a huge influence — Charlie and Gerald Mc Carthy, Con Roche, Denis Murphy, Peter Doolan and Tony Connolly.

THE SPIRIT

It's hard to define the spirit of the club. St Finbarr's always had a special magic for me — the personnel within the club and the way we played the games. We had many great characters. As to why we have been successful at both games, that too is hard to define. Coming into the early 1970s many of our personnel played both games together. We never looked on ourselves as a dual club. It was the Barrs and we gave our all at both games. Hurling was always my favourite game and I was probably better at it too.

As to great memories, I have hosts of them. The greatest for me was our first hurling All-Ireland win of 1975 against The Fenians. That whole campaign was a huge adventure. We travelled a lot that year and it was the club's first time ever playing in Croke Park and my first time playing against hurlers of the quality of Pat Delaney and Pat Henderson. Jimmy Barry-Murphy gave a roasting to Pat Henderson that day. The following day Pat Henderson starred in the Railway Cup Final against Munster when Jimmy Barry-Murphy was only a substitute for the losers. Strange!

I'd hate to single out great Barrs' people. As a group we were hard to beat. I'm still a Barrs' man to the hilt — never could be anything else. Always close to my heart and that blue jersey with Naomh Fionnbarra written in a half-moon shape on the front was always special. St Finbarr will always be our main sponsor! My own greatest moments for St Finbarr's would be the semi-final and final wins over Scotstown and Ballinasloe in football in 1980. The best club hurling game I ever played in, was the semi-final win over The Rockies in the Cork Semi-final of 1977. I had been to the US for the summer and returned on the previous Wednesday. I came on as a substitute in that epic game and enjoyed every moment of it.'

John Allen (capt.) holds the Andy Merrigan Cup aloft in Croke Park on May 31 1981 after St Finbarr's recorded a two-in-a-row of All-Ireland Club Football titles.

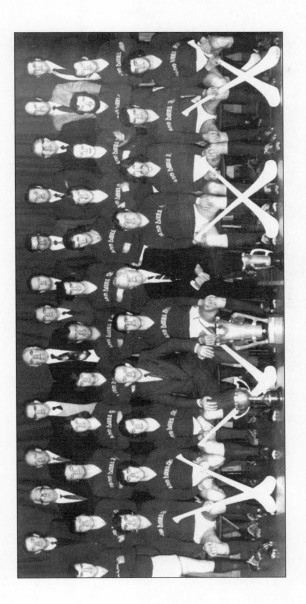

St Finbarr's, All-Ireland Club Champions (Hurling) 1975

Back row: J. Barry–Murphy, J. Twomey, M. Kenefick, J. Murphy, J. Mehigan, P. Canton, M. Finn, D. O'Driscoll, V. Riordan, D. Cremin, T. Mullane, P. Doolan.

Middle row: B. Scully, T. Maher, J. Barry-Murphy, D. O'Grady, M. O'Mahony, C. Cullinane, S. Canty, B. Wylie, B. O'Brien, C. Barrett, E. Fitzpatrick, C. Roche.

Front row: C. McCarthy, T. Butler, S. Gillen, M. Murphy, J. Power, C. Neenan, M. Archer, G. McCarthy, J. O'Shea, C. Myers.

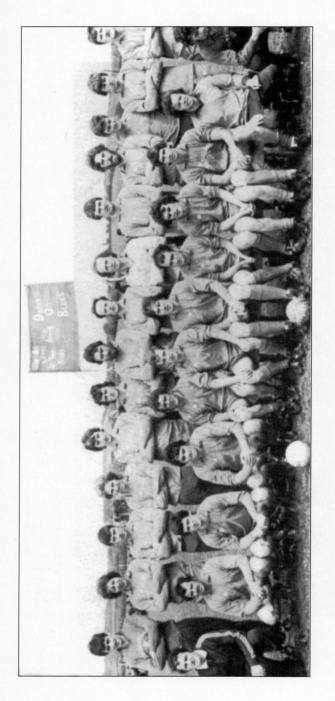

St Finbarr's All-Ireland Club Football Champions 1980

Back row: Billy Kelleher, Des O'Grady, Jerry McCarthy, Dave Barry, Richie Kenny, Finbarr O'Mahony, John Allen, Noel Aherne, Bertie O'Brien, Jimmy Barry-Murphy, Gene Desmond, Denis Burns, Donal O'Grady, Mick Lynch.

Front row: Pat Lougheed (trainer), Christy Myers, John Cremin, Jim Barry, Denny Brosnan, Michael Carey, Christy Ryan (capt.), Damian Philpott, Jamesie O'Callaghan, Finbarr Twomey, Brendan O'Driscoll, Mark Healy.

32

Nemo Top The Lot

The achievements of Nemo Rangers in the past 25 years borders on the phenomenal. The club, which was relatively new on the Cork GAA scene, won its first Cork Senior Football Championship title in 1972, and went on to win its first of six All-Ireland Club titles later that year. The club has now has amassed ten Cork Senior Football Championship titles. The name of Nemo Rangers is linked with the evolution of the club All-Ireland series and their hectic games with Austin Stack's of Tralee and St Vincent's of Dublin helped raise the tone and standard of the competition.

TITLE 1

The 19th November 1972 will always be a red letter day in the history of Nemo Rangers for it was the day of the club's first ever Cork Senior Football title success. In the final at the Cork Athletic Grounds, Nemo defeated UCC by 2-9 to 0-8. This was the end of a long wait for the victors in their second ever final, for they had appeared in the senior semi-final for the previous six years and at times felt they would never succeed. They never gave up and laid the basis for success in the first half when facing a strong wind they were only behind by a point, 0–6 to 0–5 at half-time.

Immediately after half-time they were on their way to success when a long Dinny Allen drive went straight to the net. With ten minutes to go, Séamus Coughlan made it safe with goal number two. Despite wind and heavy rain, Nemo's spirit and determination carried the day. There was no stopping the Cork club side and easy wins over Doonbeg (Clare) in the Munster Final (by 3-9 to 1-5) and over Father Griffin's (Galway) in Pearse Stadium, Salthill, on 29 April 1973 (by 0-17 to 0-9) paved the way for an All-Ireland Final showdown with St Vincent's (Dublin) at Portlaoise on Monday 4 June. The game ended in a welter of excitement at 2-11 apiece.

Paddy Downey (*The Irish Times*) captured the excitement: 'If the whole thing had been contrived you couldn't have a more tense and dramatic finish. Just picture it. There was only a half-minute to go when St Vincent's, trailing by a point, were awarded a 25 yard free. Jimmy Keaveney, however, was master of the situation and duly floated the ball over the bar. A draw was a fair result to a match which gave new stature to the three-year-old competition.' The game which started tamely, developed into a 'splendid, free-flowing exhibition' high in sportsmanship and a cliffhanger all the way. Scores were level six times including at half-time when the score stood Nemo 1-6 to Saint Vincent's 2-3.

Nemo Rangers, played their best football in the second half, powered by Frank Cogan as centre-half-back, Michael O'Donoghue and Séamus Coughlan as mid-fielders, and Kieran Collins and Jimmy Barrett as forwards. In the replay on 24 June at Semple Stadium, Thurles, Nemo Rangers won their first All-Ireland crown by 4-6 to 0-10. Two goals in each half, at decisive times, won the day for the Cork City team. In the 29th minute, Jimmy Barrett took a pass from Colm Murphy for the first and moments later Billy Cogan was in the right spot for a crossbar rebound to get the second goal.

St Vincent's started impressively in the second half but in a quick drive Séamus Coughlan put Liam Goode through for goal number three and the fourth goal, scored by Coughlan himself, put the seal on the success. In a sense it was beginners' luck for the victors. The winning team was:

Billy Morgan (capt.)

John Corcoran	Eddie Brophy	Brian Murphy
Ray Twomey	Frank Cogan	Denis O'Driscoll
Donal Barrett		Michael O'Donoghue
Kieran Collins	Séamus Coughlan	Billy Cogan
Liam Goode	Jimmy Barrett	Colm Murphy

THE SECOND TITLE

On 17 September 1978 Nemo Rangers retained their Cork Senior Football Championship crown defeating luckless St Michael's by 1-9 to 1-3. Brian Murphy played a captain's part at centre-half-back. Denis Linehan began to dominate mid-field and man-of-the-match Dinny Allen scored a marvellous second-half goal to shatter St Michael's ambitions.

On 4 February, after a four-year wait, Nemo Rangers defeated Kilrush by 0-8 to 0-5 in the Munster Final at Kilrush. Exchanges were very close and the score at half-time was 0-4 apiece. After 13 minutes of the second half Dinny Allen's penalty shot was saved by Tom Prenderville. Later on, a marvellous Billy Morgan diving save from Anthony Moloney denied the Clare lads. Denis Linehan's final point gave Nemo a hard-earned win. Earlier Nemo Rangers had beaten Austin Stack's in a replay in Tralee by 1–11 to 2-8 — yet another cliffhanger in the series of wonderful games between these superb club teams.

I was present in Tuam Stadium on 4 March 1979, for the Nemo Rangers' win over Killererin (Galway) by 3-6 to 1-6. We all stood for a minute's silence in honour of Christy Ring who had died the previous evening. The difference between the teams were two relatively soft goals, one in each half, and both vital to Nemo Rangers' win. The visitors, spurred on by mid-fielders Kieran Brady and Declan Murphy, led at half time by 1-5 to 0-1. In the second half, Noel Morgan couldn't believe his luck when facing an empty net and then when Tim Dalton scored the third goal the game was over as a contest. Frank Cogan had an outstanding game. One had to admire the determination of the visitors in green and black, and especially Kieran Collins for his decision to postpone his continental honeymoon until after the game. The same man then had to cut short this honeymoon to play in the final against Scotstown (Monaghan) on 17 March at Croke Park which Nemo Rangers won easily by 2-9 to 1-3.

This was a day of horrific weather conditions. A crowd of 4,443 paid to see the All-Ireland Club Final. 'There were times when the swirling snow almost shut off their view. Much of the snow melted as it fell, otherwise the players would have been ankle deep in it.' (Paddy Downey, *The Irish Times*.) He continued: 'With a little imagination it was easy to place the scene on a plateau somewhere north of Brooks' Range in Alaska and with that thought in mind, we would not have been surprised to see moose, caribou and grizzly

bears ambling down to the field from the Hill. Speaking of grizzly bears —
the grizzly greying head of Frank Cogan was a conspicuous sight as the
veteran thirty-five-year-old played a storming game in Nemo's powerful
defence.' The team was:

Billy Morgan

Frank Cogan	Fred Stone	Kieran Murphy
Jimmy Kerrigan	Brian Murphy (capt.)	Denis O'Driscoll

Kieran Brady   Denis Lenihan

Jimmy Barrett	Denis Allen	Tim Dalton
Noel Morgan	Kieran Collins	Colm Murphy

THE THIRD TITLE

After winning out in Cork once again, Nemo Rangers went after their third
All-Ireland title in 1982 by defeating Ballinacourty (Waterford) in
Dungarvan on 24 October 1981 by 4-14 to 1-3, Castleisland Desmonds in
Ballinlough by 0-11 to 0-2 and Kilrush in Páirc Uí Chaoimh on 6 March.
Kilrush started well in this Munster Final but two fine first half goals from
Denis Allen and Charlie Murphy saw Nemo lead at half-time by 2-3 to 0-
5. Séamus Coughlan was introduced at mid-field in the second half and he
was the trump card in a 3-9 to 1-6 win.

A very good home win followed, over Raheens (Kildare) by 1-10 to 0-7, a
great goal by Seán Hayes deciding the issue. In the final at Cusack Park,
Ennis, on 16 May 1982, Nemo Rangers trounced Garrymore (Mayo) by
6-11 to 1-8. There was a huge gulf in standards between the teams as Nemo
Rangers, led by Denis Allen, powered into a 3-5 to nil lead after 16 minutes.
This was the team:

Don Bevan

Frank Cogan	Brian Murphy	Aidan Keane
Jimmy Kerrigan	Tom Hennebry	Denis O'Driscoll

Mickey Niblock   Séamus Coughlan

Tim Dalton (capt.)	Seán Hayes	Colm Murphy
Mick Dorgan	Denis Allen	Ephie Fitzgerald

FOURTH TITLE (1984)

Nemo Rangers won the 1983 Cork Senior Football Championship title in flying style, defeating Clonakilty by 4-12 to 2-3. Then followed an easy win in December over Kilrossanty (Waterford) by 2-18 to 0-1 and a very hard earned one the following Sunday over Kenmare, by 2-6 to 1-6. A very lucky goal in the 17th minute of the second half, scored by Charlie Murphy after a series of Kenmare errors, was the difference between the teams on a cold windy and wet day. Paddy Downey (*The Irish Times*) wrote that: 'Nemo Rangers hung up all their Christmas stockings in the small mid-Cork village of Cloughduv and found them filled to their hearts' content.' In the Munster final at Limerick on 22 January, Nemo easily outpointed Doonbeg (Clare) by 3-10 to 0-3, their sixth provincial title in seven appearances. On a bitterly cold day, Charlie Murphy starred in attack and Tim Dalton had a brilliant first half at mid-field.

The semi-final and final were played on successive days on the weekend of 11 and 12 February. In the semi-final at Kiltoom on the Saturday, Nemo Rangers beat Saint Mary's, Sligo, by 1-10 to 1-7 and in Athlone on the Sunday, beat Walterstown of Meath by 2-10 to 0-5. Seán Kilfeather (*The Irish Times*) wrote that the fourth title 'was achieved with the minimum of fuss although it took two second-half goals by Ephie Fitzgerald, both engineered by arch schemer Denis Allen to kill off the Meath men'. The winning team was:

Don Bevan

Aidan Keane   Brian Murphy   Kieran Murphy

Jimmy Kerrigan(capt.) Michael Lynch   Tony Nation

Mickey Niblock   Tim Dalton

Séamus Coughlan   Seán Hayes   Colm Murphy

Ephie Fitzgerald   Denis Allen   Michael Dorgan

Substitute: Charlie Murphy for S. Hayes.

FIFTH TITLE (1989)

'Nemo the Arist ocrats' is how Noel Horgan described the Capwell-based club in the *Cork 1989 Yearbook* when writing of their 1988 County Final triumph over Duhallow by 2-8 to 0-10. Not an easy win at all, fashioned by two second-half goals from Dinny Allen, (winning a record eight Cork Senior Football Championship medals) and Ephie Fitzgerald, who gratefully accepted a goalpost rebound.

Then followed victories over Doonbeg, at Kilrush on 13 November by 3–11 to 1-4 with Tony Griffin masterly in defence, and a Munster Final win over Kilrossanty (Waterford) by 1-6 to 1-2 at Clonmel. This was a real battle and Nemo's great experience won the day. The All-Ireland Semi-final win over Parnell's (Dublin) in Ballygarvan on 19 February, 1989 was even harder still. Playing in the red and white of Cork because of a direct colours clash, Nemo Rangers, although winning by 1-4 to 0-5, had to withstand fierce pressure in the second half when Parnell's were aided by the breeze.

In the final, Nemo Rangers won pulling up against Clann na nGael of Roscommon by 1-13 to 1-3, thanks to: 'a display of accurate scoretaking by Eoin O'Mahony which inspired his colleagues and broke the heart of Clann. It was a splendid team-effort by the winners, with fine performances from Neil Creedon, Tony Griffin, Jimmy Kerrigan, Denis O'Sullivan, Eoin O'Mahony, Stephen Calnan, Stephen O'Brien, Tony Nation, Dinny Allen and Michael Dorgan' – Seán Kilfeather (*The Irish Times*). In the *Cork 1990 Yearbook*, selector Brian Barrett paid tribute to coach, Billy Morgan, for his dedication and inspiration, to his fellow selector Bernard Harrington, trainer Jim Cremin, masseurs Frank Cogan and Stephen Mulcahy, video-man Pat Lynch, Bernard Corcoran and their most efficient secretary, Bernadette Allen, who made sure there were no hitches. The team was:

Jerome O'Mahony

Aidan Keane	Neil Creedon	Michael Lynch
Jimmy Kerrigan	Tony Griffin	Dave Creedon

Denis O'Sullivan   Tim Dalton

Stephen O'Brien	Eoin O'Mahony	Tony Nation (capt.)
Stephen Calnan	Denis Allen	Mick Dorgan

Substitutes: Paul O'Donovan for T. Dalton, Seán Hayes for S. Calnan.

SIXTH TITLE (1995)

On Sunday 31 October 1993 Nemo Rangers won their tenth Cork Senior Football title, defeating St Finbarr's by 0-13 to 0-4 in a dreadful game of football. It was a different story on 28 November at Ballinlough, when the Cork champions drew with Laune Rangers (Kerry) 0-6 apiece in 'a warming and wonderful game' (Tom Humphries, *The Irish Times*) before 500 hardy souls who had braved the elements. Colin Corkery who scored 0-5 was Nemo's saviour, but on the following Sunday at Killorglin, Nemo Rangers triumphed by 0-13 to 0-7 in a game which wasn't a patch on the previous Sunday's classic. There was no rest for the winners, who on the following Sunday at Killarney easily defeated Kilmurry–Ibricane (Clare) by 1-17 to 0-4.

On Saturday 5 March, after a lengthy rest, team-manager Dinny Allen was worried during most of the game with Errigal–Ciarán (Tyrone) in the All–Ireland Semi-final at Newbridge. Tyrone ace Peter Canavan was a big thorn in Nemo's side but the latter cut loose in extra time scoring 1-5 in succession, helped by a takeover at mid-field by Stephen O'Brien and Shay Fahy and the scoring power of Colin Corkery who 'assumed a less peripheral role when moved to full-forward' (Tom Humphries, *The Irish Times*). Nemo won in the end by 1-13 to 0-11.

In the final on 17 March 1994 Nemo Rangers had an easy win over Castlebar Mitchel's (Mayo) by 3-11 to 0-8. 'Nemo's approach work was intricate and clever but when it came to shooting they were awful. Still there was never any doubt about their superiority once Stephen Calnan had the ball in the Castlebar net after ten seconds of play.' — Sean Kilfeather (*The Irish Times*). The team was:

Don Bevan

Jimmy Kerrigan   Neil Creedon   Paudie Dorgan

Kevin Cowhie   Tony Griffin   Tony Nation

Shay Fahy   Stephen O'Brien (capt.)

Joe Kavanagh   Timmy Dalton   Stephen Calnan

Peter Lambert   Ephie Fitzgerald   Colin Corkery

Substitutes: Larry Kavanagh, Niall Corkery and Aodh Quinlivan.

Let me take this opportunity to salute the very unique duo of Jimmy Kerrigan and Timmy Dalton, who played in five winning finals — a record of achievement which may never be equalled.

BRIAN MURPHY LOOKS BACK

Brian Murphy won four All-Irelands and seven County Senior Football Championship medals with Nemo, captaining the side to glory in 1979. Brian, a detective based in Kilkenny, travelled from the Marble City regularly to help the green and black. He recalls those days with pride. 'There was an amalgamation of two clubs Nemo and Rangers in the '50s. Nemo literally stands for 'no one'. The coming of Nemo Rangers as a football force began in the late 1960s and we won our first senior in 1972, mainly made up of a winning minor team of 1970 plus some experienced campaigners like Billy Morgan, Frank Cogan and Jimmy Barrett. Nemo had a phenomenal club spirit and it's hard to credit it to any one individual but if I have to name a few I would include Paddy Sullivan, who was very much involved at under-age level; great players like Billy Morgan (his dedication to club and county has been exceptional over the years); Denis McDonald; Frank Cogan, (another great player who contributed much to coaching afterwards), and Dinny Allen, another great footballer, a wonderful reader of the game and a man who scored some wonderful goals for Nemo and Cork.

My greatest memories of Nemo would centre around the comradeship of the entire squad. A lot of the lads I won a minor title with, like Denis Allen, Colm Murphy (no relation) and Denis O'Driscoll, went on to play many games together at senior level later. This generated a wonderful spirit and even though I was away in Kilkenny I was always drawn back to them. It was a well-organised club and I loved going back. As to the game I remember best, it was the All-Ireland Final in which I captained Nemo to success in 1979. It was a dreadfully snowy day and so difficult to see the players and the play at the other end of Croke Park. I was very proud of that honour. I'd link it to some great occasions in both hurling and football with Coláiste Críost Rí, my school.' (Let me interject here to acquaint readers with Brian Murphy's absolutely unique achievement of winning All-Ireland medals in Hurling and Football in all three grades; Minor, U-21, and Senior, not to mention his college and club successes; Railway Cup medals in Hurling and

Football and All-Star awards. Here you have the most honoured achiever in the GAA. Does he still follow the green and black of Nemo? According to him:

'I was sorry to see them beaten last year by UCC in the 1996 Senior Football Championship, but as always they went down with flying colours in a tremendous game. Every time I go to Cork, I always call to the Nemo Rangers' club. If you ask me why the club has been so successful, I'd have to point to the fact that we have always been well served by good managers but above all, there has always been a marvellous under-age structure in Nemo. I came through that scene myself and they are still doing it.'

Billy Morgan receives the All-Ireland Senior Football Club Shield from Noel Drumgoole after leading his club to their first title win in 1973.

Brian Murphy after receiving the cup from Con Murphy (Uachtarán) in 1979.

Nemo Rangers, Senior All-Ireland Club Champions 1979

Back row: Charlie Murphy, Kieran Brady, S. Martin, Billy Morgan, Denis
                Lenihan, Fred Stone, Seán Hayes, M. Kenneally, Jimmy Barrett.
Middle row: Frank Cogan, Kieran Collins, Tim Dalton, Colm Murphy, Denis
                Allen, Brian Murphy, Jimmy Kerrigan, Denis O'Driscoll, Noel
                Morgan.
Front row: Kieran Murphy, J. Weldon, Tom Hennebry, and L. O'Keeffe.

33
O'Donovan Rossa

SKIBBEREEN (1993)

The O'Donovan Rossa GAA club was founded in 1887 but struggled in its early years. The breakthrough for the club occurred in 1985, when they won the Cork Intermediate title, defeating Glanmire in the final and thereby bridging a 61-year gap, after being narrowly beaten in the two previous Cork Intermediate finals. The club won its first ever Cork Senior Football title on Sunday, 13 September 1992, defeating Nemo Rangers by 2-9 to 0-10 and showing far greater determination than their experienced rivals in an undistinguished game before 10,000 spectators at Páirc Uí Chaoimh. The West Cork standard bearers deprived Nemo of their tenth Cork title in 20 years with a display full of spirit and commitment and an outstanding individual performance from the cool Tony Davis at centrehalf-back.

With the assistance of the wind, O'Donovan Rossa raced into a 1-5 to 0-1 lead after 12 minutes and despite a missed penalty they led by 1-5 to 0-3 at half time. There was only one point in it with 12 minutes to go but the west Cork lads dug deep and two superb points from Joe O'Driscoll saved the day. When mid-fielder Brian O'Donovan punched a splendid goal it was Skibbereen's day and their overjoyed fans went mad in a year that was to have a fairyale ending. Earlier in the Cork Senior Football Championship O'Donovan Rossa knocked out Duhallow, the champions for the previous two years.

MUNSTER

To win out in Munster, Skibbereen first defeated Newcastlewest by 2-15 to 1-5. John Brady, the Cavan forward, started them off with a fourth-minute goal and they never looked back. Then followed a hard-earned home win over the 1992 All-Ireland Club Champions Dr Crokes of Killarney by 1-8 to 1-5 on 22 November. Once again John Brady was the star. O'Donovan Rossa's goal came in the 18th minute from their captain Michael McCarthy at full-forward. It was a bruising game which exploded in the final four minutes with three players being sent to the line. In the Munster Final proper in Killarney on 6 December, Skibbereen defeated Saint Senan's, Kilkee by 2–13 to 0-12, a victory achieved with a powerful all round display in which Anthony Davis was hugely influential at centrehalf-back and mid-fielders Brian O'Donovan and Denis O'Driscoll shone.

SEMI-FINAL AGAINST LAVEY

In the All-Ireland Semi-final at Ballinascreen (Derry) Rossa defeated Lavey, the 1991 All-Ireland club champions, by the unusually high score of 2-10 to 0-4 on 21 February, 1993 but therein hangs a sorry tale. Tom Humphries (*The Irish Times*) tells the story. 'At the end of it all Lavey formed an orange and black guard of honour and applauded their opponents off the field. It was a warm sporting gesture that belied the ugliness of the hour which preceded it. This was a game that seethed and boiled and promised constantly to spill over into all-out war. As it was we were grateful to reach the full-time whistle without too much harm being inflicted on anybody.'

Tom accorded praise to referee, Séamus Prior of Leitrim, 'for putting a cap on a match that had the potential to become uncontrollable'. After 12 minutes, having booked three (two from Lavey, one from O'Donovan Rossa) and sending two Lavey men to the line, he called the captains together and threatened them with abandonment of the fixture. Matters improved before half time and became relatively normal in the second half.

'Having travelled the length of the country to play, it might have been expected that O'Donovan Rossa would have been sluggish at the start. Not so. They rattled over three points in three minutes'. Though Lavey fought hard to contain the visitors in the first half, weight of numbers told in the end and after Don Davis placed Mick McCarthy (who scored 1-9 in all) for the easiest of goals, McCarthy himself placed John Brady for a second goal and the game was wrapped up. The whole scene called into question the home and away venue system of the club championships. It has caused problems on home grounds, where huge home followings can be intimidating and incite partisanship. This was one that boiled over far too much. The Cork side deserved credit for their forbearance in the first half. They started smartly, kept their main objective in sight at all times and triumphed well in the end.

The final pitted O'Donovan Rossa against Éire Óg of Carlow who, since their foundation in 1956, had ruled the roost in Carlow, winning the Carlow Senior Football title no fewer than 17 times. It was a real rags to riches story for the Cork lads who never looked back after dethroning Duhallow, the Cork champions of the previous two years, in Macroom in the 1992 Cork Senior Football Championship Quarter final. Éire Óg's lovely brand of flowing football and six great forwards, had captured the imagination of the whole of Carlow. I saw Éire Óg, managed by former Leinster star Bobby Miller of Laois, win both their Leinster title in Newbridge against Ballyroan of Laois and their semi-final win over Knockmore of Mayo and was captivated by their style of play.

GAME OF THE YEAR

The game was drawn, Éire Óg 3-6 to O'Donovan Rossa 1-12 and was described variously as the game of the year, a classic, an epic — certainly the high point of the club All-Irelands to date. Marty Morrissey wrote: 'The game had everything.' Garvan Ware (Éire Óg) said: 'It was the best match I ever played in.' Mick McCarthy, the Skibbereen captain said: 'The day was unique and emotional.' Noel Horgan (*Southern Star*) described captain Mick McCarthy as the hero 'for almost single-handedly rescuing Rossa's from defeat during a dramatic conclusion, in a stirring struggle, when sealing an outstanding individual display with three late points to take the game to a replay'. In all, Mick McCarthy scored 1-8, equalling Eoin O'Mahony's achievement in a previous Nemo Rangers success. John Evans at 37 years of age and a previous Cork star was striving for his first All-Ireland medal. Michael Ellard (*Evening Echo*), wrote of, 'a pulsating game that will be firmly etched in the memory for a long, long time to come'. O'Donovan Rossa were lucky to get a replay and certainly bemoaned the unavailability of John Brady.

Over 30 buses left Skibbereen on 17 March, feeding five trains from Cork's Kent Station and providing at least 5,000 of the 21,714 attendance. In fact the West Corkonians had their own St Patrick's Day Parade to Croke Park behind the Skibbereen Pipe Band. Mick McCarthy tied up the game with a point a minute from the end. The equalising point was controversial in that in its lead-up referee Jim Curran of Tyrone 'overlooked an obvious free on Éire Óg corner-back Noel Fallon'—Michael Ellard (*Cork Examiner*). The game produced four splendid goals, a number of heart-stopping near misses and McCarthy's fabulous 1-8. Quite extraordinarily both teams played best against the stiff breeze blowing into the Railway end. Just before half time Mick McCarthy scored a vintage goal to keep Skibbereen in the race and a further point from a free to leave it all square and the advantage of the breeze to follow. Then Éire Óg took over and a brilliant Anthony Keating goal seemed to set them for the title but then came McCarthy's three points and both teams had to fight another day. Club Chairman Noel Kearney said afterwards: 'We came within an ace of losing it but we never threw in the towel.' In the vastly relieved Skibbereen dressing-room player-manager Gene O'Driscoll, who had to leave the field with a muscle injury, said it all: 'We got out of jail out there.'

THE REPLAY

The replay in Limerick's Gaelic Grounds on 28 March saw O'Donovan Rossa's win by 1-7 to 0-8, a game which finished controversially. Michael Ellard (*Cork Examiner*) began: 'The emotional opposites of pure unbridled joy and deep anguish were very much in evidence at the boiling sporting cauldron of Limerick's Gaelic Grounds when the titanic duel for the AIB All-Ireland Club Football Championship was finally and dramatically decided.' A disallowed goal for Éire Óg after three minutes of extra time saw the end of the Carlow side's noble efforts. Referee Jim Curran ruled that a number of Éire Óg players were inside the square when Joe Hayden's 35-yard free ended in the Skibbereen net.

The Skibbereen defence was much improved on the drawn game with veteran John Evans a power house at full-back. Half-backs, Ian Breen, the man-of-the-match, Tony Davis and Gene O'Driscoll were quite outstanding. It was 0-2 each at half time. It was still 0-5 each with 15 minutes to go when Pat Davis scored the most important goal of his career.

Éire Óg fought back to cut the deficit to one point before a Michael McCarthy point after a jinking run put the winners two points up with three minutes to go. Then followed seven minutes of pure tension as Éire Óg tried everything to win and the West Cork men held on for glory before the greatest ever attendance at a club game (estimated at 25,000 but nearer 30,000 as quite a number were allowed in free to avoid crushing at the turnstiles).

In the column *Gleanings of the Gael (Southern Star)* the writer told it all: 'It's hard to be dispassionate about this marvellous achievement, neutral and all as we are supposed to be. This was a victory for every no-hoper, for every team written off before the championship begins. It will stand as a beacon to all who hardly dare to dream of success. It can be done.' One of Skibbereen's greatest supporters was Bishop John Buckley and they were led out in the replay by mascot Revlin Minihane in the club's red colours (because of a clash Skibbereen played in Munster's blue). The club donated the ball used in the replay to its father figure, Noel O'Driscoll, father of players Joe and Denis, and the man who handled the logistics of the great transport exodus of O'Donovan Rossa fans for the major occasions. Skibbereen never witnessed a night like 28 March 1993. It was 1.30 a. m. before the team finally arrived in the town after many wonderful receptions along the route starting in Inishannon.

MICK MCCARTHY REMEMBERS

I visited Skibbereen on 25 August 1996 and attended a Kelliher Shield game between the local team and Glanmire. Once again Mick McCarthy put on a goal-scoring exhibition in an easy win for the home team. Noel O'Driscoll and son John, the club PRO, were there to greet me. After the game the 1993 captain reminisced on the glory year of 1992–1993. Mick is proud of the club's GAA ground with the most modern floodlit facilities, and its well appointed dressing-rooms. 'We went senior in 1985 and from there spent seven hard years chasing the Cork Senior Football title often falling at the first hurdle. We were rank outsiders in 1992 starting off after early winter training and the usual format. This time we had a lot of young players coming through and I felt if we got on a roll, we could be dangerous. We took every game as it came, heartened by the leaven of experience of some players from the Intermediate success of 1985 like Tony Davis, Denis

O'Driscoll, John Evans, Ian Breen and myself. We had all looked up to John Evans as we grew up and he was still with us. We had seen and admired him playing on great players like Mikey Sheehy and John Egan, more than holding his own on Cork teams which tended to lose to Kerry then. Years were running out for him then but he kept battling on.

'Winning the Cork title was something I'll never forget. There were incredible scenes at Páirc Uí Chaoimh. The whole town got behind us. It was like a fairy tale. We always had a great football tradition in Skibbereen though never winning a senior title. Holding the Cup brought tears to my eyes and I'm not the most emotional of people. The homecoming was like a royal one. We had never seen scenes like that even when I was part of a team which brought the Sam Maguire to Skibbereen. The odds on us at the start of the Championship were 33/1 and a few of our real hard core supporters put together £500 and had the faith in us to lay it on.

'We kept going on, beating Dr Crokes, then the long journey to Lavey. We'll never forget that trip and getting a win there was phenomenal. What spurred on our team was that we couldn't let our huge support down after travelling the length of the country behind us. Whole families came on a one day trip. It was a very tough first half but there were no hard feelings afterwards. The drawn final was an action filled game. Éire Óg came at us and got goals at great times. We came back and got in front. They came back and there wasn't a foul deed in the whole game. We were lucky to draw that one. In the replay we had to defend stoutly at the end when they were unlucky again, having a goal disallowed in lost time. At this stage we were the toast of the whole county after winning and the crowds in Limerick were huge. When we returned with the Andy Merrigan Cup, we were received in Inishannon, Bandon, Clonakilty, Rosscarbery and Leap. It was late when we got to Skibbereen. Winning that All-Ireland meant an awful lot to the town. It lifted the whole scene for all the younger teams and we will win another county title someday. The young lads who followed us in 1992–1993 will want to emulate us.

'No club wins an All-Ireland accidentally. A lot of our team came out of St Fachtna's De La Salle College in Skibbereen and the lads of my age group lost an All-Ireland colleges title to St Jarlath's College, Tuam in a replay in 1983. We also lost a minor All-Ireland Final to Derry the same year with some of our club lads involved. Some of the young lads of our All-Ireland winning team had been on the winning St Fachtna's Hogan Cup team of

1991. So St Fachtna's contribution to our success was immense. In my time there Joe O'Neill was the man, but there was a deep interest in gaelic football ingrained in all of us. We were very fortunate to have Gene O'Driscoll as our player-manager. He joined us from Caheragh a few years before. He was a fine motivator — our trainer and full-back. I still get the same old kick out of playing for Skibbereen. I got three goals tonight and I'll keep at it as long as they keep me. We had a great backup from our officials always. We've had some great players in the past like Noel O'Driscoll, Dr John O'Keeffe and Dermot O'Donovan. If I have to give you the greatest thrill from any of the games of that year it has to be the goal I got in the first half in Croke Park in the drawn final. I had played in Croke Park before and never thought I did myself justice. This time the goal was special. We were out of the game at the time and it was slipping away. So it came at the right time. That would have to be my favourite score of all time.' The winning team was:

Kevin O'Dwyer

John Evans   John O'Donovan   Frank McCarthy

Gene O'Driscoll   Anthony Davis   Ian Breen

Denis O'Driscoll   Brian O'Donovan

Brian Carmody   Joe O'Driscoll   Don Davis

Pat Davis   Mick McCarthy (capt.)   Neville Murphy

Substitute: Mick McCarthy for G. O'Driscoll

Anthony Davis, O'Donovan Rossa's star half-back for club and county.

O'Donovan Rossa, All-Ireland Club Champions 1993

Back row: Diarmuid O'Donovan, Gary Minihane, Brian Carmody, Denis O'Driscoll, John O'Donovan, Ian Breen, Kevin O'Dwyer, Gene O'Driscoll, Brian O'Donovan, Anthony Davis, John Evans, Mick McCarthy.

Front row: Darragh Whooley, Don Davis, Pat Davis, Joe O'Driscoll, John Brady, Neville Murphy, Frank McCarthy, Mick McCarthy (capt.), Gearoid Davis, Barry Casey, Martin Bohane.

34
Burren In Mourne

O'er the Corrag Road,
With their precious load,
Came the team,
With the Cup held high
And Bullock Hill
Echoed loud and shrill
As we cheered
Till our throats ran dry,
And McKinley stirred,
'Neath the cromlech old,
In the light of the moon's bright sheen
For the All-Ireland crown was brought home to the Pound
By the men of the Burren 15.

(M. Harty)

Danny Murphy, former Down Chairman and current Ulster Vice-President is a Burren man. It was he who met me at the Carrickdale Hotel just inside County Down on a balmy September day and conducted me on a tour of the football kingdom of Burren starting with the Flagstaff Viewpoint overlooking Carlingford Lough and the Burren parish. Danny takes it up: 'The present Burren St Mary's Club was formed in October 1949 though Gaelic football was played in the area for decades beforehand. We never looked back and since then have won ten Down Senior Football titles (the 10th last Sunday) when we were very proud to bring off a unique minor and senior double for the club, never achieved in Down on the same day before.

Besides John "Shorty" Treanor won a record ninth Down Senior Football Championship medal. No club has won more than ten titles, so "Shorty's" achievement is phenomenal. He was only a youngster in 1981 when we bridged a gap of 15 years after our first ever in 1966. That first one was a great time for the club but it had its own downside in that the club had a long frustrating argument and debate with the County Board over the outcome of it all but we finally had the championship guaranteed to us by a decision of Árd Comhairle in Croke Park. That was the beginning of the tremendous dominance of Down football by the Burren club in the past 25 years.

'As to the reason for our success there are many factors. We were one of the first clubs in Down to organise a solid juvenile section and we have always worked at producing good under-age players. There is a tremendous loyalty and passion for the area among the people of Burren. Probably the most important factor behind the present club strength was the late Seán Murdock because Seán, way back in the 1950s and 1960s, ran a small family building business and was instrumental in keeping a lot of young Burren lads at home and in trades. We kept the young people in Burren. They married, built homes and raised families here. The population of Burren has increased significantly from about 700 in the 1970s to about 3,000 today. Seán's contribution was that he gave a sense of purpose to Burren. Everything was done with a view to improving the community as well as the club and it became practically institutional over the years. Seán sadly died just as 1985 ended and he wasn't alive for our first All-Ireland triumph of 1986.

'I suppose our first ever senior title in 1966 was a huge achievement. We had men then like the McGoverns, Johnny and Frankie, Séamus Doyle, Aidan Woods, Jack and Mickey McMahon, Colm and Brendan Curtis in 1966 who broke the mould and set the scene. We had lost the 1953 final to Warrenpoint by 1-0 to 0-1 (scoring an own goal). My most abiding memory of all the Burren years had to be our defeat of Nemo Rangers in Cork in 1988. Never did I witness such a migration of Burren people and to the other end of Ireland at that. The spirit of our team that day and our win are things no Burren person will ever forget.'

Danny took me to that great Gaelic football nursery St Colman's College, Newry to meet the team-manager of the two All-Ireland Burren teams of 1986 and 1988 — namely Ray Morgan where the portals of the impressive corridors are graced with football photos old and new. Then we went on a tour of the 12 townlands which comprise and surround the village of Burren, high in the hills between Warrenpoint and Mayobridge, a distinctly rural area of narrow roads and many houses. Then in darkness we saw St Mary's GAA ground and complex, the first ever floodlit ground in Ireland (opened in 1968), with its floodlights first switched on in 1975 and since updated to a most modernised floodlit park in January 1995. No club I've seen has better facilities in this area.

THE 1986 TITLE

Burren won the Down Senior Football title for the third successive year, defeating Loughlinisland by 0-10 to 0-5. They followed this up with wins over Glenullin (Derry) and Augher (Tyrone) before defeating Scotstown of Monaghan for their third successive Ulster crown at the Armagh Athletic Grounds by 0-6 to 1-2. For ten tense minutes after Brendan Beggan had scored the equalising goal for Scotstown, late in the second half, it looked as if Burren would have to settle for a draw. Six times they roared upfield only to see their efforts go wide of the posts. The winner came in extra time from Larry Fitzpatrick, his first point in the championship and went in off an upright. Burren led 0-4 to 0-1 at half-time.

On 23 February 1986 Burren travelled to Portlaoise and outclassed the 1982 title-holders by 2-13 to 0-6. At all times Burren looked the fitter side and led by 0-7 to 0-2 at half-time. The home side were decisively beaten in the final quarter. With the score 0-10 to 0-5 Tony McArdle, the man of the match, shot a Burren goal completely flatfooting the Portlaoise defence and when he repeated the dose in the 57th minute it was all over. Burren had qualified for their first All-Ireland Final on 16 March in Croke Park against the All-Ireland champions, Castleisland Desmonds of Kerry. Burren came and conquered, beating the Kerrymen by 1-10 to 1-6. Martin Breheny (*Irish Press*) takes it up: 'When Kerry teams lose All-Ireland finals the rest of the country rejoices. That does not reflect an anti-Kerry bias — it's just nice to see other parts of the country grab some of the football glory. Predictably most neutrals in the 10,176 attendance were happy to cheer Burren to what captain Tommy McGovern described as 'our finest hour'. Despite the narrow margin Burren were clearly the better side. Leading by eight points with six minutes to go, the winners were pegged back when Willie O'Connor scored 1-2 but semi-final hero Tony McArdle pointed in the last minute to put Burren out of reach.

'Burren achieved their ambition with a mixture of determination and energy which was admirable, though the quality of the fare was just adequate. Playing with wind advantage, Burren led 0-4 to 0-1 at half-time having shot eight wides. They then increased their strike-rate thanks mainly to the intelligent forward play of John Treanor, Tony McArdle and man-of-the-match Vincent McGovern. It was Treanor who scored Burren's goal with a cracking left-footed shot in the 42nd minute. Years of hard work had brought its final rewards and all the players were heroes in their supporters eyes.' The *Armagh–Down Observer* under a banner headline 'High Kings of Ireland' paid tribute to Burren's 'flawless exhibition of the basic skills of Gaelic football. Burren's way with football makes it seem a simple game to play, an enjoyable one to watch.' The writer selected Brendy McGovern as star of stars. This was the team:

Declan Murdock

Brendan McKiernan   Aidan Murdock   Malachy Murdock

Kieran McConville   Willie McMahon   Brendan McGovern

Tommy McGovern (capt.)   Paddy O'Rourke

Larry Fitzpatrick   John Treanor   Pat McKay

Jim McGreevey   Vincey McGovern   Tony McArdle

Substitute: Charlie Doyle for Jim McGreevey.

THE 1988 TITLE

In defeating old rivals Bryansford by 0-12 to 1-6 in the 1987 County Final, Burren were creating a record of five consecutive Down Senior Football titles. Then followed a win in a replay against Aodh Ruadh of Donegal at Ballyshannon. John Treanor saved them the first day in Ballyshannon with a point from a free in injury time but in the replay at the same venue the following Sunday, Burren won by 2-7 to 1-7 thanks to two Tony McArdle goals in the 33rd and 38th minutes. In the Ulster Final on 15 November at Ballybay, Burren won a record fourth Ulster crown, defeating Kingscourt (Cavan) by 0-8 to 0-6 in a close encounter played in difficult conditions. The losers led by 0-5 to 0-4 at the break but Burren hit a purple patch early in the second half started by a quick John Treanor point.

Then followed one of Burren's greatest triumphs — over Nemo Rangers in Midleton on 21 February 1988 by 1-5 to 0-6. The *Irish Independent* report read: 'Burren had too much all round power for Nemo in a very competitive semi-final. The turning point of the game came two minutes after the break when Denis Allen was robbed 30 yards from the Burren goal. A long delivery from Vincent McGovern found Ronan Fitzpatrick for a fine goal. Just three minutes later Allen was sent to the line and from then on a game which was delicately balanced started to go Burren's way. In truth the winners should have won by more, for a succession of missed chances might have cost them dearly as Nemo Rangers came like lions in the end.'

THE FINAL

In the final on St Patrick's Day, Burren defeated Clann na nGael (Roscommon) by 1-9 to 0-8. Paddy McEvoy in the *Mourne Observer* picked Burren 'as a team apart amongst all the clubs in Ireland. After captain Vincent McGovern had hoisted the Andy Merrigan Cup aloft, he led the Burren players and supporters in a spontaneous rendering of *The Mountains of Mourne*. Once again Burren proved as immovable as the very mountains of their homeland.

'Despite Tony McArdle's sixth-minute goal, the tough and resilient western opponents worked their way back into the game until they drew level midway through the second half. At this stage Ray Morgan introduced Paul Fegan and swopped Pat McKay with Brian Lavery at mid-field. The transformation was evident. Fresh and stormy, Fegan's arrival renewed the adrenalin in weary Burren legs. A few deft touches from Tommy McGovern, *Shorty* on song, Tom Fegan and Ronan Fitzpatrick rising to the occasion like veterans, four points during the last few minutes and the All-Ireland Cup was on its way to a McGovern sideboard.' In tribute to Burren's second success in three years from 3,200 clubs wrote McEvoy: 'Burren's success is the success of a community where men and women have worked steadfastly from limited resources to achieve it.' And, of the team itself: 'It is a combination of skill and commitment which we are unlikely to see again in our lifetime.' The team was:

Declan Murdock

Brendan McKiernan   Aidan Murdock   Malachy Murdock

Kieran McConville   Larry Fitzpatrick   Brendan McGovern

Tommy McGovern   Brian Lavery

Tony McArdle   John Treanor   Pat McKay

Ronan Fitzpatrick   Vincent McGovern (capt.)   Tom Fegan

Substitute: Paul Fegan for B. Lavery.

RAY MORGAN REMEMBERS

Meeting Ray Morgan, former Down player, head of the PE department in St Colman's College, Newry, and coach to so many St Colman's triumphs, was a privilege in itself. He talked of his Burren involvement, how injury cut short his playing career though never dampening his enthusiasm. 'I got my love of Gaelic football while I was a student here in College through my great friend Father John Treanor. He made a fantastic impression on all the footballers who went through this school.

'I came back to teach here in 1970 and my football coaching began then under Father Treanor. In all I have coached St Colman's to four Hogan Cup triumphs having taken over the senior squad in 1971, with Dan McCartan (the GAC man) taking over the juniors. We won our first of the four in 1975 with many of those juniors involved. As I said, my Burren involvement began funnily enough with Father John Treanor, a native of Burren and another bloodbuddy of his, Seán Murdock. In my college days our team often played Burren on our own pitch and we knew them well. They helped to toughen up our football and we were never in awe of other college teams. Father Treanor prevailed on me to take over in Burren in 1977, to help them overcome the psychological barrier of winning a county title. I was very impressed with them staightaway, earthy people like my own people in Annaclone, no airs or graces to them, just wanting me to lead them up the mountain. They gave me effort from the word go and we reached the County Final, losing to Bryansford. Things didn't go well after that and I departed in 1980. Johnny McGovern and Jackie McManus took over and guided Burren to three county titles. In 1985, I took a team which had won three county and two provincial crowns since I left. They still had to climb Everest, having lost to Walterstown (Meath) in 1984 and to St Vincent's (Dublin) in February 1985.

'Seán Murdock it was who prevailed on me to return, "to do the job for me" as he put it, to win the All-Ireland. They wanted to win an All-Ireland Club title. They would have followed me anywhere in quest of that. It was close against Scotstown in the Ulster Final. That night Seán Murdock told me the big battles lay ahead and we would do it. Unfortunately he didn't live to see these games. The man who guided us all had gone. At our first training session after Christmas Tommy McGovern led the panel in prayers for Seán and then vowed that this All-Ireland would be won for him. We travelled to Portlaoise the night before the semi-final staying in the Montague Hotel. Nothing was spared. Portlaoise never knew what hit them. We just blitzed them. In the final we had to counter the precision Mick O'Dwyer type football of Castleisland Desmonds. So we defended one against one, forced them to kick the ball rather than allowing them to dictate a short passing game and it worked. Disbelief was the first feeling. To come with a small parish team from South Down and win an All-Ireland in Croke Park was incredible. Also we had great satisfaction and pride in ourselves for doing it with flair and playing our own style of football. We had done it for Seán Murdock.

'We lost to Castleblaney Faughs in 1987 but we set off again to climb Everest again in 1988. Experience was helping us now. We came out of Ulster and had to play Nemo Rangers in the semi-final in Cork. At the time we were going badly and we had little hope. An altercation with the County Board over the training arrangements for our county team members helped steel our resolve and focus our minds on Nemo. We withdrew our players from the county panel and all hell broke loose. Everybody in Down seemed against us and it was the catalyst that got us going. Nobody was going to down us. Everything lifted. That win over Nemo is the game everyone remembers now. At half-time with some of them still down, Tom Fegan in a moment of exhortation put his fist through a roof panel and that got everybody going. Second half, we took the game to them and played them off the field. If we hadn't taken on the County Board we'd never have beaten Nemo. Some of the supporters didn't get home till mid-week!

'In a hard-won final we played Clann na nGael. Lucky enough Tony McArdle's goal gave us a lifeline. In the second half the introduction of Paul

Fegan gave us great space and we finished off very strongly to win. As to my greatest memory of it all it has to be our first semi-final win over Portlaoise for sheer flair, aggression, ability. They were a coach's dream.'

Burren, All-Ireland Club Champions 1986
Back row(L to R): Paddy O'Rourke, Tony McArdle, Jim McGreevy, Pat
McKay, Declan Murdock, Aidan Murdock, Brendan McKiernan,
Malachy Murdock.
Front row: John 'Shorty' Treanor, Willie McMahon, Brendan McGovern,
Tommy McGovern, (capt.), Kieran McConville, Larry Fitzpatrick,
Vincent McGovern.

35
Loughgiel Shamrocks

ULSTER'S SOLE TITLE

One of the final chapters in this book is dedicated to the mighty men of Loughgiel Shamrocks, who won for the North its one and only Senior Hurling All-Ireland title in 1983, defeating St Rynagh's (Offaly) in a replay at Casement Park, Belfast, on 25 April by 2-12 to 1-12. I visited this small parish of 1,700 people on a beautiful September day. Nestling in the hills of North Antrim, this peacefully rural spot is steeped in hurling tradition. The present Antrim team-manager Dominic McKinley met me first in his home village of Dunloy, another hurling stronghold, some eight miles away and brought me to meet the men behind the scenes and see for myself the excellent club grounds which was the Father Healy Memorial Park which was officially opened in 1955 and has the finest turf I've seen in any club pitch. The groundsman responsible for keeping the field in such condition is local enthusiast Bobby McIllhatton, who spends much of his time caring for it, and as the present Chairman of the club Harry Connolly says, 'is the pride of our club'. Just a short distance away is another club field with an equally good playing surface — opened in 1990 called the Father Barrett GAA Park; this one also is attended to dutifully by groundsman Bobby.

My main port of call was the Pound Bar, the focal point of this area, literally the home of the GAA in Loughgiel. Liam McGarry, its owner, is the father figure of the club, an absolute enthusiast for hurling. He talked of the great hurling men of Loughgiel down the years: 'I saw Loughgiel win the 1938 Antrim title with men like Sammy Mulholland, John Curry, Brendan and Dan Carey, Patsy McIllhatton, Edward McCarry, Mick O'Connell, many of them fathers of the men of 1983. The hurling tradition was handed down from *glún* to *glún*. Our best period was in the 1960s when we won the Antrim title four times. All final victories have been celebrated here over the years. We are very proud of our two pitches. Croke Park doesn't look any better than Father Healy Park. Father Healy was born down the road here and was our parish priest. The greatest player we ever had was Jim McKee. Later, people here would talk of Sammy Mulholland but even Sammy himself talked of Jim. The greatest night we ever had was the night we brought the Tom Moore Cup home in 1983.'

ROUTE TO SUCCESS

In pursuit of the dream, Loughgiel won their fourteenth of fifteen Antrim Senior Hurling Championship titles, defeating Ballycastle McQuillans by 5-9 to 3-8 in the final after surviving a strong challenge from Cushendall earlier by 3-7 to 1-11. Founded in the 1920s, the club set off on its journey outside Antrim with wins over Clontibret O'Neills (Monaghan) by 3-15 to 0-6 and another hard-earned win in the Ulster Final over Down champions Ballygalget by 1-9 to 0-9. They had achieved the Ulster title success twice before in 1971 and 1972. Now came the biggest question posed to date, but a home venue at Father Healy Park with the Tipperary champions Moycarkey-Borris on 13 February 1983 would be a bonus.

TWO SENSATIONAL GOALS

Two sensational goals inside 60 seconds at 11 minutes from time ripped the form book to shreds as Loughgiel brought off a sensational win over Moycarkey–Borris by 2-7 to 1-6. The Antrim team had been very much cast in the customary role of lambs to the slaughter but, despite a poor start when county star John Flanagan scored a great goal for Moycarkey after only 15 seconds, the home team survived immense pressure and were only three points in arrears at half-time.

And so it continued until super-sub Paddy Carey goaled first from a goalmouth scramble to be followed seconds later by a brilliant Aidan McCarry goal. Now Loughgiel became a devastating force, changed utterly from the previously ragged side which had been satisfied with a potential slender beating. Two fine points by Brendan Laverty and Martin Coyle put Loughgiel five in front. Moycarkey could only manage a consolation point from John Flanagan and Loughgiel Shamrocks were in the final. Goalkeeper and captain Niall Patterson was brilliant in goal once again and the half back line of Éamonn Connolly, Paddy McElhatton and Aidan McNaughton was outstanding. The whole country sat up and took notice. Michael Fortune (*Irish Press*) wrote that the result was probably surpassed only by Antrim's All-Ireland Semi-final defeat of Kilkenny in 1943.

WRANGLING

There was a great deal of wrangling before Loughgiel knew who their opponents would be in the All-Ireland Final. The semi-final between St Rynagh's, Banagher and Kiltormer (Galway) had been a tempestuous affair of sending offs and objections which caused the postponment of the final. St Rynagh's, the winners, held on to the game at Central Council level and the final was fixed for Croke Park on Sunday, 18 April. Again the Antrim champions surprised everybody except themselves by drawing the game 1-8 to 2-5 for Rynagh's. Paddy Downey (*The Irish Times*) described it: 'The long delayed final ended in a draw some six or seven seconds after Pádraig Horan sent a 52-yard slightly-angled free wide. Thus did fortune smile on Loughgiel but the Antrim side deserved whatever luck was going for they played with admirable pluck and a great deal of skill.' The men from the North, after holding St Rynagh's scoreless for 29 minutes, deserved to be more than 1-4 to 1-2 ahead at half-time.

Slackness in defence conceded a goal before the break and the same fault gave Rynagh's their second major score and the lead for the first time within two minutes of the restart. Loughgiel didn't panic and fought back to level the scores three minutes from time. Man-of-the-match was goalkeeper and captain Niall Patterson, one of the great characters of hurling. Aidan McNaughton starred at left-half-back. Aidan McCarry levelled the scores 1-7 to 2-4 in the 52nd minute. Rynagh's edged ahead and three minutes from time substitute Paddy Carey Jnr scored from an angled 21 yard-free to gain parity for the third time in the game.

THE REPLAY

Inexperience according to Peadar O'Brien (*Irish Press*) was the factor which cost Loughgiel dearly in the drawn game. Would they get over that in the replay at Casement Park, Belfast the following Sunday? Cardinal Cathal

Daly, a native of Loughgiel, visited the team's dressing-room before the game and this certainly helped to fire up the Loughgiel side who startled the whole country by winning the replay 2-12 to 1-12.

Two goals at identical periods in each half of the replay paved the way for success before 10,000 delirious supporters. The first goal came after 22 minutes with the scores pretty even, Rynagh's having taken the lead 0-5 to 0-4 after an Aidan Fogarty '70'. Brendan Laverty was the scorer, Paddy Carey the maker. This was Laverty in all his glory — bursting through in a fine solo dash, then a deft flick of the wrist for a super goal. The winners led 1-7 to 0-7 at half-time. It remained a touch-and-go situation for much of the second half but Loughgiel were never headed. Every score Rynagh's got was followed by a Loughgiel one. There is nothing as soul-destroying as this. Then came the goal which decided the game. Aidan McCarry, was the scorer and Dominic McKinley the creator. Now Loughgiel led by 2-10 to 0-11 and they held on to win for the North, a deserved first timer, with a display of first time hurling, reminiscent of a Munster team at its best. Then the place went mad. All the Loughgiel players were mobbed. Once again Niall Patterson was a star supreme with Paddy McElhatton brilliant at centre-half-back. Mick O'Connell at mid-field had his finest hour. In the forwards, Brendan Laverty and Aidan McCarry were the torchbearers in a team of heroes. The most telling tribute came from the *Irish News* report: 'For years we have heard that Antrim hurlers are second-class. That myth is now dead. For years Antrim had soldiered on to disprove it. Yesterday the myth exploded.' The team was:

Niall Patterson (capt.)

Martin Carey	P. J. Mullen	Seán Carey
Éamonn Connolly	Paddy McElhatton	Aidan McNaughton

Mick O'Connell   George McKinley

Aidan McCarry	Brendan Laverty	Dominic McKinley
Paddy Carey Snr.	Paddy Carey Jnr.	Séamus McNaughton

MEMORIES

Club Secretary, Niall Patterson, father of goalkeeper Niall, said afterwards, the whole area was dazed by the achievement. 'Loughgiel is a small parish of some 300 families almost all of whom are connected with the club. Hurling is the traditional and predominant game here. Many of our players work in Belfast but they all made sacrifices to train under trainer Danny McMullan a P.E. teacher in Ballymoney and a great servant to the club.'

Dominic McKinley, left-half-forward on the 1983 team relived that glorious time with me. 'We always kept the game as simple as possible. Our style is based on ground hurling — play the ball quick and fast. Hurling was always the game here, Gaelic football never got going despite a few attempts. It's hurling or go to chapel. I came from a big family of 13, six girls and seven boys and we all played it together. The girls still play camogie for the club. My father and mother took great pride in seeing us going out to play hurling. Winning the first Antrim medal in 1982 was special to me. As we went on in 1982–1983 we tended to get better and better. In fact before the championship we got a right going over from Niall Patterson, the Secretary, after a poor Feis Cup loss to Glenariff. We played exceptionally well in the Antrim Final, starting off brilliantly. I scored the first one that day and helped set the tone.

Niall Patterson was extra special because of his size. A great goalie and his weight never hindered him. People will tell you a good club team is based on families and at that time we had a lot of family connections in it — the Careys, McKinleys, McNaughtons, McCarrys and the Lavertys which gave us a solid foundation. Brendan Laverty was a genius, but after doing something special he often took a rest for a while. He could do anything with a ball. Aidan McCarry another exceptional forward. Séamus McNaughton had his best ever year that year.

The day we beat Moycarkey–Borris was a wet sticky day, typical of February. It wasn't a day for frills. It was probably the proudest ever day in the village. Mick O'Connell and my brother George set the basis at mid-field (I was dropped for that game but trained hard to get back in for the final). We trained very hard under Danny McMullan, often in the snow. We often did 30–36 laps. Paddy McElhatton was 35 at the time and he did all those laps too. We had got to the final and we meant business. St Rynagh's had a strong experienced team but they failed to put us away in the end. In the replay at Casement Park, Bishop Daly came to meet us and that helped us a lot. We got great support that day from the whole of Antrim and Ulster. It was an ecstatic scene afterwards. There wasn't as much hype then as now but the scenes then were unbelievable. We were all carried off the field and the Belfast people were especially happy for us. Antrim had made the breakthrough in hurling on a national stage. Our journey home to our home of hurling — the Pound Bar — was unreal.'

Brendan Carey, one of the old-timers who won an Antrim Senior Hurling Championship medal with Loughgiel in 1943 recalls Sammy Mulholland as 'the best forward he ever saw in Loughgiel. A wonderful left-corner-forward. He'd have got his place on any team. The biggest thrill I ever got was when we beat Rossa in 1953. "Stout" McDonnell, "Butler" Mullaney were the big ones. I'm very proud of our field and we put some work into that field. We were working at it from 1953 on.'

Danny McMullan

Danny McMullan is retired from teaching now. He first trained the Loughgiel team in 1963, winning the final against Dunloy Cuchulainns, a local derby. 'I trained them to win three-in-a-row 1966–1968, two-in-a-row 1970 and 1971 and then I took a break. One day big Paddy McGarry, Liam's father, called me over as he sat outside the Pound Bar and he asked me would I 'take the wee hurlers for another year' and how could I refuse. That's how it began. The success we got in 1982–1983 was both phenomenal and unexpected. We started off from very moderate beginnings. There were many young players with a splattering of experience but hardly enough. The whole thing gathered momentum as we moved on. In the first round at home to St John's we struggled here at home. We did better against Cushendall. The team gave a great exhibition of all that is good in the game in the County Final and hopes rose after that. We didn't find it easy to beat Ballygalget. Nothing went right and Mick O'Connell saved us that day. The win over Moycarkey–Borris was for me the best defensive display Loughgiel ever gave, with Paddy McElhatton a tower of strength in front of solid full-back P. J. Mullen.

'Michael O'Connell, though doubtful, was the star of the drawn final. We were lucky to survive but we deserved a draw. Rynagh's were very sporting and generous to come to Belfast for the replay but county Offaly in general has always been generous. We were confident of winning if we stayed with them in the replay. St Rynagh's lifted their game for the replay but we did likewise. We decided to play the wings and we tended to break their hearts. They were all heroes. The chances we spurned in Croke Park were utilised in Casement. We gave away two silly goals in Croke Park. My team-talk was perhaps the best I ever gave. That may sound boastful but it's as I saw it. After winning it I gave a huge sigh of relief and everybody else went mad. I tend to hide in the background and savour the joy alone. For me the enjoyment afterwards was to stand back and watch young and old enjoy themselves — Antrim and Loughgiel people. That was my joy. Brendan Laverty as a hurler was a genius and he delivered the goods when we needed it always. For instance in the Casement replay he caught the ball off an opponent's stick as he was picking the sliothar up and laid it in the back of the net and Damian Martin said, 'What a goal!'. He did the same against Ballycastle and in Croke Park. He had a gift. They called him God in Ballycastle because whenever he took the notion he could do it.'

Loughgiel, All-Ireland Club Champions 1983
Back row: *Aidan McNaughton, Brendan McGarry, Martin Coyle, Aidan McCarry, Éamonn Connolly, Séamus McNaughton, Dominic McKinley, Gerard McKinley, Brendan Laverty, Paddy McIntyre, Martin Gillen, Paddy O'Connell.*
Front row: *Paddy Carey Jnr., Martin Carey, P.J. Mullen, Mick O'Connell, Paddy McElhatton, Niall Patterson, Seán Carey, Paddy Carey Snr., Robin Clarke, Harry Carey, Seán Laverty, Dominic McMullen.*

$\underline{\qquad} 36 \underline{\qquad}$

Baltinglass In 1990

BALTINGLASS BEACON IN 1990

Baltinglass's All-Ireland Club Football success in 1990 didn't happen overnight. For some years beforehand the club had earned a fine reputation for itself with some stirring battles in Leinster. I attended one such game against Parnell's (Dublin) on their own home ground on October weekend 1988. That game ended in a draw and there was a mighty home attendance present to cheer on the local team. The club didn't win a Wicklow Senior Football title until 1958 but for many years now has become Wicklow's top football club, being thwarted in 1995 by An Tóchar for a nine-in-a-row of Senior Football Championship titles. When I visited the club on Saturday, 10 August to meet Club Chairman Séamus Kelly, a Cavan-born Gárda, who has been a buoyant force behind the rise of Baltinglass, I was conducted on a tour of the town and the fine club premises and fields of which the club is very proud. I got the feel of the spirit of the place and why in 1990 this club from Wicklow, with no tradition of winning All-Irelands behind it, shone a beacon far and wide for all aspiring clubs.

COUNTY FINAL

It began for Baltinglass on 1 October 1989 with a hard-earned 1-8 to 0-4 County Final win over Saint Patrick's. Though reduced to 14 men after captain Brian Fitzpatrick was sent off, it was Baltinglass who finished strongest and when Robert McHugh took a superb Kevin O'Brien pass and shot to the net, Baltinglass had won a three-in-a-row of titles to equal a previous achievement in 1967. Then followed wins over Longford Slashers and Ferbane (Offaly) and a Leinster Club Final date with Dublin champions Thomas Davis at Newbridge on 26 November. Tom O'Riordan (*Irish Independent*) did justice to the event 'This is what it is all about — two unfashionable clubs giving their all in search of sporting history. That one side and then the other looked set to win the Leinster Club Football title for the first time was in keeping with a game that had everything and provided first class entertainment for an attendance of 6,000. The game ended all square 1-6 each in a welter of excitement as Robert McHugh converted a real pressure kick from an awkward angle virtually on full time.' The replay at the same venue a fortnight later was eagerly awaited and equally exciting. This time Baltinglass triumphed by 1-9 to 0-11, coming from behind to win where they had failed in replays so often in the past. Being led by 0-10 to 1–4 with eleven minutes left Baltinglass came back point by point. First it was mid-fielder Billy Kenny, then Tommy Murphy, and the equaliser from Kevin O'Brien after a superb catch by Raymond Danne. This was followed by two Robert McHugh points before Thomas Davis halted the rot with a Paul Nugent point. But the Wicklow men held out for their first Leinster crown. Both Seán McGoldrick (*Irish Press*) and Paddy Hickey (*Irish Independent*) lauded Seán O'Brien at corner-back for a brilliant display in defence and the fighting qualities of the winners who started very well then faded before finishing in glory. Jack Boothman was a proud man presenting his last trophy as Leinster Chairman to the winning captain Brian Fitzpatrick. Local balladeer and supporter Andy Sinnott composed a song entitled *Murphy's Machine* the chorus of which ran:

> *Now the game it was over we had waited so long*
> *There were tears to be seen in the eyes of the strong.*
> *All we had hoped for had now come to pass*
> *And the great Leinster trophy it was ours at last*
> *There was singing and dancing that night in the town*
> *And the pubs they were packed and never closed down*
> *There were bodhráns and banjos to add to the ball*
> *And the Rathvilly Band could be heard overall.*

CASTLEHAVEN

Next on the agenda was the visit of Cork champions Castlehaven to Aughrim on Sunday, 18 February and to the surprise of all the pundits Baltinglass delighted a huge home support by winning 1-5 to 0-6. The winners started brilliantly and a scoring blitz of 1-4 in the first 11 minutes, when aided by the wind, set them up for success. It was a masterly defensive performance in the second half which saved the day as Castlehaven, despite being reduced to 14 men, plied on an unrelenting barrage. Once again Seán O'Brien was the rallying force ably helped by Hugh Kenny at full-back and centre-half-back Pat Murphy while Dan Leigh was excellent in goal. Baltinglass, who led by 1-5 to 0-2 at half-time, had their goal scored in the eighth minute by doubtful starter Paul Kenny, twin brother of Hugh. Meeting them in the final on St Patrick's Day were the Roscommon champions Clann na nGael, experienced campaigners who had lost the previous three finals. Once again the Wicklow lads were underdogs, a position that player–manager (and local veterinary surgeon) Tommy Murphy rather liked as he quietly prepared his charges for the fray.

THE FINAL

Baltinglass won their first final convincingly by 2-7 to 0-7 while once again Clann na nGael couldn't do it on the day. In the marchround beforehand, Tommy Murphy shook the hand of fellow-vet and former UCD mate Tony McManus. Playing against the breeze in the first half, Baltinglass withdrew Tommy Murphy from the full-forward line as a third mid-fielder with the two wing-forwards Paul Kenny and Liam Horgan playing very deep, Raymond Danne was getting good mid-field possession and playing a quick through ball to his forwards while the speed of Robert McHugh and Kevin O'Brien proved a menace. This was in sharp contrast to Clann, who overplayed the ball completely at times. The McHugh–O'Brien combination set up Con Murphy for his first goal in the 19th minute and from a Kevin O'Brien centre he went on to score goal number two before the break to leave Baltinglass leading by 2-2 to 0-5 and the wind still to aid them second half. Clann did rally in the second half and got as close as two points but four successive Baltinglass scores between the 37th and 45th minute sealed Clann's fate. Seán McGoldrick (*Sunday Press*) gave special praise to 'Seán O'Brien who kept a right rein on Tony McManus, Hugh Kenny and Pat Murphy both outstanding in defence, mid-fielders Raymond Danne and Billy Kenny while Con Murphy with a personal tally of 2-3 emerged with the scoring honours and was ably supported by Kevin O'Brien Robert McHugh and his brother Tommy'. The winning team was:

Dan Leigh

Seán O'Brien   Hugh Kenny   Tom Donohue

Brian Fitzpatrick (capt.) Pat Murphy   Bryan Kilcoyne

Raymond Danne   Billy Kenny

Paul Kenny   Robert McHugh   Liam Horgan

Con Murphy   Kevin O'Brien   Tommy Murphy

Substitute: Billy Timmons for Paul Kenny.

The homecoming with the Andy Merrigan Cup was described thus in *The Nationalist:* 'There was a street carnival atmosphere as people thronged the town square enjoying themselves as they chatted about the exploits of the men in green and white. Indeed much of the population of the Garden County appeared to be compressed into the town square.'

SÉAMUS KELLY

Séamus came to Baltinglass in March 1970 and started playing with the club in 1971. Hailing from Bailieboro, County Cavan, he brought a great football interest with him. He won five Wicklow Senior Football Championship titles with the club and his greatest joy of all came when winning an Intermediate title in 1982. He became Secretary of the club in 1975, continuing in that position for 13 years and became Chairman the year the club All-Ireland was won. 'Baltinglass is a small country town of about 1,200 people and we represent about nine or ten townlands plus the town itself. It is very agriculture-based with a little industrial estate of three or four good factories employing about 100 people in all.' I interviewed Séamus in the spacious boardroom of the club premises situated beside the beautifully appointed club pitch, with a number of adjoining practice pitches serviced by spacious dressing-rooms. An ideal club setting with all necessary amenities. Was it always thus? 'When I came here first the club organisation wasn't marvellous. We had no under-age structure as such so we took the bit between our teeth and our present Secretary Martin Coleman and myself, and others, got juvenile affairs here going. Training became much more organised and in 1976-1979 we won four County Wicklow U-21 titles in a row. Those teams included Con Murphy, Brian Fitzpatrick, Kevin O'Brien and Robert McHugh. The Kennys came later. We began to see a future for Baltinglass outside Wicklow. The first real indication came in 1985 when we lost in a replay to Portlaoise at Athy. We lost in 1988 in a replay to Parnell's.

'Then came 1989–1990. Tony Norton was classified as team-manager and Tommy Murphy acted as trainer. Tommy Murphy was the arch motivator. He'd be the first in to open the gates for training and the last to leave night after night. The same five fellows were involved with the team for five years Tom Whelan, Ken Browne, John Farrell, Tony Norton and Tommy Murphy. First of all beating Thomas Davis was a great thrill. Then Castlehaven in Aughrim before 10,000 people in dreadfully wet conditions. In the final we won it well. We had incredible scenes when we brought home the Cup. One little thing about the final. The whole team party met in the Ashling Hotel on the morning of the game. I arranged a Gárda escort for our bus to Croke Park and we got there post haste. I remember Seán O'Brien sitting in the front of the bus with his eyes popping out as we careered along, getting to Croke Park in six minutes on a busy St Patrick's Day!'

QUINN'S

'Liam Quinn and his family have always been great supporters. Indeed we got support from the whole town. We didn't have a sponsor then – that day had still to come. Quinns are our sponsors now. Winning the All-Ireland didn't really surprise me. Remember we were trying since 1985 and getting closer all the time. Our best football that year was against Ferbane in Athy. We won that one by 14 points. Kevin O'Brien is our best-known player and has given us great service. Brian Fitzpatrick, our captain, was a Gárda in Dublin and never missed a night's training. We usually train three nights a week. At the moment we are training for yet another County Final which is to be held shortly against Rathnew. The old spirit is alive as ever.

'Martin Coleman our Secretary is a great worker. Our whole development has been phased. The dugouts and press-box were opened in 1983 and our new boardroom complex was completed through Fás three years ago. We don't have a bar as we are too far out of town for that. It was always my dream to have a spacious comfortable place for a meeting. The seven acres adjoining were acquired for £23,000 not long ago. We needed to do little development on it and it is a superb acquisition. We lit a beacon for the whole country when we won that title.

'Before I conclude I'd like to pay tribute to some stalwarts from the past. First of all Johnny Kenny, father of Hugh, Paul and Bill, former player and Secretary of the club for years. He was a great man in so many ways. Seán O'Toole was club Treasurer for 32 years - honest as the day is long. Former county player Ken Browne another stalwart and like Johnny Kenny on the first title winning team of 1958, was Club Chairman at a crucial stage in our development. Tony Norton, another former club and county star. Also Godfrey Timmons TD former player and our President, another top supporter.'

CON MURPHY

Con Murphy, brother of trainer Tommy was the scoring hero of the final. He remembers: 'All my birthdays came on the one day. I was proud of my 2-3 but it was a 20 man achievement. We won it on 17 March, 1990 a day the whole town will never forget. Tommy, my brother and trainer has been with the club for 20 years now. That was the pinnacle of his career and a reward for hard work done by him. All the players were really delighted for Tommy. He spent a lot of time and effort, training, managing and motivating us. About the goals in the final, I took a pass from Robert McHugh and scored from 20 yards luckily enough. Then just before half time, Kevin O'Brien lofted a high ball in and it broke off Tommy to me and I let fly with my right foot (which I'm not noted for at all, the citeog being my norm) and again that one went in. It was from closer range but came just on the stroke of half time, a great time to get a goal against the wind.

At half time Tony Norton and Tommy made sure we kept our feet on the ground. I'm still playing and we are in the County Final again this year. A lot of people thought we were gone for years after last year's defeat. Since 1990 we had some great battles with Éire Óg who have gone so close twice. Winning that All-Ireland was the best thing that could ever happen for Baltinglass. The whole town and county were on a high for some time afterwards. It gave everybody in the town a marvellous lift and a confidence that what we did once could be done again. It was one of the happiest days of my life.'

Baltinglass, All-Ireland Club Champions 1990

Back row: Peter Timmons, Billy Nolan, Donal Buckley, Thomas Donohue, Paudge Doody, Seán O'Brien, Pat Murphy, Hugh Kenny.

Middle: Tony Norton, Martin Coleman, John Farrell, Simon Murphy, Tommy Murphy, Billy Kenny, Raymond Danne, Paul Kenny, Tom Fox, Ken Browne, Séamus Kelly, Tom Whelan.

Front row: Brian Kilcoyne, Con Murphy, Kevin O'Brien, Robert McHugh, Brian Fitzpatrick, Dan Leigh, George Bradley, Liam Horgan, Billy Timmons.

Action in a snowstorm as Nemo Rangers and Scotstown battle with the elements in the 1979 All-Ireland Club Football Final.

AIB GAA All-Ireland Football Club Championship Silver Jubilee Award Winners.

Back row: Mike Sheehy, Jimmy Kerrigan, Éamon O'Donoghue, Tony Hanahoe, Billy Morgan, Brian Murphy and Tom Prendergast.
Front row: Donie O'Sullivan, Kevin O'Brien, Jack Boothman, President GAA, Hugh Cawley, General Manager AIB Bank,
Hugh Kenny and Ger Power.
Absent at the time of awards were: Brian Mullins, John O'Keeffe, Pat Spillane and Jimmy Barry-Murphy.

AIB GAA All-Ireland Hurling Club Championship Silver Jubilee Award Winners.

Back row: Denis Coughlan, Tony Maher, Francis Loughnane, Ger Fennelly, Tony Doran, Conor Hayes and Joe Cooney.

Front row: Liam Fennelly, Neilly Patterson, Jack Boothman, President GAA, Hugh Cawley, General Manager AIB Bank, Joe Hennessy and Charlie McCarthy.

· Absent at time of presentation were: John Horgan, Frank Cummins, Gerald McCarthy and Ray Cummins.